# Foreign Courts
## Civil Litigation
## in Foreign Legal Cultures

# Oñati International Series
# in Law and Society

GENERAL EDITOR

Terence C. Halliday

BOARD OF GENERAL EDITORS

Johannes Feest
Peter Fitzpatrick
Hazel Genn
Rogelio Pérez Perdomo
Hubert Rottleuthner

TITLES

*Totalitarian and Post-Totalitarian Law*
**Edited by Adam Podgorecki and Vittorio Olgiati**

*Foreign Courts: Civil Litigation in Foreign*
*Legal Cultures*
**Edited by Volkmar Gessner**

*Family Law and Family Policy*
*in the New Europe*
**Edited by Jacek Kurczewski and Mavis Maclean**

Oñati International Series
in Law and Society

# Foreign Courts
## Civil Litigation
## in Foreign
## Legal Cultures

Edited by Volkmar Gessner

A Series published for
THE OÑATI INTERNATIONAL INSTITUTE
FOR THE SOCIOLOGY OF LAW

DARTMOUTH
Aldershot U K • Brookfield USA • Singapore • Sydney

Published by
Dartmouth Publishing Company Limited
Gower House
Croft Road
Aldershot
Hants GU11 3HR
England

Dartmouth Publishing Company
Old Post Road
Brookfield
Vermont 05036
USA


**British Library Cataloguing in Publication Data**
Foreign courts : civil litigation in foreign legal
    cultures. - (Oñati international series in law and society)
    1.Actions and defenses 2.International Law
    I.Gessner, Volkmar
    341.7'8

**Library of Congress Cataloging-in-Publication Data**
Foreign courts : civil litigation in foreign legal cultures / edited
    by Volkmar Gessner.
        p.    cm. — (Oñati international series in law and society)
    Includes bibliographical references and index.
    ISBN 1-85521-808-9. — ISBN 1-85521-812-7 (pbk.)
        1. Conflict of laws. 2. Actions and defenses. 3. Judgements.
    4. Conflict of laws—New York (State)—Statistics. 5. Judicial
    statistics—New York (State) 6. Conflict of laws—Germany-
    -Statistics. 7. Judicial statistics—Germany. 8. Conflict of laws-
    -Italy—Statistics. 9. Judicial statistics—Italy. I. Gessner,
    Volkmar. II. Series.
    K7040.F67      1996
    340.9—dc20                                                        96-8125
                                                                          CIP

ISBN 1 85521 808 9 (Hbk)
ISBN 1 85521 812 7 (Pbk)


Printed and bound in Great Britain by
Hartnolls Limited, Bodmin, Cornwall

# Summary of Contents

# Table of Contents

# List of Figures and Tables

# Acknowledgements

No empirical research is possible without the support of many people. Foremost we wish to thank the New York County Clerk, Mr. Norman Goodman, the presidents of the *Landgericht* Bremen, the *Landgericht* Hamburg, the *Amtsgericht* Bremerhaven, and the Civil Court of Milano, as well as the chancellery and archive officers of these courts, for the formal authorization to access the court files and their substantial cooperation with our research project.

We are grateful to Terence Halliday (Chicago) and José Antonio Azpiazu (Oñati) for putting so much energy into the production of this book. We further wish to thank the Isvaran Consultancy of Madras, India, namely Balkrishna and Kalyani Isvaran, for the tremendous work of entering and processing the data. Kalyani also provided the entire content analysis for the LEXIS judgements. Eva Munz in Bremen further assisted us with the statistical analysis and with setting the tables into a publishable format. Martin Novar in New York spent many nights at the computer doing the LEXIS research. Damiano Carcano in Milano assisted with the court file research there.

The many New York law firms who have been so kind as to give us some of their valuable time for an interview will be named in a further volume planned on lawyers. Here we only wish to mention the law firm of Thomas Ré & Partners, New York, for their invaluable support.

Dieter Martiny and Jürgen Samtleben of the *Max Planck Institut für ausländisches und internationales Privatrecht*, Hamburg, have extensively reviewed and commented on the German and New York parts and provided us with many valuable ideas. Of course, the responsibility is all ours.

The German Volkswagen Foundation, within its programme "Law and Behaviour", gave a major research grant to the *Zentrum für Europäische Rechtspolitik* at the University of Bremen, which provided the indispensable financial support for this project.

# Introduction

VOLKMAR GESSNER

## I. Global Approaches in the Sociology of Law

The study of global aspects of law and legal institutions with a sociolegal frame of reference and with sociological methods looks overambitious and unmanageable.[1] This explains why little has been done empirically so far and few internationally composed research teams have been successful. Theoretically, sociology of law tends to concentrate on municipal law and eventually to generalize national legal phenomena (legalization, informalization, materialization, decentralization, and so on) without taking global legal interaction between states, between firms, or between individuals, or the legal activity of international organizations as an object of analysis. The law of the world society does not appear in our textbooks and is left to highly sophisticated but sociologically uninformed discourses among lawyers and economists. Legal sociology sometimes gives the impression that it adheres to a description of the world-system as lawless and spontaneous—not in Ovid's idealizing manner[2] but, rather, in Hobbesian understanding.[3]

The hesitation about studying legal practices outside or above the nation-state is unjustified, first, because such practices are becoming more and more important and, second, because from a theoretical, as well as political, point of view, it seems unreasonable to know so little about them. Notwithstanding, while entering this new field of research, some peculiarities have to be taken into account and many caveats must be made explicit.

---

1   Some parts of this introduction have already been published in the *Journal of Law and Society* 22 (1995): 85–95.

2   Ovid, *Metamorphoses*, No. 89 and 90: *Aurea prima sata est aetas, quae vindice nullo, sponte sua, sine lege fidem rectumque colebat.*

3   Max Weber "solves" the problem of the historical existence of *Weltreiche* without Leviathan by discovering the cohesive role of prophets, priests, and religions in general, cf. Max Weber, *Wirtschaft und Gesellschaft* (Köln/Berlin: Kiepenheuer & Witsch, 1956): 346ff.

First, in the national context most legal interactions take place (in a horizontal relationship) between individuals and between firms on the one hand and (in a vertical relationship) between those actors and the state. This picture, familiar to everyone reading statistics about legal activities (in the courtroom, in lawyers' offices, in state administration), changes dramatically as soon as we leave this context and approach the international arena. States appear globally as actors in horizontal relationships (in conflicts based on international public law and as members of multinational consortia in large investment projects in conflicts based on private law) as well as in vertical relationships (in migration cases, customs, import control, credit insurance, and so on). Individuals are hardly visible as legal actors, the only exception being some transborder claims for divorce, child support, and succession. In their role as consumers they completely refrain from legal action across borders even where a single market (as in the European Union) has been created.[4] Most interesting is the role of big and multinational enterprises and the banking sector. Although they are, economically seen, by far the most important actors, they tend to shove their legal claims into the background and work on the basis of mutual trust or economic dependence. It is then mainly the medium-sized firm that, on the one hand, lacks the dominant position to make state law superfluous and, on the other hand, is strong enough to go into the global market and to use all necessary legal means in order to pursue economic interests. The medium-sized firms are the clients of international law firms who elaborate complex contracts, use international arbitration, and eventually even bring lawsuits to national courts. The role of small firms in global legal interaction generally seems to be more difficult to define since their participation in the global (legal) market depends very much on the support structures (chambers of commerce, consulates, governmental legal information services, and so on) they find in their home country.

4        Cf. Coopers & Lybrand Europe, *Handling of Cross-Border Consumer Disputes—Final Report for the Commission of the European Communities* (1990). Even if U.S. consumers are said to sometimes take foreign enterprises to U.S. courts in order to claim exorbitant and often punitive damages based on product liability, these cases cannot be used to generalize the role of consumers in the global legal arena.

A different mixture of actors and their different uses of law as a means of pursuing interests has obvious consequences for sociolegal analysis; most nationally verified hypotheses about actors' choices and preferences are of little value globally.

Second, whereas in most national studies legal sociology can make use of the class variable in order to explain legal phenomena, this makes little sense on the global level. The class variable can in a certain respect be replaced by north-south or centre-periphery classifications, which are trade-based labels.[5] Other classifications in use[6] are income-based, resource-based, quality of life-based, or block-based, but are all state-centred and cannot be used in a theoretically fruitful manner for nonstate actors such as firms. Even for state conflicts their explanatory power is limited due to the universal activities of multinational enterprises and financial actors who often are more powerful and influential than state governments. One is inclined to define the relative weakness of parties for every single case, taking into account that parties who are really weak simply do not participate in global legal interaction. But this renunciation of the use of stratificatory variables would be a self-denial of sociology and should not be accepted too quickly. In a functional perspective stratificatory variables define the chances of the actor to pursue his/her interests—and these chances obviously are unequally distributed in the world of cross-border legal interaction. First one may distinguish between economic and all other interests and—due to the absence of welfare state considerations within the global legal infrastructure—give the former more chances of realization. Within the category of economic interests, it is obviously the transnational enterprises that dominate the global markets (their share of world trade being estimated at nearly 50%[7]) but that, due to their powerful position, rely to a smaller degree on legal structures than less powerful groups of actors. At least in civil matters the relevant stratification for legal behaviour then begins below the multinational or transnational enterprise and is defined as the chance to mobilize or create law through the

---

5    Immanuel Wallerstein, *The Modern World-System* (New York: Academic Press, 1974).

6    Cf. Leslie Sklair, *Sociology of the Global System* (New York: Harvester Wheatsheaf, 1991).

7    Allen Asher, "Global Action for the Age of Uncertainty", *Consumer Affairs* 131 (1994): 28–35.

use of the global legal infrastructure and, in particular, access to one of the big (predominantly United States) law firms. The legally relevant global stratification is a function of a network between repeat players, where contacts to important banks, diplomats, international law firms, and arbitrators are helpful—just as the success of global criminal behaviour is a function of a Mafia network.[8] A fruitful classification would then consist of membership vs. nonmembership in the international legal network: small firms and individuals are typical nonmembers, larger firms may become members when they fulfil certain entrance conditions and tests of trustworthiness.

Third, in the national context only anthropological studies are confronted with the problem of legal diversity when they deal with traditional customary law in the new states of Asia and Africa. In other areas of the sociology of law, the conflict of laws has never become a major issue. This obviously will have to change as soon as the global level becomes the object of systematic sociolegal observation; sociolegal categories that compare legal systems not only descriptively but with explanatory power have to be elaborated. Little can be learned in this respect from comparative law[9] where, after a century of research, no scientific classification of legal orders in the world is offered except the concept of legal families[10]— telling us that some legal systems are more related to each other than others. A decisive step forward is taken by those legal sociologists who develop legal indicators for a more informative com-

8     In relation to the last aspect, cf. Umberto Santino, "The Financial Mafia: The Illegal Accumulation of Wealth and the Financial-Industrial Complex", Contemporary Crises 12 (1988): 203–43.

9     Cf. René David, Les Grands Systèmes de Droit Contemporains (Paris: Dalloz, 1950); René David and J.E.C. Brierley, Major Legal Systems of the World Today (London: Stevens, 1968); Konrad Zweigert and Hein Kötz, An Introduction to Comparative Law (Amsterdam: North-Holland Publishing Co., 1977).

10    For a critical discussion cf. Lawrence Friedman, The Legal System: A Social Science Perspective (New York: Russel Sage Foundation, 1975), 202; Richard Abel, "Law Books and Books About Law", Stanford Law Review 26 (1973): 175–228; Inga Markovitz, "Hedgehogs or Foxes?: A Review of Westen's and Schleider's Zivilrecht im Systemvergleich", American Journal of Comparative Law 34 (1986): 113–35.

parison,[11] but they do not yet generate hypotheses about behavioural consequences of the differences by which legal systems are characterized. Questions such as "What advantages and handicaps does a German lawyer bring into global legal interaction in comparison with a United States lawyer?"[12] or "Why do plaintiffs prefer to sue in Germany instead of suing in their home country?" cannot yet be answered by the legal indicators' research. It does certainly not make much sense to fight for legal pluralism—as is in vogue now—without entering a discussion about the problems created by the diversity of legal systems. Legal science, at least, is critical about the consequences of legal pluralism and makes enormous efforts in order to unify or harmonize law.[13] It seems plausible that global legal interaction is substantially facilitated by these efforts, but it would be interesting to hear the legal pluralists' response to this position. Recent research on the problems caused by the dramatic increase of European Law within the European Community may be a good start for a discussion around social consequences of the unification or harmonization of national legal systems.[14] Legal diversity certainly complicates research on glo-

---

11   William Evan, *Social Structure and Law* (London: Sage, 1990), 156ff.; Adam Podgorecki, "Social Systems and Legal Systems—Criteria for Classification", in *Legal Systems and Social Systems*, eds. Adam Podgorecki, Christopher J. Whelan, and Dinesh Koshla (London: Croom Helm, 1985), 1–24; Samuel Krislov, "The Concept of Families of Law", in *Legal Systems and Social Systems*, 25–38.

12   The differences between U.S. adversary justice and European managerial justice described by John H. Langbein ("The German Advantage in Civil Procedure", *University of Chicago Law Review* 52 (1985): 823–86) lead to a very different professional experience for lawyers in each system. The greater responsibility of the U.S. lawyer in civil litigation certainly capacitates him/her more for the complexities of international dispute resolution.

13   René David, "The International Unification of Private Law", *International Encyclopedia of Comparative Law II* (Tübingen: Mohr, 1971): 5–579.

14   Cf. Richard Münch, *Das Projekt Europa—Zwischen Nationalstaat, regionaler Autonomie und Weltgesellschaft* (Frankfurt/Main: Suhrkamp, 1993); Volkmar Gessner, "Wandel europäischer Rechtskulturen", in *Lebensverhältnisse und soziale*

bal legal interaction, but it will have also a salutary effect on those
sociolegal approaches that formerly talked simply about "the law",
"the legal system", "the profession", and so on, without taking
into account the different shapes of these phenomena in the world.
The specific characteristics of laws that come into play and compete with one another in the global arena have to be taken much
more seriously than is done in the national context.

Fourth, due to the dominant national focus and the lack of
mental distance from one's own national legal traditions, legal
sociology so far has not been able to describe specific legal cultures as complex phenomena (or is at best still working with hun-
dred-year-old Weberian categories).[15] Thus it lags behind neigh-
bour disciplines, such as psychology (intercultural communication),
political science (comparison of political cultures), administrative
science (models of public administration and bureaucratic intervention), and economics (business cultures, business environment,
international management), where the specific characteristics of
national cultures are sometimes compared in almost universal approaches.[16] As long as the legal cultures of the world cannot be

*Konflikte im neuen Europa—Verhandlungen des 26. Deutschen
Soziologentages in Düsseldorf 1992*, ed. Bernhard Schäfers (Frank-
furt/New York: Campus, 1993). The theory of international regimes tends to neglect these social consequences, cf., e.g., Thomas
Gehring, *The Theory of International Regimes and the European
Community* (Paper presented at the XVIIth World Congress of
the International Political Science Association, Berlin, 1994).

15    It seems fair to mention that some "exotic" legal cultures, such as
the Japanese one, have been described quite frequently and that
the *International Encyclopedia of Comparative Law*, vol. II, offers many interesting insights into a comparison of legal cultures.
Cf. also a recent small brochure by Erhard Blankenburg and Freek
Bruinsma, *Dutch Legal Culture* (Deventer: Kluwer, 1991).

16    The possible contributions of these cultural comparisons for le-
gal sociology are discussed in Volkmar Gessner and Angelika
Schade, "Conflicts of Culture in Cross-Border Legal Relations:
The Conception of a Research Topic in the Sociology of Law",
*Theory, Culture and Society* (1990): 253–77; Volkmar Gessner,
"L'Interazione Giuridica Globale e le Culture Giuridiche", *Sociologia
del Diritto* 20 (1993): 61–78; Volkmar Gessner, "Global Legal In-
teraction and Legal Cultures", *Ratio Juris* 7 (1994): 132–45.

adequately described, explaining global legal phenomena by cultural variables remains extremely speculative and arbitrary and leads some researchers to totally reject culture as an independent variable. This is contrary to actual tendencies in sociological theory and to sociolegal traditions taking values and the social construction of reality seriously (in disputing processes, in legal decision-making, and so on).

Legal-cultural differences that may affect global legal interaction are to be studied on different levels: (1) the normative level; (2) the level of professional and scientific interpretation of norms (supreme court decisions, legal science); (3) the level of the implementation of norms by institutionalized actors (lower courts, public administration, interest groups); and (4) the level of individual actors (lawyers, enterprises, citizens). A comprehensive view on a legal culture as a complex social phenomenon obviously must take all these four levels into account[17] in order not to remain on the superficial, and mostly inadequate, level of national prejudices. Some legal cultures realize legal objectives on the normative level, others in the phase of implementation, others leave the regulatory initiatives and the struggle for justice on the level of organized or unorganized actors. It is therefore completely misleading to compare legal cultures only on the first two levels of statutes and professional and scientific legal opinions.[18]

Some good examples exist for the value of the cultural approach in the field of international lawyering, where the common-law lawyer is usually compared either with the Japanese lawyer or with the continental (civil-law) lawyer, who differ in their legal education, societal role, professional regulation, and cultural values. In situations of cross-border interaction this often leads to misunderstandings between both groups of professionals and to the dominance of the former due to their more creative approach in contract drafting and dispute resolution.[19]

17    This is the subject of a forthcoming textbook by Volkmar Gessner, Armin Höland, and Csaba Varga, *European Legal Cultures* (Aldershot: Dartmouth, forthcoming).

18    For an excellent critique of comparative law for its lack of complexity, cf. Markovits, "Hedgehogs or Foxes".

19    Arthur T. von Mehren, "The Significance of Cultural and Legal Diversity for International Transaction", in *Jus Privatum Gentium—Festschrift für Max Rheinstein* (Tübingen: Mohr,

Fifth, a description of what might be called a global legal culture seems to raise less problems than the comparison of different legal cultures around the globe. This developing culture of the world-system has been described by Luhmann as "cognitive", a behavioural pattern of readiness to learn, to accept the nonfulfilment of expectations, to adapt to new circumstances instead of insisting on contractual stipulations and statutory rules.[20] The complexities of the world require a more flexible and more understanding attitude towards the other party than is usual and adequate in the local or national context. Legal literature on private and public international relations, in spite of its preference for normative structures, sometimes alludes to this cognitive legal culture. The *pacta sunt servanda* principle may in specific circumstances be subordinated to the *clausula rebus sic stantibus*, mediation of state conflicts is preferred to adjudication, flexible rules and customs of international trade may be recognized and then replace national law. Similar tendencies are found on the behavioural level. Legal sanctions are neither offered nor required by the actors, contracts are adapted or simply put aside instead of taken as basis for legal claims, contracts are in many instances replaced by gentlemen's agreements in order to clearly define relationships as socially but not legally binding. Economic and political science literature, and even some legal practice books, therefore put much more emphasis on the problems of negotiation than on those of legal implementation and enforcement. Global legal culture may be seen in a permanent tension with national legal cultures, which try to reproduce globally what they conceive as normal and natural behavioural patterns.

1969), 247–57; Laurent Cohen-Tanugi, *Le Droit sans l'état* (Paris: Presses Universitaires de France, 1985); Danian Zhang and Kenji Kuroda, "Beware of Japanese Negotiation Style: How to Negotiate with Japanese Companies", *Northwestern Journal of International Law and Business* 10 (1989): 195–212. The classical comparison is still Dietrich Rüschemeier, *Lawyers and their Society* (Cambridge, Mass.: Harvard University Press, 1973), whereas too few comparative insights are to be found in Richard L. Abel and Philip S. Lewis, eds., *Lawyers in Society* 3 (Berkeley: University of California Press, 1989).

20    Niklas Luhmann, "The World Society as a Social System", *International Journal of General Systems* (1982): 8.

## II. Comparison of International Litigation

1. Our study of court files in three German first instance courts, of court files in one Italian first instance court, of court files in one New York court, and of judgements in all New York courts presented in this volume is part of a wider project on cross-border legal interactions. Our focus is on major actors who participate in global legal exchanges, one of the basic assumptions being that most such exchanges remain outside the system of national courts and even outside national legal systems. On the national level, state-produced norms (Law) are dominant and autonomously created norms are complementary. In the international arena, we assume the reverse relationship. Due to this complementary function of law and legal institutions, courts cannot be in the centre of legal sociological curiosity.

On the other hand, national and international legislators have made enormous efforts to facilitate the use of law in the international arena, and legal science has important branches like private international law and comparative law where the basic assumption concerning the role of courts and of law for conflict resolution is not at all different from the national model. The abovementioned assumption of a reverse relationship between law and autonomous orders in the international field does not seem to be shared by legal scholars and legal decision-makers. Rather, the use of private international law, of international conventions, and of unified law in judicial decisions is seen as the culmination of all these efforts.

In view of these divergent perspectives, an empirical study of the real contribution of courts to the resolution of international cases is at least a first step in understanding what might be called the normative order of the world society. One open question to be answered by empirical data is the quantitative relevance of domestic courts in the resolution of international disputes. Also of interest are qualitative aspects, namely the way domestic courts handle international cases. Finally it could be assumed that courts at least play a role in minor cases that are not taken into account by the associations and institutions of global trade but, nevertheless, have to be resolved. Hence also the characteristics of cases taken to domestic courts are to be described.

Astonishingly enough, no one has undertaken such a study so far. Miles of book shelves deal with norms to be applied *if* an international case is taken to court. But the simple questions of *whether* this is done, under *which* conditions, and with *what* results is not asked—probably because it is a dusty and time-con-suming task to collect these data in court archives. As legal soci-ologists we did not refrain from these adventures and we were more than compensated by what we learned.

2. Before a case enters the courtroom, most cultural aspects of the dispute are filtered out. If the relationship between the parties has been complex and value-loaded, it has already been reduced by their lawyers to a legal relationship where only some elements are selected and thematized. The relationship is then further re-duced to a claim if a lawsuit is formulated and taken to court.[21] This legal reductionism is observable in every single dispute in-volving only one culture but—and this is one of our assumptions—will probably be even more dramatic if the parties of the dispute are members of different cultures and different legal cultures. Their value conflict, their conflict of behavioural patterns, their conflict-ing views on what they understand as social reality, and their con-flicting theories explaining this reality may be disregarded in or-der to present a case that the judge can subsume under his/her legal categories.

This process of abstraction from social realities notwithstand-ing, cultural elements may influence the lawsuit. Parties may or may not be litigious and may or may not prefer a settlement to a judgement; they may or may not be willing to wait years until a final decision is made; they may or may not apply economic crite-ria of cost and benefits to a lawsuit; they may or may not insist on getting their legal judgement confirmed by the judge's authority. Of course, lawyers and judges also bring in their own legal-cul-tural background, which may be very different from the back-ground of the judges and lawyers in the home country of the for-eign party of the international case.

Unfortunately, background phenomena are difficult to study empirically, and quantitative methods are particularly ill-suited to uncover the "cultural shadow" of legal behaviour. Our studies nevertheless try to give evidence of the invisible and do not hesi-tate to generalize from scarce data, even if this seems speculative. In the very beginning of research in a field of action, errors of interpretation and even some excursions into speculation may be tolerated.

21    William Felstiner, Richard Abel, and Austin Sarat, "The Emer-gence and Transformation of Disputes: Naming, Blaming, Claim-ing", *Law and Society Review* 15 (1981): 631–54.

3. The courts that are the objects of our research are localized in Germany, Italy, and the United States, representing three legal cultures distinguished in legal sociology mainly by the social role attributed to law. In Germany there is little question that the value placed on law-abiding behaviour is very high indeed. This respect for law was, according to Rueschemeyer, one of the meeting grounds between modernized authoritarian traditions and the Rechtsstaat ideals of the liberal opposition throughout the nineteenth century, and this attitude still prevails in the second half of the twentieth century. He explains the professional behaviour of lawyers mainly by their legal-mindedness.[22] Münch speaks of the "proverbial law-abidingness" of the Germans, which is attributed to specific intermediary institutions between state and citizen.[23] As regards the United States, Rueschemeyer quotes William Hurst: "People in the United States of all social levels and at all times mingled respect for the law and for doing things in a legal way with an unashamedly practical attitude toward the law as an instrument. They would use it when it effected a purpose and otherwise dispense it more or less openly".[24] Using law as an instrument means that the goals that guide social behaviour are different from law and are mainly to be found in economic interests. Different yet again is the Italian situation, which, according to Olgiati, is characterized by "a deep separation between the so-called 'legal country' and the 'real country'".[25] Members of the latter organize their relationships according to the convictions of the political groups to which they belong or according to the rules, orders, and directives given by economic, professional, cultural, and religious organizations, always consciously escaping from the positive "official" law.

In their data analyses the authors of the three studies included in this volume had to take this variance of the role of law in soci-

22    Dietrich Rueschemeyer, *Lawyers and Their Society* (Cambridge, Mass.: Harvard University Press, 1973).

23    Richard Münch, *Das Projekt Europa—Zwischen Nationalstaat, regionaler Autonomie und Weltgesellschaft* (Frankfurt/Main: Suhrkamp, 1993), 161.

24    Rueschemeyer, *Lawyers and Their Society*, 86.

25    Vittorio Olgiati, "Legal Systems and the Problems of Legitimacy—The Italian Case", in *Legal Systems and Social Systems*, ed. Adam Podgorecki, Christopher Whelan, and Dinesh Khosla (London: Croom Helm, 1985).

ety into account. The German study therefore uses law as the main independent variable: first of all behavioural patterns in the data are explained by the existence of legal norms. It is assumed that the actors are guided by legal norms if their behaviour is in harmony with what the law expects. The New York study uses the same approach as regards judges but not as regards lawyers. In this respect it follows Max Rheinstein, who observed that in the United States,

> law is a set of rules and principles which tell judges how they have to decide those disputes which private individuals choose to submit to them for decision. . . . In such a view, law is addressed to the judges rather than the individuals. The norms by which individual human beings are expected to direct their behaviour are primarily those of religion, ethics, and social convention.[26]

One must, of course, add to Rheinstein's guiding principles the economic interests of the individual citizen, of the legal profession, and of commercial companies. The Italian study mostly refrains from using law as an explanatory variable and puts the emphasis on "bargaining", which seems to be the dominant pattern in Italian legal culture.

In the "continuous struggle between the 'culture-boundedness' of system-specific categories and the 'contentlessness' of system-inclusive categories",[27] we have chosen the first alternative. The attempts by legal sociologists to generate universal theories on the causal relationship between law and social behaviour do not seem to have been successful. On the contrary there are overwhelming indicators that this relationship is culture-specific. This has led us to not use law as an independent variable throughout our cross-cultural analysis.

4. The concept of court may also be culture-specific, but this is not the case among the three countries compared in our study. In spite of many procedural differences between common law and civil law, the courts as state institutions for professional conflict resolution are comparable units.

This institutional comparability notwithstanding, our empirical methods had to be adapted to the specific circumstances of

---

26    Cited in Rueschemeyer, *Lawyers and Their Society*, 87.

27    Neil J. Smelser, *Comparative Methods in the Social Sciences* (Englewood Cliffs: Prentice Hall, 1979), 178.

"court cultures": of access to documents, of the contents of court files, of the duration of proceedings, of the form of pleadings, of the style of reasoning, and of the way cases are put into the archives. As explained in the methodological parts of each of the three studies, these circumstances fostered some kinds of information and excluded others. Only the German study allowed a comparison between the handling of domestic cases with international cases, while only the New York study allowed a computerized content analysis of judgements. The Italian study, on the other hand, is weak as regards hard data but offers cultural specificities of court interaction, which form an interesting contrast to the "northern" way of civil litigation.

In addition, our focus on "civil cases" did not lead to identical samples due to slightly different competences of the chosen courts as regards family matters, labour cases, and administrative disputes. Some courts (as in Germany) have by statute created special chambers for commercial matters and, in addition, define autonomously some other matters (like car accident, patent, or landlord-tenant cases) as being within the competence of some of the civil chambers. This specialized jurisdiction was not found either in Italy or in New York.

Taken together, all these differences mean that quantitative comparisons between our samples were nearly impossible. Therefore, in spite of much hard data, only soft comparisons can be made.

## III. The Project and the Book

This volume is the first product of an ongoing project on structure and culture of cross-border legal interaction, which brings some ten lawyers and legal sociologists together for empirical research. In the beginning we did not have a set purpose as regards the practical utility of the knowledge produced, nor did we intend to engage ourselves in legal policy and law reform. But hard data are scarce in the field of international lawyering and litigation. Many of our correspondents in legal practice showed enormous interest in our findings and interpretations, which has led us to satisfy their curiosity and has in turn helped us to a better understanding of this field of legal practice. In addition to these daily contacts with practitioners, we were approached by the Commission of the European Community asking us to study cross-border litigation within the European Union. We interrupted the basic project for half a year and carried out this important task for European legal policy-making. The data from our court studies in

Germany and Italy were of use, but more data on the costs of cross-border litigation had to be collected. Again, this exercise helped us in developing our theoretical understanding.

The book will, we hope, reflect what we have learned without concealing the many aspects we still cannot adequately explain. The data are full of real surprises that others may be able to interpret in legal, economic, or sociological discourses. In particular, we would hope to stimulate more empirical research in the field, which certainly requires major legal-sociological attention.

All parts of this book are closely related to each other and follow the same assumptions, which have been elaborated in intensive discussions during the course of some three to four years. Our instruments of data collection, as well as the data evaluation, have been coordinated, and the final reports went through several discussions and revisions.

The logic of the presentation needs little explanation. The first chapter deals with the institutional approach chosen as being most appropriate for what we conceive of as the global arena of interaction. It is not ambitious in itself (and may even seem superficial to lawyers) but aims at briefly describing the structural and cultural environment with which actors of cross-border exchanges are confronted and have to cope. The chapter is intended as a map and, at the same time, as a list of problems and hypotheses.

The middle chapters resume the court data using a nearly identical structure of topics under scrutiny in order to help the reader make whatever comparison he/she is interested in. In these papers we resisted the temptation to confront every single piece of data with the results of the other two country reports—this would have been overambitious in this early stage of empirical research of international litigation.

The final chapter attempts a broader view of the material and resumes some aspects that might help to define the present and future role of domestic courts for conflict resolution and norm creation in world society.

# 1 The Institutional Framework of Cross-Border Interaction

VOLKMAR GESSNER

## I. Choice of Theoretical Approach

Our interest in the institutional framework of cross-border legal interaction needs some qualifications as regards the focus on the world society and its regulatory structure.

### A. World Society as a Point of Reference

The legal regulations for and legal behaviour of international and cross-border exchanges are part of what is called world society[1]—the only conceivable reference point for attempts to explain global regulatory processes and to criticize their results. In a system's theoretical approach the international legal system is a functional prerequisite of global interaction by providing behavioural patterns and models for decision-making. But world society, though already a social fact, is poorly conceptualized by sociology.[2] Whereas the majority of social scientists still think of extrasocietal matters in terms of international relations, it was a decisive step forward to conceive of world society as a stage where not only states play their roles, but also migrants, churches, media, merchants, interest groups, and Mafiosi.[3] What remains unknown is their interrelationship, their position in a global structure, and their cultural orientations. According to Luhmann these actors communicate in globally differentiated systems—which has made world society the only possible one, because communica-

---

1    John W. Burton, *World Society* (London and New York: Cambridge University Press, 1972); W.L. Hollist and James N. Rosenau, "World Society Debates", *International Organisation* 31 (1981): 1.

2    Kurt Tudyka, "'Weltgesellschaft'—Unbegriff und Phantom", *Politische Vierteljahresschrift* 30 (1989): 503–8.

3    Leslie Sklair, *Sociology of the Global System* (New York: Harvester Wheatsheaf, 1991).

tion processes have made "societies" and shared cultures obsolete.[4] This position is hardly shared by Wallerstein, who reduces
the world-system to utilitarian preferences of economic actors and
to contracts and division of labour as their most prominent forms
or goals.[5] Two decades of discussion on Wallerstein's "economic
reductionism" led to more and more complex sociological approaches,[6] in particular to the increased use of political and cultural variables and to the consideration of noneconomic actors in
the process of "structuration" of the world order.[7] It is clearly this
post-Wallerstein sociology that allows legal sociologists to build a
global frame of reference for their empirical observations. Global
legal actors at all levels create global social structures, but they are
at the same time following economic (utilitarian), political (ideological), and cultural patterns, which are still, contra Luhmann, of
basically intrasocietal origin.

## B. Institutional Analysis

The process of "structuration" of the world order could be
made the sole object of analysis, and important empirical studies,
mainly in political science, international relations research, and
peace research, have been carried out in this direction. In legal
sociology there is a recent interest in the contribution of the legal
profession to the construction and definition of an international
regulatory arena.[8] In particular the "legal field" of international

4    Niklas Luhmann, "The World Society as a Social System", *International Journal of General Systems* (1982): 8.

5    Immanuel Wallerstein, *The Modern World System* (New York: Academic Press, 1974).

6    Cf., e.g., Roland Robertson, *Globalization—Social Theory and Global Culture* (London: Sage, 1992); Albert Bergesen, "Turning World-System Theory on its Head", *Theory, Culture and Society* 7 (1990): 67–81.

7    Anthony Giddens, *The Consequences of Modernity* (Stanford: Stanford University Press, 1990).

8    Yves Dezalay, *Marchands de droit—La restructuration de l'ordre juridique international par les multinationales de droit* (Paris: Fayard, 1992); Yves Dezalay, "Multinationales de l'expertise et 'dépérissement de l'état'", *Actes de la recherche en sciences sociales*, 96–97, (March 1993):3–20; Alain Bancaud and Yves Dezalay, "Des 'grands prêtres' du droit au marché de l'expertise juridique", *Revue Politiques et Management Public*, 12, (June 1994): 203–20.

arbitration has been made the object of research by Dezalay and Garth, who interviewed no less than 250 arbitrators all around the globe in order to describe the competition for business and legitimacy between civil-law and common-law jurists, between academics and practitioners, between "grand old men" and "technocrats".[9]

The Dezalay/Garth analytical tool of a "legal field" (Bourdieu) seems well chosen for this particular object of study, which is very recent (the beginning of international arbitration as a major method for commercial dispute resolution is said to be the oil crisis in the 1970s), extremely personalized (the authors give names and biographies of most actors in the field), and in an early stage of institutionalization. Bourdieu's anthropological approach, where all structures are symbolic and subject to individual definitions and recreations, and where the strategies of players for obtaining "symbolic capital" prevail over objective constraints, may explain characteristics of the world society that are of a tribal nature, for example, the Mafia, *opus dei*, the scientific community, or—as is the case here—the arbitration club.

But world society on the whole has more institutional than tribal aspects and would be misconceived by generalizing anthropological concepts to either state or individual (commercial) behaviour. Global exchanges require more and more complex devices, which sociologists describe on the level of (national) societies as "social institutions", that is, as relatively stable action patterns that reduce the uncertainties with respect to the behaviour of other individuals in the process of human interaction. Social institutions help the actor in making choices and, at the same time, act as constraints by executing formal and informal sanctions against deviant behaviour. They are considered even by the most critical approaches in sociology as indispensable coordination mechanisms.

A sociology of the world society, and particularly a legal sociology of the world society, will have to deal primarily with social institutions in the above-mentioned sense. Insofar as global exchanges are economic exchanges—and this is certainly true for

9    Yves Dezalay and Bryant Garth, "Merchants of Law as Moral Entrepreneurs: Constructing International Justice from the Competition for Transnational Business Disputes", *Law and Society Review* 29 (1995): 27-64; Yves Dezalay and Bryant Garth, *Dealing in Virtue: International Commercial Arbitration and the Construction of a Transnational Legal Order* (forthcoming).

most cross-border interactions—this emphasis on institutions is strongly supported by the recent work of Douglass C. North, making use of established sociological knowledge for classical economic theory.[10] Their explanation of economic success by rational choice is criticised by pointing to incomplete information on the actor: "The costliness of information is the key to the costs of transacting, which consist of the costs of measuring the valuable attributes of what is being exchanged and the costs of protecting rights and policing and enforcing agreements".[11] These transaction costs are a function of the institutional framework of legal rules, organizational forms, enforcement, and informal patterns of behaviour. In our context it is important to note how much importance North attributes to effective third-party enforcement in the historically most advanced form of exchange, the impersonal exchange. Courts reduce transaction costs and hence contribute to economic growth.

This strong support from sociological theory as well as from new institutional economics justifies our focus on institutions in the global arena. Whereas this volume concentrates on formal constraints (legal rules and courts), a forthcoming publication will deal with informal constraints created by the actors of (mostly, but not exclusively, economic) transnational social systems.

As one of the central hypotheses of this project we could then formulate that the analysis of legal and nonlegal (which encompasses cultural) institutions uncovers the most relevant characteristics of the developing global legal culture. It answers questions about use or avoidance of legal processes, types of disputes, and ways of decision-making, as well as the attitudes and strategies of legal actors. This volume in particular attempts to give a fair description of the role of courts in cross-border litigation.

## II. The Coordination of Cross-Border Legal Interactions

A review of legal and social-science literature on the international legal arena allows the formulation of three (not necessarily exclusive) assumptions on the problem of order in the world society: (1) world society is structured by state regulations and

10    Douglass C. North, *Institutions, Institutional Change and Economic Performance* (Cambridge, England: Cambridge University Press, 1990).

11    North, *Institutions*, 27.

international conventions; (2) world society is structured by semiautonomous institutions and regulations; and (3) world society is for the most part unstructured, resulting in anomic situations. We will try to combine these divergent views into a picture of differentiated action patterns and develop hypotheses on the role of the national courts therein.

## A. State Ordering of Private Cross-Border Relations

Export trade is characterized by constitutional insecurity.[12] There is no world state protecting the fulfilment of contractual obligations. The insecurity of transactions leads to transactional costs and welfare losses.

But transborder interactions are frequent and—in spite of the absence of a central order—regulated by a variety of mechanisms. Export trade moves valuable goods across the oceans, millions of people travel every year in other countries, and some people even marry foreigners. In legal language contracts and torts, consumer debts, inheritances, child support, and property claims across national borders are abundant—in a situation of legal insecurity, political instability, and cultural diversity. It can easily be assumed that legal sociological theories of legal behaviour and of the functions of legal institutions are of little help on the global level and that cognitive categories, such as private ordering and personal trust on the one hand, and categories of power and exploitation, such as fraud, abuse, hostage-taking, and kidnapping on the other hand, become dominant explanatory variables.

One step taken by all states to protect the fulfilment of the obligations of cross-border contracts is the formulation of *private international law*. This branch of law applies to transactions extending over more than one legal system and determines in an individual case the law applicable to the dispute between the parties and the jurisdiction of the courts that have to adjudicate upon the issue. These two questions do not coincide: it is conceivable that according to the rules of private international law the dispute has to be heard by the national courts but that these courts have to apply foreign law (or vice versa).

It is generally admitted among practitioners that private international law contributes little to solving the dilemma of the inse-

12    Hans-Jörg Schmidt-Trenz, *Außenhandel und Territorialität des Rechts* (Baden-Baden: Nomos, 1990).

curity of international contracts. First, the private international laws of the respective home countries of the actors may contradict each other. Second, even if jurisdiction and applicable law are clearly defined between the respective legal systems, one of the actors has to submit his/her case to a foreign legal order normally unknown to him or her. Unknown rules may create even more insecurity than the absence of rules where the actor is simply referred to his/her power potential.

Only the first of these two problems may be resolved by the ongoing activities of harmonizing private international law, such as the EEC Convention on the Law Applicable to Contractual Obligations (adopted in 1980), the Convention on Jurisdiction, and the Enforcement of Judgements in Civil and Commercial Matters (adopted in 1968). International actors belonging to the contracting countries get some security concerning the choice of law and jurisdiction. What decision will be given in his/her case can be calculated only by the actor whose national law and jurisdiction will be applied. His/her opponent has little chance to defend his/her position. He/she has to get access to one of the few international law firms capable of giving legal advice in foreign law. He/she then has to hire a local lawyer in the other country willing to accept the additional burden of international cases. And he/she will have to act in court proceedings completely unfamiliar to him/her. These are barriers few foreign parties of legal conflict will be able to surmount.

Private international law also leads to very problematic situations for judges if they have to apply foreign law. If the application of foreign law cannot be avoided, it must be proved (in Germany *ex officio*,[13] in the U.S. ex parte[14])—often at considerable inconvenience and expense.

The access to information on foreign law was to be facilitated by a European Convention prepared by the Council of Europe and signed on 7 June 1968. But experiences with this information service (offered by the Ministries of Justice) show its very marginal relevance: in 1980 the German Ministry of Justice received three requests about German law, seven in 1981, and eleven in 1982. Requests from German courts about foreign law were trans-

---

13      I.e., by itself. The common-law equivalent would be the concept of *sua sponte*.

14      I.e., by party submission.

mitted in nineteen cases in 1980, in thirty-five cases in 1982, and in thirty cases in 1983.[15] If courts are advised by an expert or experts on the subject, their knowledge, skill, and experience can vary considerably. The point of law may be doubtful in the foreign law, there may be different opinions about it, or it may be not discussed at all. Yet the forum court has to find the rule of decision there. The judge most likely will examine a foreign legal system through and under the influence of his/her own legal system and will fail to appreciate the different methods of the foreign courts and lawyers.[16]

Thus, private international law is understandable as an attempt of legal science to avoid systemic gaps in legal regulation, but in practice it contributes little to resolve the insecurity problem of cross-border legal relations. It refers the parties either to one or to the other legal system in question without taking into account the specific character of international legal relationships. International commerce strongly opposes private international law. It prefers its own methods and objectives for the litigation of disputes, "worked out case by case and legislation by legislation, rather than as the brainchildren of jurisprudential system builders".[17]

Another, more promising step to reduce insecurity in international private relations is the elaboration of *international uniform law*. According to Bonell[18] it is no longer possible to count the number of international conventions, uniform laws, codes, and rules of conduct that either seek to replace the corresponding domestic law through the appropriate ratification procedures or through immediate applicability or that offer only model rules, the introduction of which is left to the discretion of the national legislators. *The Digest of Legal Activities of International Organi-*

---

15   Günter Ott, "Die gerichtliche Praxis und ihre Erfahrungen mit dem Europäischen Abkommen vom 7.6.1968 betr. Auskünfte über ausländisches Recht", in *Festschrift für Karl Firsching*, ed. Dieter Henrich and Bernd von Hoffmann (Munich: Beck, 1985), 209–32.

16   Jan F. G. Baxter, "International Business and Choice of Law", *International Comparative Law Quarterly* 36 (1987): 92–115.

17   Baxter, "International Business and Choice of Law", 113.

18   Michael Joachim Bonell, "International Uniform Law in Practice—or Where the Real Trouble Begins", *American Journal of Comparative Law* 38 (1990): 865–88.

*zations and Other Institutions*, published regularly by UNIDROIT, mentions 38 international organizations active in the unification process. Unified law is of special importance in the following areas of private law:
- letters of credit and cheques,
- product liability,
- international transport by air, sea, and land, and
- patents and author rights.

Some of these conventions have reached universal application; others are at least signed and ratified by most industrialized countries. Of special importance is the unification of law within the European Economic Community, which already affects most parts of private law, economic law, and procedural law.

Some of the unified law has been specially created for the cross-border situation,[19] e.g., the United Nations convention on Contracts for the International Sale of Goods (CISG), ratified so far by 34 national parliaments, representing most of the highly industrialized states.

Some critics say that the unification of law thus far achieved applies more to marginal areas,[20] that it has only created tiny islands of unified law in a sea of national legislation,[21] and that it is fractional, and isolated, lacks any systematic overall concept, and is random and unduly involved.[22] But these problems may be transitional, and the European Community at least puts enormous energy in achieving homogeneity of legal structures within the member states. The problems are rather to be found on a sociolegal level, namely in the behaviour of judges and private actors.

19   Baxter, in his critique of international business litigation, fails to recognize this development, which fulfils his demands.

20   Peter Schlechtriem, "Bemerkungen zur Geschichte des Einheitskaufrechts", in *Einheitliches Kaufrecht und nationales Obligationenrecht*, ed. Peter Schlechtriem (Baden-Baden: Nomos, 1987), 27–36.

21   Hein Kötz, "Rechtsvereinheitlichung—Nutzen, Kosten, Methoden, Ziele", *RabelsZ* 50 (1986): 1–17.

22   Peter-Christian Müller-Graff, "Privatrecht und Europäisches Gemeinschaftsrecht", in *Staat und Wirtschaft in der EG*, ed. Peter-Christian Müller-Graff and Manfred Zuleeg (Baden-Baden: Nomos, 1987), 17–52.

First, in spite of provisions of international conventions or uniform laws requiring the national judge or private arbitrator to take into account their international character, there is the risk that uniform law will be interpreted differently in each state. Legal education and the social background of judges, their socioeconomic status, their political role, and their attitudes show such a variance within the realm of every uniform law that its uniform interpretation and application will be the exception rather than the rule. Lower court judges have no access to information about foreign court decisions, and even supreme court judges do not take foreign practice into account. The interpretation of uniform law follows the patterns of domestic legal reasoning. To avoid this dilemma the European Court of Justice may be used according to Art. 177 Treaty of Rome as a supranational organ ensuring uniform interpretation of EEC regulations and directives. Thus far, however, only a few hundred cases have been submitted to this procedure, and some member states virtually never make use of it. Hence, it can easily be assumed that EC law is interpreted differently by courts in the European Community.

Second, most uniform law is private law and therefore dispositional. It is an offer to private actors and particularly to business circles to submit their relations to a single normative order. But unexpectedly this offer is often not accepted:

> Entire generations of specialists have devoted their energies to working out uniform rules, seeking in each case to find solutions which best meet the practical needs of the time. But once a convention has finally been approved, there is a serious risk of it remaining a dead letter in practice since those to whom (and for whose benefit) it is principally directed, i.e., the economic operators actually involved in the trade sectors in question, take no notice of it or, when it is brought to their attention, do everything in their power to escape its application.[23]

This frustrating experience has led to various speculations as to the reasons why international actors avoid uniform law. Businesses in developing countries seem to be afraid of unequal distribution of power or, rather, feel they need more favourable regulations to compensate for their unequal bargaining power in contracts with industries of northern countries. But parties within a

23   Bonell, "International Uniform Law in Practice", 868.

north-north relationship are also contracting out of uniform law. They complain that business associations have not had enough opportunity to participate in the elaboration of the respective uniform laws.[24] These authors assume that the contents of uniform laws are unsatisfactory and therefore unattractive for business circles. This, however, is only part of the truth. Rather, the reason uniform law does not play the role aspired to by the respective legislators and legal comparativists is to be found in the development of a separate legal culture of international transactions with autonomous rules and its own infrastructure for advice and decision making. In spite of the claims of states and legal science that law must always have the last word in conflict resolution, state actors have, in fact, little to say in the social system of worldwide trade. This leads us to the aspects of private ordering to resolve the insecurity problem as an alternative to governmental activities.

## B. Private Ordering of Cross-Border Relations

In situations of insecurity rational actors make a particular effort to avoid risks. This aim structures the behaviour of every person or enterprise who steps into the no-man's-land of cross-border interaction. People refrain from marrying a foreigner, from investing money, or from buying valuable goods abroad—except for cases where special mechanisms of trust have been established. These mechanisms deserve the interest of sociologists of law because they are the result of imaginative private ordering. Our exercise of mapping the structure of this field comprises main actors and important organizations who take part in this semiautonomous order.

Legal science has given this private order a name—*lex mercatoria*[25]—but is sceptical about the idea of its complete au-

24    Allan Farnsworth, ed., "International Uniform Law in Practice", in *Acts and Proceedings of the 3rd Congress on Private Law* held by the International Institute for the Unification of Private Law (Rome: UNIDROIT, Oceana Publications, 1988) 547–59.

25    Clive M. Schmitthoff, "Das neue Recht des Welthandels", *RabelsZ* (1964): 47–77; Aleksander Goldstajn, "The New Law Merchant Reconsidered", in *Law and International Trade—Festschrift für Schmitthoff*, ed. Fritz Fabricius (Frankfurt/Main: Athenäum, 1973), 171–85; Harold J. Berman and Colin Kaufmann, "The Law of International Commercial Transactions (lex mercatoria)", *Harvard International Law Journal* 19 (1978): 221–75.

tonomy from state regulation and state coercive power.[26] Economic analysis of law takes it more seriously and applies its mathematical potential to calculate its costs and benefits.[27] Unlike legal science this approach considers private protection of international transactions to be sufficient—but, at the same time, too costly— and recommends a mix between self-regulation and legal protection of commercial cross-border transactions.[28]

The structural dominance of large enterprises is nearly self-evident. They have normally long since established stable relations with other (large) enterprises abroad. A mix between trust and interdependence provides enough self-produced security to solve problems without conflicts. Transactions are planned and fixed in detailed contracts, but the purpose of this drafting effort is organizational rather than legal because judicial enforcement or even arbitration is rarely necessary. The use of legal advice is more frequent than at the time when Stewart Macaulay made his study on "non-contractual relations in business". In-house corporate legal departments have grown rapidly, but problems are also handed over to large law firms. The rest of the autonomous or legal infrastructure of the international arena plays no role between large enterprises.

A special case of close cooperation between large enterprises is the multinational company, a cluster of companies registered under—and owing their identity to—various national laws, joined by links of common ownership and operating in accordance with a common management strategy. The legal construction of multinational companies may vary considerably: the subsidiary of such a company may be seen as an extension of the nationality of the parent company, as a foreign enclave in the host country's economy; alternatively, its links with the parent company may be almost

26    Cf., e.g., Otto Sandrock, "Internationales Wirtschaftsrecht und 'konsensuale Wirtschaftsregulierung'?", *Zeitschrift für das gesamte Handelsrecht und Wirtschaftsrecht* (1988): 66–87; Volker Triebel and Eckart Petzold, "Grenzen der Lex Mercatoria in der Internationalen Schiedsgerichtsbarkeit", *Recht der Internationalen Wirtschaft* (1988): 245–50.

27    Hans-Jörg Schmidt-Trenz, *Außenhandel und Territorialität des Rechts—Grundlegung einer Neuen Institutionenökonomik des Außenhandels* (Baden-Baden: Nomos, 1990).

28    Schmidt-Trenz, *Außenhandel und Territorialität des Rechts*, 313ff.

invisible, and it is regarded as no different from the purely domestic companies operating in the host economy.[29]

The economic links, however, profit as much as possible from the advantages of an economy of scale, from the exploitation of lower costs of capital and labour and from access to national markets and sources of raw materials. In addition—and this aspect is of special interest in our context—the network of commonly owned companies is a security system against the risks of international trade, a private order of trust and honesty. If the bulk of their commercial transactions takes place "within the family", the absence of legal enforceability of contractual obligations is irrelevant. Contracts are fulfilled because of a common interest. The inevitable frictions are resolved smoothly without having to sue or to seek a law firm's advice.

Law firms have acquired a decisive and growing importance in the international arena. Major transnational law firms, composed of lawyers familiar with different legal systems and specialized areas of law, offer their negotiation and deal-making capacities, their drafting techniques, and their creativeness in developing new forms of investments and financial instruments. Together with corporate tax accountants, financial advisors, and management consultants, they occupy a strategic and intermediary position in the field of economic power in the world market. Because this market is dominated by the English language, American capital and common-law reasoning, United States law firms play the most influential part.[30] They gained substantial experience in international business transactions during the 1950s and 1960s when American corporations had a near monopoly in international business. And they offer a unique style of commerce-oriented creative lawyering that is particularly suited to the facilitation of transnational business deals. According to Crabb, in 1982, 50 of the largest 200 Ameri-

29    Michael Hodges, "Functionalism and Multinational Companies", in *Functionalism*, ed. A.J.R. Groom and Paul Taylor (London: University of London Press, 1975), 225–37.

30    Yves Dezalay, "The Big Bang and the Law: The Internationalization and Restructuration of the Legal Field", *Theory, Culture and Society* 7 (1990): 279–93; Roger J. Goebel, "Professional Qualification and Educational Requirements for Law Practice in a Foreign Country: Bridging the Cultural Gap", *Tulane Law Review* 63 (1989): 443–523.

can law firms had one or more offices abroad (most of them in England and France, and some in Hong Kong, Belgium, Japan, Saudi Arabia, and other countries).[31] The "Big Six" American accountancy firms have formed networks of national practices bound together with different degrees of cohesion.[32] With the creation of the European Economic Community, Europe becomes a most attractive arena for international lawyering. Whelan and McBarnet mention in particular the

> Eurolink for Lawyers, an international legal network which after only one year of operation covered fourteen European countries (fifty cities) and the USA. It includes ninety firms, one third of which are British, employing 2000 commercial lawyers. Members have access to a data base to find an associate in another country. Through such networks, smaller firms may obtain the benefits of the large firm without the need for formal integration in an elaborate internal organization.[33]

The role of banks in international business became central with the development of instruments like documentary credit. This creative invention, described by English judges as "the life blood of international commerce",[34] guarantees payment of cross-border sales:
• The buyer (the credit applicant) fills in a standard application form requesting his bank to issue its irrevocable credit in favour of the foreign seller (the beneficiary).
• The buyer's bank issues its documentary credit in accordance with the applicant's instructions. This constitutes an independent undertaking of the bank, and is enforceable against it even if the buyer cannot reimburse the bank.

31    Kelly Charles Crabb, "Providing Legal Services in Foreign Countries: Making Room for the American Attorney", *Columbia Law Review* 83 (1983): 1767.

32    Christopher Whelan and Doreen McBarnet, "Lawyers in the Market: Delivering Legal Services in Europe", *Journal of Law and Society* 19 (1992): 49–68.

33    Whelan and McBarnet, "Lawyers in the Market", 53.

34    Cited in Clive M. Schmitthoff, *Export Trade* (London: Stevens, 1986), 336.

• The issuing bank usually asks a bank in the seller's country with which it has a correspondent relationship (the advising bank) to notify the credit to the beneficiary.

• The credit may be made payable at the counters of a bank in the seller's country (the nominated bank) or, more rarely, at the issuing bank. In some cases the nominated bank adds its own payment obligation by confirming the credit. This gives the beneficiary a direct right against a bank in his own country.

• The seller ships his goods and presents his documents to the bank for payment. The credit may provide for payment to be made immediately or at a later date. It may also call for the beneficiary to present a bill of exchange as well as the commercial documents.

• The paying bank sends the documents to the issuing bank and obtains reimbursement. Often it is entitled to obtain immediate reimbursement from a third bank designated in the credit.

• The buyer collects the documents from the issuing bank and takes possession of the goods. He may have been required to make a cash deposit in advance with the bank or may have to reimburse it before receiving the documents. Alternatively his bank may be affording him time to repay.

The two banks normally involved in every transaction are bound by contracts with the importer and the exporter. These contracts are protected by the national legal systems. The unprotected contract relationship between buyer and seller residing in different legal orders is the highly insecure part—the exchange of goods against an equivalent amount of money across borders—replaced by an equally legally unprotected but socially protected relationship between two banks. This social protection follows from the relatively small number of bank institutions in the world market and the stable business relations between them.[35] This situation is demonstrated by

---

35    Schmidt-Trenz, "Außenhandel und Territorialität des Rechts", 264.

Figure 1.1: The Organization of Cross-Border Payment
Through Documentary Credit

The establishment of stable business relations between the banks involved in this payment procedure requires enormous efforts of negotiation, drafting contracts, setting up organizational structures, and permanent risk control (ranging from the risk of the individual credit to a highly sophisticated country risk assessment). After the recent breakdowns of important international banks, it has also become crucial to be cautious in choosing the partner bank in the foreign banking sector.

Medium-sized enterprises are at the centre of attention of the international business community, because their commercial power, organizational capacity, experience, and information are not sufficient to compensate transactional insecurity across borders by their own means. As already shown, banks offer the most valuable service. In addition a number of other institutions offer advice and information:

• Trade associations employ a specialized staff to study the export trade for all important products of the branch and work out general sales conditions, which provide a detailed regulation of those aspects that assume particular importance for the particular type of sale concerned.

• National chambers of commerce and binational chambers of commerce (these latter representing the interests of a national trade in another country) publish information sheets on export and import trade law and give general and individual advice on legal questions or refer to competent lawyers. They also answer questions about informal rules and commercial customs, thus strengthening the private ordering of commercial actors.

• National information services on export and import trade complement the information service offered by the chambers of commerce. In contrast to the aforementioned institutions, they are state-run (e.g. the German *Bundesstelle für Außenhandelsinformation* and the *Mexikanische Handelsmission,* both located in Cologne).

• The International Chamber of Commerce (ICC) in Paris goes far beyond advice and information and must be viewed as one of the most important actors in the international commercial arena. Among its most important activities range the elaboration of INCOTERMS (International Rules for the Interpretation of Trade Terms) like cif (cost, insurance, freight) and fob (free on board), thus avoiding differences in interpretation of contract clauses in different legal systems and cultures. Standardization efforts have been especially successful in the fields of documentary credit (Uniform Customs and Practices for Documentary Credits), debt collection (Uniform Rules for Collections), contract guarantees (Uniform Rules for Contract Guarantees), adaptation of contracts, force majeure and hardship clauses, and so on. The ICC offers a Court of Arbitration and other dispute settlement measures. Through congresses and seminars the rules of international trade are continuously discussed, adapted and amended.

• Of special importance as a quasi-international legislator is the United Nations Commission on International Trade Law (UNCITRAL), whose objective is to further the progressive harmonization and unification of the law of international trade. After having prepared successful texts such as the UNCITRAL Arbitration Rules and the Convention on the Carriage of Goods by Sea it worked out the above-mentioned Convention on Contracts for the International Sale of Goods (CISG) in 1980. It governs all export contracts unless parties opt out expressly.

Last but not least insurance institutions offer a reduction of the risks of international trade. First, as an incentive for export trade, many industrialized countries offer a state or quasi-state insurance against "political" risks (HERMES in Germany, for example, or guarantees by the British Export Credits Guarantee Department). Second, commercial and transport risks are insured with commercial insurers. Third, some business communities have created their own "private" insurance mechanism. The most prominent examples are the Protection and Indemnity Associations or P.&I. Clubs organized autonomously by ship owners "for the purpose of protecting each other . . . against such losses, claims and demands . . . as cannot be covered by ordinary insurance".[36] Conflicts are rare, but if they arise the situation is similar to the documentary credit arrangement: an international case is nationalized and made legally enforceable.

This by no means complete picture of the infrastructure of international trade describes the legal, quasi-legal, or customary environment of cross-border interactions among medium-sized enterprises. These institutions, rules, and dispute settlement measures all have become crucial for global economic exchange.

Small firms may, of course, also take advantage of the autonomous infrastructure of the business community and do so to a certain degree.

Private individuals are best described by the picture of isolated nomads with no autonomous infrastructure ready to assist them in cross-border contacts. Partners of binational marriages may get some advice from private associations, but their conflict-solving potential is close to zero. Such "normal" problems as custody of children, child support, divorce, and inheritance become extraordinarily complicated in the cross-border situation and no lawyer—in view of the generally low amounts at stake—is willing or able to handle them properly. In special situations international conventions on the state level try to compensate for the weakness of individual noncommercial actors, e.g., in cases of child abduction ("legal kidnapping"), where a central authority in every signatory state pursues the claims of the parent whose right of custody was violated by the ex-spouse. Consumers, according to a recent study commissioned by the European Communities,[37] are completely disoriented in cases of cross-border complaints and, in most cases, probably will give up their claims. Those national organizations that attempt to deal with these complaints report:

• difficulties in contacting the foreign supplier, initial tracing problems and subsequent refusal to respond to correspondence,

• lack of knowledge of applicable law, problems of private international law,

• where foreign law applies, lack of knowledge of its provisions and its underlying legal system and case law,

36  Cited in Hanno von Freyhold, "Das autonome Recht der P. & I. Clubs", (unpublished paper, Bremen, 1990).

37  "Handling of Cross-Border Consumer Disputes", *Final Report for the Commission of the European Communities*, October 1990.

• poor chances of enforcement, due to low level of collaboration with foreign equivalent organization,

• unavailability of legal aid. Legal aid schemes are generally
inapplicable for nonresident consumers and for actions in foreign
courts,

• inability to communicate due to foreign language deficiencies. The problem applies to communication with foreign suppli-
ers or manufacturers, to foreign consumer organizations and the
comprehension of foreign consumer law.[38]

This complete lack of private ordering of such sporadic claims
arising from family problems, consumer problems, inheritances,
environmental damage, and so on, is no surprise for those familiar
with M. Olson's Theory of Collective Action.[39] Individuals who
are rarely confronted with cross-border relations have no incentive to create protective instances. If claims in a foreign country
occur more frequently, the necessary infrastructure is quickly created: such is the case in automobile accidents where insurance companies have made adequate arrangements.

### C. Main Structural Characteristics of the International Arena of Private Actors

In our description of the international arena of private actors, legal sociologists may discover something like an autopoietic
system or a postmodern societal organization. Until there is empirical evidence of efficient self-regulation and low efficiency of
state intervention, these theories do not seem to contribute too
much to our understanding of social processes in the area of global contracting and dispute settlement. Thus far we can only observe a specific mix of state and private ordering, which cannot be
found with similar characteristics in any national legal system.
The direct impact of state rules seems to be weak but it must be
taken into account that most parts of the private infrastructure
are governed by national regulations, such as lawyers by the national laws of legal professions, chambers of commerce by public
law, or insurance companies by state insurance law.

Due to the aforementioned fact that private ordering does not
reach all international actors, namely small firms and noncom-

38    "Handling of Cross-Border Consumer disputes", 185.

39    Mancur Olson, *The Logic of Collective Action: Public Goods
      and the Theory of Groups* (Cambridge, Mass.: Harvard Univer-
      sity Press, 1965).

mercial actors, there is obviously some elitist flavour in the famous *lex mercatoria*. If the international arena is conceived as a
self-regulatory system, this refers only to a relatively small circle
of economically important actors—and their behaviour was self-
regulatory for many centuries. What is really new is not self-regulation but the typical mix of state and private ordering and the
appearance of more and more actors in the international arena
who do not belong to the international elite.

If the focus is on the new actors in the international arena, a
revised version of anomie theory seems to offer the most appropriate set of hypotheses.[40] A modern conception of anomie refers
to situations of low social integration where little knowledge is
shared commonly or where institutionalized typifications of behaviour are scarce. These situations may, in the international arena,
lead to withdrawal (avoiding cross-border contacts), conflict stag-
ing (scrupulous use of power and influence), or, as a cognitive
response to anomie, to private ordering. This last aspect has at-
tracted the interest of lawyers and legal sociologists, but the deviant forms of reaction to anomie still seem to prevail and must not
be neglected. The world society offers the actor a great variety of
structured and unstructured areas, and, as will be shown in the
next section, structural integration may be counterbalanced by
cultural diversity.

## D. Cultural Elements in Cross-Border Relations

The functionalist paradigm of international integration,
assuming increasing support for coordination and community
building after having taken the initial steps toward global networks,
left little room for discussions of how loyalty to a new and common world order would be developed. Economic rationality creates, it was assumed, an automaticity to convergence and integration.

During the 1970s the belief in the convergence of industrial
societies weakened. It became clear that structural similarities are
not necessarily accompanied by cultural rapprochement and that
cultures change slowly. International organizations and even the
European Community, which was founded mostly on the conver-

40    For an elaboration of this aspect, cf. Volkmar Gessner and
      Angelika Schade, "Conflicts of Culture in Cross-Border Legal
      Relations: The Conception of a Research Topic in the Sociology
      of Law", *Theory, Culture and Society* 7 (1990): 253–77.

gence hypothesis, had to recognize the stubbornness of national differences. Even if formal institutions are equalized, the informal ways of using them differ. For example, formal law in France protects the rights of the individual against the state much better than does formal law in Great Britain or the Netherlands. However, few French citizens have ever won court cases against the state, whereas this happens quite regularly in the Netherlands and Britain. Such informal legal-cultural realities are quite resistant to change.[41] The dominant aspect of the international arena is therefore cultural heterogeneity, which may lead to misunderstanding and conflict in all kind of legal relationships.

Convergence, however, cannot be discarded entirely. Within the immense cultural plurality of the international arena, one can easily detect relatively integrated communities that share not only institutional arrangements but also values and attitudes. Applied to our context of cross-border legal relations, there are, in the picture of Kötz,[42] not only islands of unified legal structures but also islands of common legal cultures. Some sociologists have called them "third cultures":

> As men continue to associate across societies while engaged in common enterprises, they incorporate into the efforts of their in-group, standards for interpersonal behaviour, work-related norms, codes of reciprocity, styles of life, networks of communication, institutional arrangements, world views, and on the individual level, new types of selves. These composite patterns differentiate a third culture from the culture it transcends.[43]

National borders become nearly insignificant for these communities. A detailed description of dispute resolution mechanisms in the diamond trade exemplifies the most effective institutionalization a "third culture" is able to attain.[44]

---

41    Geert Hofstede, "The Cultural Relativity of Organizational Practices and Theories", *Journal of International Business Studies* 14 (1983).

42    Kötz, "Rechtsvereinheitlichung", 1–17.

43    John Useem et al., "Men in the Middle of the Third Culture", *Human Organization* 22 (1963): 179.

44    Lisa Bernstein, "Opting Out of the Legal System: Extralegal Contractual Relations in the Diamond Industry", *Journal of Legal Studies* 21 (1992): 115–57.

Finally, even when cultural diversity is the dominant characteristic, some common regional or even common global orientations
towards cross-border interaction or at least trends towards such
orientations may be found. Speculations range from a greater ag-
gressiveness of actors in the international arena to the predominance of more flexible attitudes or, expressed in sociological terms,
fears of anomie or hopes for empathy.

These three aspects—the conflict of culture, the third culture,
and the universal culture—will be discussed briefly in relation to
our assumption that formal and informal, legal and autonomous
forms of institutionalization prevail in the international arena.

Legal literature is reluctant to admit conflicts of culture in cross-
border legal relations with the only exception being studies on
Japanese law.[45] Japan may indeed be of particular interest to demonstrate how a modern industrialized society can prosper with a
community-oriented nonindividualistic legal culture. But the discussion of how Japanese legal values influence legal behaviour of
Japanese businessmen in the international arena can easily be generalized to other legal cultures, as von Mehren notes:

> To operate effectively in transactions involving more than one legal
> system requires a kind of insight and feel that perhaps few lawyers
> have . . . . The parties may hold different conceptions of "contract"
> even though both understand the terms of the agreement.[46]

These questions of mutual misunderstandings are treated extensively by authors in the fields of international management and
international marketing"[47] probably because culture shock is con-

---

45    Cf., e.g., Guntram Rahn, *Rechtsdenken und Rechtsauffassung in
      Japan* (Munich: Beck, 1990); Danian Zhang and Kenji Kuroda,
      "Beware of Japanese Negotiation Style—How to Negotiate with
      Japanese Companies", *Northwestern Journal of International Law
      and Business* 10 (1989): 195–212.

46    Arthur von Mehren, "The Significance of Cultural and Legal Di-
      versity for International Transactions", in *Jus Privatum Gentium—
      Festschrift für Max Rheinstein* (Tübingen: Mohr, 1969), 247–58.

47    Vern Terpstra, *International Marketing* (Hinsdale, Ill.: Dryden
      Press, 1978); Philip R. Cateora and John M. Hess, *International
      Marketing* (Homewood, Ill.: Irwin, 1979); Rabindra N. Kanungo
      and Richard W. Wight, "A Cross-Cultural Comparative Study of
      Managerial Job Attitudes", *Journal of International Business Stud-*

sidered an important cost factor in international business transactions. Among the dimensions of cultural diversity elaborated by this kind of research, "uncertainty avoidance" seems to be of special significance for sociolegal interests.[48] In "weak uncertainty avoidance cultures" risks are taken rather easily and planning of the future is not taken too seriously. "Strong uncertainty avoidance societies", on the other hand, try to create security by all possible means, formal rules and institutions being among the most important ones. If, for example, India belongs to the first group and Germany to the second, contract drafting between firms from each of these countries will have a different cultural background. The German firm will probably insist on a detailed regulation of the business relationship and will also insist on its complete performance, whereas the Indian firm will show a more relaxed and flexible attitude towards drafting and fulfilment. The same applies to public legal security regulation (safety of products, environmental risks, safety of transport) in both countries.

Legal orientations and attitudes of international actors belonging to a third culture seem to be too specific to allow generalizations. The international cocaine Mafia or the dealers in war material have obviously quite different norms in common than the enterprises which are members of the Cotton or Coffee Stock Exchange or the COTIF (*Convention relative aux transports internationaux ferroviaires*). They all probably share the view that conflicts should be resolved by autonomous procedures and that state intervention should be avoided. It is also to be expected that the independence of third cultures from national legal cultures is only relative and that often there is even a dominant influence of one of the legal cultures. Systems approaches or even autopoietic theories, if applied to third cultures, would certainly exaggerate the autonomy of these business communities, but their aim to bridge cultural differences by creating a necessary minimum of common orientations is certainly achieved.

ies 14 (1983): 115–29; Nancy J. Adler, "A Typology of Management Studies Involving Culture", *Journal of International Business Studies* 14 (1983): 29–47.

48    Geert Hofstede, *Culture's Consequences: International Differences in Work-Related Values*, (Beverly Hills and London: Sage, 1980); Geert Hofstede, "The Cultural Relativity of Organizational Practices and Theories", *Journal of Business Studies* 14 (1983): 75–89.

As regards universal attitudes towards cross-border interaction, the prevailing assumption in the literature seems to be that actors liberated from domestic social control behave aggressively and unscrupulously. This is the anomie hypothesis, which is indeed confirmed by much empirical data.[49] The opposite view supports Luhmann with his idea of the cognitively oriented "world society".[50] Empirically this assumption is only supported for long-term relationships and third cultures where renegotiations of contractual agreements are more frequent than normative sanctions. But this is true also for domestic legal behaviour. The trend towards cognitive rationality is also observed by scholars in the field of International Relations Research who believe that networking leads to mutual understanding and the reduction of the risk of war. Whether these hypotheses can be applied to private legal behaviour in the international arena is rather doubtful.

It is not by chance that some authors link the development of a universal legal culture closely to the ethical standards of the legal profession. It is the transnational lawyer who works out sophisticated contracts and new financial instruments, who participates in negotiations and arbitration procedures, and who represents national and foreign clients in court. He/she either imposes his/her own legal culture or rather tries to understand the foreign legal mind in order "to bridge the cultural gap".[51] Legal education, at least in the United States, seems to foster the second alternative by teaching comparative law and by facilitating legal practice abroad. But there is also a tendency to dilute the conception of professionalism and to eliminate the incompatibilities, which, on the national level, justify the existence and the privileges of this group of individuals.[52] Dezalay observes this disappearance of the "gentleman lawyer" in the international practice and the uprising of a new generation of "yuppie lawyers", highly competent businessmen

49    Gessner and Schade, "Conflicts of Culture in Cross-Border Legal Relations", 269.
50    Niklas Luhmann, "The World Society as a Social System".
51    Cf. Goebel, "Professional Qualification and Educational Requirements for Law Practice in a Foreign Country", 443–523.
52    H. Patrick Glenn, "Private International Law and the New International Legal Profession", in *Mélanges en l'Honneur d'Alfred von Overbeck* (Fribourg. Editions Universitaires Fribourg, Suisse, 1990), 31–45.

who sell law as a technical know-how to everybody and for every purpose.[53] Attempts are made to develop a transnational form of professional governance that will meet the needs of transnational practice, for example, the Code of Deontology of the Advocates of the European Community, adopted in Strasbourg in 1988.

A second arena where transnational legal culture is defined is the operation of transnational corporations. Following disclosures in the mid-1970s about payments made by Lockheed and other companies to government officials, the United States called for the preparation of an agreement to outlaw corrupt practices by transnational corporations. In 1976 OECD adopted a normative Declaration on International Investment and Multinational Enterprises. This spelled out obligations for transnational corporations in eight areas: general policies, disclosure of information, competition, financing, taxation, employment, industrial relations, and science and technology. The regulatory power of such codes of conduct or model statements remains to be seen.

Legal integration is so far exclusively treated by comparative lawyers with their disciplinary limitation of being normative as regards the goals and descriptive as regards the methods. Theory-building has never been the domain of comparative law. Hence, in spite of considerable research resources spent for problems of legal integration, we know next to nothing about social processes in the arena of private cross-border interactions and about cultural phenomena such as values and behavioural patterns. Theory-building must from the outset refrain from romantic ideas of stateless order of the world society but rather focus on new forms of legal interaction, of influencing behaviour and of dispute resolution, and observe in all cases both private and state regulation.[54] In par-

53    Dezalay, "The Big Bang and the Law", 279–93.
54    Thomas W. Wälde offers more examples of the intertwining of state and economy in international relations; cf. Thomas W. Wälde, "Rechtsformen der Verflechtung von Staat und Wirtschaft im Bereich internationaler Wirtschaftsbeziehungen: Zwischenstaatliche Kooperationsabkommen und Modellverträge internationaler staatlicher Organisationen", in *Rechtsformen der Verflechtung von Staat und Wirtschaft, Jahrbuch für Rechtssoziologie und Rechtstheorie* 8, ed. Volkmar Gessner and Gerd Winter (Opladen: Westdeutscher Verlag, 1982), 372–90.

ticular theory-building must take into account the great variety of arenas where cross-border interactions take place.

### III. Institutional Framework for International Litigation

Historically, one has to go far back in order to find special courts for international matters. In the Roman Empire the *praetor* had jurisdiction only in cases originating from a Roman citizen. An additional court was created to deal with foreign actions: the *praetor peregrinus*. This judge had to apply the *jus gentium*, not the *jus civile*, if one of the parties of the lawsuit was not a Roman citizen. This "universal" *jus gentium* (albeit of Roman origin and not a product of international conventions) was a precursor of modern uniform law and succeeded in avoiding the conflict of laws situation. When in 212 A.D. the Roman citizenship was extended to all free men of the Roman Empire, this judge disappeared (and the *Corpus Juris Civilis* did not have to deal with conflicts of laws either).

Medieval Europe was again split into a great number of jurisdictions where only local law (*lex fori*) was applied. With the beginning of long-distance trade around the tenth century, more and more institutions were set up, which in modern language could be called international commercial tribunals. Merchants of long-distance trade offered their goods at fairs and markets and developed their own norms and customs, which were enforced on the spot by merchant judges.

The "law merchant" was a case-law system applied on the continent as well as in England where it replaced the common law in the staple courts and the pie-powder-courts.[55] In addition special rules were created by maritime trade and enforced by admiralty courts in England and similar institutions in the Hanse cities of northern Germany, and in Italy, Spain, and France. A unique characteristic of these courts was their "international", or, rather, multicultural, composition: the judges sitting in panels frequently came from different cities, regions, and countries (and probably knew some Latin as their common language, because they also used the term *lex mercatoria* for the law they created and applied). This international jurisdiction seems to have been competent, speedy, and highly recognized.

55    J. H. Baker, "The Law Merchant and the Common Law Before 1700", *Cambridge Law Journal* 38 (1979): 295–322.

This institutionalization of international commercial litigation waned at the end of medieval Europe when Europe became divided into national states. In modern Europe these merchant courts disappeared or became transformed into state courts. The *lex mercatoria* was transformed into state law, and the judges had to go through their country's legal education and lost completely their universal perspective. Private international law had to bear the burden of nationalizing international cases by defining the applicable (national) law and the competent (national) jurisdiction for every single legal situation.

The steps taken in the twentieth century to cope with international cases in judicial proceedings consisted mainly in bilateral and then multilateral conventions for recognition and enforcement of foreign judgements in civil and commercial matters (culminating in the Brussels Convention of 1968 and the Lugano Convention of 1988, now embracing most European countries). Other conventions try to facilitate the service of process and the taking of evidence abroad, the legalization of documents, the custody of children, and so forth. But the basic pattern that courts are national institutions with virtually no knowledge of other legal systems and other legal cultures remains unchanged and is even strengthened by the increasing number of statutes produced by legislative bodies in all modern legal orders.

Institutions, according to North, reduce transaction costs by reducing the uncertainties of economic exchange. But they may be ineffective and then even increase transaction costs. This could be true for national courts in international matters: they may be inexperienced, inadequately organized for this type of case, or even biased against foreign parties. They may or may not be able to consider foreign elements of the cases, understand other legal systems and legal cultures, or be familiar with the impressive number of uniform laws and international conventions briefly described above. These questions define a research programme for legal sociology to which we attempt to contribute in this volume.

## Abstract

World society, although poorly conceptualized by sociology, is the only conceivable reference point for attempts to explain patterns of global interaction. The article attempts to provide a brief overview of legal and legal-cultural patterns—or "institutions" in the sense of Douglass C. North—that structure the international arena for nonstate actors: private international law, unified law, and the norms of the law merchant.

Their success in reducing legal uncertainty is estimated to be rather limited due to the reluctance of state and economic actors in recognizing their legitimacy or practicability. This does not necessarily lead to anomic situations but certainly to great regulatory gaps with the effect of unequal distribution of opportunities for actors to step into the global arena. Some multinational enterprises or members of third cultures, such as banks, insurance institutions, or diamond traders interact without any problems in the global market. Others, such as small enterprises or private individuals, suffer from legal uncertainty. The article discusses the support structures created for such "anonymous" actors, one being domestic courts. Their dilemma of having to decide international cases in a national context, with domestic legal education and little information about foreign legal developments, has led to various attempts on the level of bilateral or international conventions in order to at least facilitate their tasks when foreign parties appear as litigants. The article ends by questioning the ability of domestic courts to reduce transaction costs and by formulating empirical questions for this new field of legal sociological research.

## The Author

Volkmar Gessner. Degrees in Law and Sociology. Prior practice as lawyer and as judge. Currently Professor of Comparative Law and Sociology of Law at the University of Bremen, Germany. Research areas (mainly empirical) lie in the fields of litigation in national and international contexts, alternating forms of dispute resolution, legal culture and globalization of law. Heavy involvement also in policy research for the German government and the European Commission.
*Address*: ZERP, Universitätsallee GW 1, 28359 Bremen, Germany.
*e-mail*: VGESSNER@ZERP.uni-bremen.de

# 2  Cross-Border Legal Interactions in New York Courts

HANNO VON FREYHOLD

## I. Introduction

### A. New York as the Marketplace for the International Legal Business

Studying the handling of cross-border interactions in New York seemed a particularly interesting and challenging task. New York[1] is an important marketplace for international commerce, finance, insurance, and many other areas. New York has a high foreign population percentage, and a large number of international business enterprises from all over the world are represented in one way or another, having headquarters, subsidiaries, branch offices, or agents in New York. Almost every country has a mission to the U.N. located in New York. Within the other boroughs of New York and neighbouring New Jersey,[2] there are three major com-

---

[1]   Technically, there is the state of New York with a population of 18 million, having its capital in Albany, New York; the city of New York, consisting of the five boroughs of Brooklyn, Bronx, Queens, Staten Island, and New York City, with a total population of 8.5 million; and there is New York County, i.e., New York City, or New York, N.Y., which is the island of Manhattan, with a population of 1.5 million. The greater metropolitan area of New York with neighbouring New Jersey and Connecticut (tri-state area) has a total population of 18 million. *Source*: U.S. Bureau of Statistics, *Statistical Abstract of the United States: 1992* (Washington, D.C.: U.S. Government Printing Office, 1992, 112th ed.). Generally, herein, the term "New York" is used for New York City.

[2]   The airports and seaports are jointly administered by the "Port Authority of New York and New Jersey".

mercial international airports that also serve as gateways to the
U.S. as well as major seaport facilities in the near vicinity.

All these activities create legal needs, which lawyers come to
meet. It is no surprise that the number of lawyers in total and per
capita is unusually high in New York, second in the U.S. only to
Washington, D.C.[3]

Yet there is more to New York as a legal marketplace than only
being a major business place. As shall be described, New York
lawyers not only serve parties in New York but worldwide. Quite
a number of large international business deals that have no connection to New York are negotiated and contracted by New York
lawyers.[4] Furthermore a number of standard contract forms, particularly in maritime trade,[5] as well as individual contracts, contain New York law and jurisdiction (or arbitration) clauses. Thus,
New York law firms have developed a special expertise in international business transactions,[6] which, conversely, has had an influence on the law commonly used for these transactions and which
has led to further utilization of these law firms.

Furthermore, advanced by these law firms, the New York leg-
islature and courts have developed laws that are particularly inviting for international business. New York has an exceptionally
strong doctrine in favour of freedom in contracting, including, but
not limited to, the organization of companies and their internal
structure and the personal liability of officers and directors. Only
the state of Delaware, which has traditionally attempted to derive
an income from corporations incorporating in that state, com-

3    Barbara A. Curran, et al., *The Lawyer Statistical Report: A Sta-
     tistical Profile of the U.S. Legal Profession in the 1980's* (Chi-
     cago: American Bar Foundation, 1985).

4    See John Flood, *The Legal Profession in the United States*, 3rd
     ed. (Chicago: American Bar Foundation, 1985); Yves Dezalay,
     "The Big Bang and the Law: The Internationalization and
     Restructuration of the Legal Field", *Theory Culture & Society* 7
     (1990): 279–93.

5    Such as charter parties and bills of lading, see, e.g., the standard
     forms: New York Produce Exchange Form, Vegoilvoy, Asba-
     tankvoy, NORGRAIN.

6    Erwin Cherovsky, *The Guide to New York Law Firms* (New York:
     St. Martin's Press, 1991), 6.

petes with New York in the attraction of subsidiaries.[7] In both states, liberal organization, limitation of liability for officers, and a low minimum franchise tax are attractive incentives.[8] Due to ease of procedure and the access to infrastructure, New York is especially attractive for small foreign corporations to form subsidiaries, as the procedure of organization is a little less expensive in New York, and, if business actually needs to be done from New York, the incorporation of a subsidiary eliminates the need of obtaining a licence to do business in New York as a foreign corporation which would otherwise be required. In addition, labour laws in New York are favourable to employers and afford freedom of contracting as well as a "hire and fire at will" doctrine. Delaware, on the other hand, is probably more interesting for large corporations as the franchise tax does not increase with volume and because the laws are still more liberal in terms of organizational structure and the limitation of liability for officers and directors.

New York's jurisdictional rules have an exceptionally "long arm" but also favour, more than other jurisdictions within the U.S. and maybe in the world, the recognition of foreign law, foreign judgements, and arbitration awards. New York laws also give foreign lawyers easier access to take the New York bar exam,[9] to

7      More than 600,000 new corporations were incorporated in the year 1991. The highest number of new incorporations were in Florida (80,000), followed by New York (70,000), California and Texas (35–40,000 each), and Delaware, Illinois, and New Jersey (almost 30,000 each). *Source*: U.S. Bureau of Statistics, *Statistical Abstract of the United States: 1992*. The large number for Florida is due to the high number of estate-tax shelters in the state.

8      For a short description in German, see, Werner Walbröl, "Gesetzlicher Rahmen und wirtschaftliche Bedingungen in den USA für Beteiligungen und Kooperationen deutscher Unternehmen", in *Handbuch der Internationalen Unternehmenstätigkeit*, ed. Brij Nino Kumar and Helmut Hausmann (Munich: C.H. Beck, 1992); For fundamentals, see Carlos L. Israels and Alan M. Hoffman, *Israels on Corporate Practice*, 4th ed. (New York: Practising Law Institute, 1983).

9      In the United States, only Washington, D.C., provides for an almost similar access to the bar. See Curran, et al., *The Lawyer Statistical Report*.

appear before court in one or the other capacity, or to join a New York law firm than most other jurisdictions in the world. This enables large law firms to employ foreign lawyers and add their expertise, and foreign lawyers to take the New York bar exam. When these foreign lawyers return to their countries, they will most likely favour New York law and jurisdiction clauses whenever they have to resort to a jurisdiction other than their own.

Finally, New York has one of the most developed legal systems in the U.S. The highly developed economy, together with the lawyers, create a demand for constant adaptation of the law to progress, and such developments often serve as a role model for other states and even abroad. Strict product liability and parts of the business corporation laws and the procedural codes—to mention a few—have been adopted elsewhere after being introduced in New York.

In effect, the factors mentioned have made New York an important marketplace for international legal services. So far, however, little research has been done on the actors and the actual handling of international matters in New York.

## B. Transborder Interactions

The title of this chapter needs some explanation. There are few terms that sufficiently describe interactions between individuals and corporations of different residence or nationality. The subject of interest here is exactly this kind of "cross-border" interaction. *International*, in legal language, commonly is used to designate activity among nation-states, as in the U.N. and other settings. In common language, however, *international* has a broader meaning, which includes both aspects; for example, an international telephone call, international trade, or international air transport are rarely matters between the governments alone. Furthermore, in civil-law countries it is common to term "conflicts of law" as "private international law". Thus, while *cross-border* or *transborder* are the more precise and appropriate terms, *international* shall also be used herein interchangeably.[10]

An international matter is, for the purpose of this study, a matter where cross-border activities are involved or anticipated or

---

10    See also Gary B. Born and David Westin, *International Civil Litigation in United States Courts: Cases and Materials,* 2nd ed. (Deventer and Boston: Kluwer, 1992) for their terms.

where at least two actors reside or have their place of business in different countries, whereas an international case is a case where at least two actors reside or have their place of business in different countries and which has become pending in a court or other formal forum.

Thus, for the purpose of this empirical research, international matters and cases have been restricted to legal transactions between actors residing in different countries. Whereas many civil-law countries' conflict of law rules use nationality as one potential aspect governing the applicable law, there are two reasons not to distinguish parties according to nationality. The nationality of a party, whether individual or corporate, is rarely mentioned in court records and thus cannot practically be determined in any empirical research of files or judgements.

Second, the insignificance of nationality makes a distinction according to nationality in any case not worthwhile: a party that is domiciled or resident in a jurisdiction has sufficient ties to that jurisdiction to be considered local for all means but a few. Many of the migration-related legal problems are of an administrative nature, and where the interaction is with persons or institutions at the (new) place of residence, the interaction sphere is domestic rather than with an international character. A local resident of foreign nationality can be served upon easily, has approximate knowledge of the language and customs and the means to participate sufficiently in a proceeding at least equally to a national, and by his or her residence has willingly accepted to be subject to the court's jurisdiction and laws. In addition, the United States' conflict of law and jurisdictional rules give little regard to the nationality of a party. Thus, for all practical purposes a foreign national resident is no different from a native.

It is the cases that involve business and private transactions, service of process, participation, and enforcement across borders that are truly international and that are the subject of this study.

## C. Fields of Interaction

A description seems necessary to divide the fields of potential cross-border legal interactions. There are basically two different approaches to define the fields of interaction, based either on a particular field or on the type of actors and their relationship. Both shall be examined in turn.

If one distinguishes by fields, one takes into account that cross-border legal interactions are generally caused by four different

activities. First, *trade* of merchandise, know-how, services, and fi-
nances is the most significant aspect of cross-border legal interaction; second is *internationalization*, the expansion of business activities by creation of dependants; third, *migration*; and fourth,
*travel* as its own activity, for tourism, business, education, or any
other temporary purpose. The borderlines between the categories
are not entirely clear, and they are partially dependent. Travel creates trade of services, internationalization is a strategy to promote
trade and creates migration by employees, and migration requires
travelling, and leads to further travelling for family reasons.

The other distinction focuses on the actors and the place of
action, which may be personal interaction, interaction between
business partners in an office, an attorney-client interaction, or
interaction in court. This approach focuses, inter alia, on the role-
playing performed by the actors involved.

Both approaches are used, throughout this study, where they
seem to explain particular patterns.

## 1. Trade

As mentioned, international trade is extensive and growing. Due
to the importance of the financial values involved, trade is also
one of the most important fields of legal interaction, domestically
and internationally. Thus, it is also one of the most important fields
in which legal norms are developed.[11]

Furthermore, the normative concepts of trade are quite similar
all over the industrialized world. Thus it is no wonder that commercial laws and trade laws are not only similar, but are areas
with quite significant developments in terms of international conventions, which attempt to further harmonize the laws, at least
where international trade is concerned.

As a result, one should expect largely *harmonized* legal norms
and a significant extent of *legal security* in cross-border legal interactions based on commercial trade. On the other hand, this
legal security may be overshadowed by remaining *cultural insecurity* with regard to the actors involved. It is the minor differences
in the law, in spite of overall similarity, different use of law, per-

---

11    See Volkmar Gessner and Angelika Schade, "Conflicts of Culture
      in Cross-Border Legal Relations: The Conception of a Research
      Topic in the Sociology of Law", *Theory, Culture and Society* 7
      (1990) 253–77.

sonal behaviour in communications, and, in particular, distance, which may create difficulties.

## 2. Internationalization

Connected to, but different from trade is the internationalization of extraction, agricultural and industrial production, and sales and services. Certain areas such as commodity trade are handled almost exclusively by TNCs or other international conglomerates. Industrial insurance business is handled worldwide by agents or subsidiaries. Production of mass goods is channelled worldwide through subsidiaries, joint ventures, and licensing/franchising.[12]

Regardless of the type of transaction of this kind, a characteristic feature is usually their singularity. The organization of a subsidiary, a joint venture, or licensing of production is ordinarily a rare event for any entity. Even as regards name, sales, or service franchises, more than a few hundred franchisees rarely are contracted with by a single party. The legal issues are usually involved and the agreements are accordingly complex. All these activities create a need for complex legal structuring handled by sophisticated in-house legal departments or international law firms, often on both sides of the transaction.

The legal issues may be complex, involving monetary aspects as well as intellectual property and reputation, be they legally protected or not. Yet the singularity of the transactions allow for negotiations and adjustments for the interests of both sides, if such sides exist. Moreover, most of these transactions are designed for longevity—for several years—and it is in the interest of both parties to promote mutual benefit, a factor that should lead to understanding and to successful renegotiations in the event any circumstances change. These factors should lead to a certain degree of *security* in general and to the nonnormative reaction of renegotiations where differences occur.

However, the duration, the intensity of contact, and the financial sums involved with regard to these relationships bear particular risks. The potential sources for differing interests or just cultural misunderstandings are higher than in single transactions. In

---

12    An aspect that may be politically problematic is the farming out of labour-intensive manufacturing from industrial countries to low-wage areas.

addition, it is more difficult for the parties to walk away from each other once a conflict arises. The nonnormative reaction of abandoning is not available. Where settlement fails, normative reaction is likely.

Contracts, and complex contracts in particular, are said to contain definition clauses, performance clauses, risk/liability clauses, and procedural clauses. In the event of irresolvable conflict, the two latter parts of the structuring contract meet their test by a legal system. The security is replaced by *insecurity*.

### 3. Migration

Migration is the most important source of individual cross-border legal problems. These problems begin with travel and transport and immigration, continue with employment law, tax, social security, housing, and other aspects of the transition between the countries involved, and may continue for the immigrant's entire life, regardless of whether the immigrant stays, moves further, or returns to the "home" country.

A swift look at the law of conflicts of law, statutes, and cases reveals the intricacy of the legal issues of matrimonial, family, child custody, and estate law for migrants. From a legal point of view, a migrant is never at home anywhere. The legal insecurity resulting from this situation creates legal needs that must be met.

Unfortunately, legal services are expensive, and usually the individual must foot the bill. Furthermore, whereas corporations usually have contacts or even standing relationships with lawyers, individuals generally have problems of access to legal services, more so in a foreign country. Also, not all lawyers are qualified to deal with said intricacies, and the problem of selection is added. While people may often be incompetent in many legal fields of their own culture, a foreigner is even more so. Legal *insecurity* is the result. Also, while conflicts are generally avoided, many of the above legal aspects, because of either the law or the stakes, do not allow for amicable out-of-court resolution. This does not mean that these conflicts, which take place within the host country, are necessarily of an "international" nature.

Only over time, as the migrant becomes part of the new society, are some of the obstacles eased and does security become available. Often there is a group to which the individual can turn for emotional assistance and practical advice and thus a certain degree of *security*.

## 4. *Travel*

The most important aspects of travelling do not usually create transborder legal interactions or conflicts. In most cases, particularly tourism, the contracting for the travelling itself is made in the traveller's home country, subject to domestic laws, jurisdiction, and enforcement. Where foreign entities provide services, the travel is through agents and subsidiaries and is a trade activity or an internationalization activity that need not concern the traveller. Even third-party services performed for the tourist abroad are often held by courts to be included in the original travel contract, and are noninternational.[13] Thus, many aspects of travel are domestic, and thus *secure and normative.*

Being temporarily in the foreign country the traveller does not have the time to fully adapt his or her normative expectations. Yet the traveller might easily realize, beforehand or through actual frustrations, the different culture in the foreign country and the resulting different norms. Furthermore, the rather temporary stay in the foreign country makes it virtually impossible to make any legal claim or even commence action while there, and pursuing the claim from home is met with severe difficulties. In such cases, transborder legal interactions resulting from travelling are subject to *insecurity.* Thus, cross-border legal interaction is avoided, and many legal disputes are of a very involuntary nature, such as car accidents and the like.

## 5. *Summary*

In all fields that are sources for transborder legal interactions, there are areas of relative security and others of relative insecurity. The specific mechanisms thereof, the strategies employed in moving the borders towards more security, and the factors that defeat this goal are the subject of this study.

## D. Legal Interactions and Institutions

Legal interactions (actually, the legal part of interactions) take place when the actors believe that their interaction is of legal consequence and that rights and obligations are created that can be dealt with in categories of legal institutions.[14] Thus, where norms

---

13  See the German discussion, e.g., OLG Frankfurt, NJW-RR 1989, 1018, OLG Stuttgart NJW 1990, 1081.

14  Roger Cotterell, *The Sociology of Law: An Introduction* (London: Butterworths, 1984), 3, fn. 2.

are involved—many of which are legal norms—legal institutions become involved in the resolution of frustrations. In transborder interactions, regardless of which norms are eventually violated, the law and legal institutions that become available for the frustrated actor for sanctions may be from the country of either of the actors or even from a third country. The legal institutions may have different norms than the ones an actor has expected, or, if the actor attempts sanctions through legal institutions that are based on the actor's own norms, these legal institutions may lack any reasonable means of enforcement. Whichever way the actor chooses, it could mean that sanctions are really not available for such norms and little remains that is not anomic. In addition, in transborder interactions we are faced in part with the unusual situation that social control is at a minimum, which is quite irritating for the parties involved. On the other hand, this could also be a situation where we could find law in its purest sense: only law and no social control.[15] However, it also seems that if, in fact, there is law, the matter is rarely ever brought to court and offenders are rarely brought to justice. A subject of this study shall therefore also be the reaction of the law and legal institutions to transborder interactions.

Lawyers, courts, and state institutions, assigned the official role of organizing and structuring legal interactions and of resolving conflicts arising out of the same, can be summarized as legal institutions. It should be noted that harmonized law or international treaties between nations are not autonomous but a part (which could possibly be called an enhancement) of legalized fields of action.

The courts—the judicial branch—are usually regarded as the ultimate institutions that interpret and guard the normative law. Whatever conflict, whatever contract, the availability of the courts and their interpretation of the law is the penultimate step to enforcement. As self-help justice is commonly regarded as inappropriate in our societies, the courts, and ultimately the enforcing agencies, have the role of enforcing legal norms. Thus, in the context of our study, it must be asked whether the courts are adequately performing this function. Even though most conflicts are never brought to court, the potential result if the dispute were in fact

15    See Volkmar Gessner, *Global Approaches in the Sociology of Law, Problems and Challenges* Journal of Law and Society 22 (1995):85–95.

brought to court guides the actors to some extent in their out-of-court resolution, even as early as in contract drafting.[16]

In economic terms, in order to adequately perform their functions, it is generally assumed that courts must be available, expedient, and cost effective, and must provide adequate and calculable results. To be inadequate, the opposite is true, they would be unavailable, time consuming, expensive, or provide inadequate or risky results. All of these factors are somewhat dependent on each other and are relative to each other. An extremely time-consuming procedure is also expensive and may amount to unavailability of justice, yet even high expenses may be justified if the result is rewarding. Thus, in a purely economic analysis, these factors have to be taken into consideration. Yet these factors are also relative to the circumstances and the parties. It cannot be predetermined, unless the specific circumstances are known, whether a speedy and negative resolution or a positive but time-consuming resolution is more favourable. Furthermore, under some circumstances some parties, particularly defendants, may prefer losing a case late to losing it earlier, if legal costs do not play a role.

One more aspect needs to be discussed. While it is the aim of this study to analyse the adequacy of the courts for transborder legal interactions, there may be some doubts as to the domestic adequacy as well. To further discuss this issue would be beyond the scope of this thesis. However, some of the results of this study may contribute to the discussion in that area.

Lawyers take roles both as legal institutions, when they interact within legalized (normatively controlled) fields of action, and within autonomous (nonstate) fields of interaction. Nonstate stable norms may be produced by autonomous institutions, such as trade associations, organizations and arbitrators, on a macro level. A contract may constitute an autonomous ministructure of norms. Yet, in court, lawyers are part of the state-controlled legal normative system and can be expected to adapt their behaviour accordingly. This may cause particular problems with their clients, which, however, will remain beyond the scope of this court-based study and needs to be analysed in further research.

16  Shadow of the law discussion in Marc Galanter, "The Radiating Effects of Courts", in *Empirical Theories About Courts*, ed. Keith O. Boyum and Lynn Mather (New York and London: Longman, 1983), 117 et seq.

In the broadest sense, this study is guided by two main assumptions. On the one hand, it assumes that cross-border legal conflicts are different from domestic legal conflicts. On the other hand, it assumes that the general infrastructure of the law deals inadequately with said differences and that various structures and institutions have developed that attempt to solve these conflicts in a more adequate fashion. These attempts can generally be divided into two different strains. One strain can be termed "techniques to circumvent the legal structure", while the other can be termed "the attempt to redefine the legal structure". This study, however, will only touch on these strategies as it is devoted to the legal structure itself and, more specifically, to the courts and procedures therein.[17]

What the study will be looking for in particular is signs of lack of norms, of lack of enforcement, of low-norm situations, of insecurity, and of strategies to deal with these problems.

With regard to anomie, the *lack of norms* is the first aspect to be shown. A theoretical discussion would map the normative and the nonnormative areas from a legal perspective. The analysis of cases and judgements would show the extent to which legal institutions are able to find adequate solutions to the conflicts before them.

The *lack of enforcement* could be shown by the analysis of cases and would be reflected by extremely long procedures, a high number of withdrawals, and a low number of judgements, particularly judgements in favour of the plaintiff. In addition, interviews with practitioners as well as practice literature in this area should reflect statements that counsel against litigation and emphasize the difficulties of international litigation and the enforcement of judgements, if any.

As discussed, in the context of transborder legal transactions the *low-norm situation* should be reflected by a marked insecurity about the norms that will guide such transactions. Either partner in such a transaction would necessarily be insecure about the other party's expectations as well as about the other party's compliance. In a court-based study, these items are difficult to find.

To examine the extent of *insecurity* involved, further evidence is necessary to prove the existence of insecurity. The sources and

17    Keith O. Boyum, "Introduction: Toward Empirical Theories About Courts", in *Empirical Theories About Courts*, ed. Keith O. Boyum and Lynn Mather (New York and London: Longman, 1983), 1 et seq.

reasons for the insecurity have to be described in more detail. Interviews with primary and secondary actors must be weighed in
light of professional displays of competence. Language used by
judges in written decisions, and to some extent the legal literature's discourse, can show the legal system's reaction and its attitude towards the specific situation.

With regard to circumvention strategies, by design, these will
only be found in court where they fail. To find those (hopefully
rare) events should be rather rewarding, indeed.

As to solution strategies and the development of autonomous
law and an independent third (legal) culture, the practice of the
main actors in this area is decisive—and these are not the courts.

The empirical studies more specifically outlined below include
a court file analysis and a judgement analysis. Where useful, the
results of interviews with a random selection of New York attorneys and the author's own experience at a New York law firm that
specialized in international legal transactions shall assist in inter-
preting the results.

## E. The Study

Several empirical studies described more specifically below
were undertaken to examine the practical aspects of transborder
legal relationships and shed new light on the legal and scholarly
discussions. The overall goal of this study was to research and
describe the handling of international legal transactions in New
York. The assumptions were to be examined in a variety of empirical studies. Successes and failures to adequately solve the particular problems of international legal transactions needed to be
determined and evaluated and the reasons analysed in light of legal and scholarly discussions.

### 1. Court File Analysis at the New York
### Supreme Court

In this part of the study, court files in a New York court were
analysed in order to determine how matters involving foreign parties are handled by the judicial system, whether there would be an
effective dispute resolution, and whether there would be any difference between matters involving only domestic parties and matters involving a foreign party.

The New York Supreme Court handles approximately 30,000
civil matters of first instance every year, exclusive of appeals, matrimonial matters, tax matters, and some matters brought by or

against the city of New York.[18] In order to determine the amount of time consumed for different stages of the proceedings, as well as the ultimate resolution of such proceedings, it was decided that the basis for the study should be a few years back in time. For practical reasons (accessibility of files, avoiding disturbance of day-to-day court operations) the year 1986 served as the basis for the study. In 1986, 29,973 general civil matters were filed.[19] On a random basis a sample of 2200 cases was taken using the court's file number assignment system, which assigns numbers on a continuous basis by the date and time the case is filed with the court.[20]

Since no record, except for the files, is kept with regard to the parties' residence, there is no way to determine whether any party to a proceeding is foreign, except by actually reviewing the file. The files are kept in order of their filing number in the form of an open envelope, which, in the standard case, includes:

• a pink file number purchase invoice form, which states the names of the parties and their attorneys, the date of filing, and the date of service if the same was accomplished before filing;

• a summons form, stating the full name and address of the parties, their attorneys, and the alleged basis of the venue; in addition, the summons form may include a simplified complaint if the same is not filed additionally in the form of a verified complaint;

• a verified complaint, stating the facts of the case and the request for judgement against the defendant(s); and

• an affidavit of service of process of the summons and complaint on the defendant(s).

18    *Ninth Annual Report of the Chief Administrator of the Courts* (Albany, N.Y., 1987); the official data mention 40,000 cases, which includes cases by and against the city, tax certiorary, and some other nongeneral civil matters.

19    By the author's own observation in the archive.

20    Until recently, it was not necessary in most cases in New York courts to file a lawsuit with the court prior to service of the summons and complaint to the defendant(s). A plaintiff had the option of commencing action by service on the defendant(s). At any time, prior to or after such service, a file number could be "purchased" by either side, but no papers needed to be filed at the same time. Such filing of papers (and the purchase of a file number) would only be needed if one side wished to move the court for any action.

In addition the file may contain the defendant's response, motion papers, memoranda of law, transcripts of hearings, and supporting documentation to such papers as well as court orders and decisions.

However, summons and complaint are not always filed, the parties' residence is not always indicated on the file number purchase invoice form, and the residence of the parties is not always mentioned in a complaint or indicated on the summons, if any. Frequently, even at the place on the form usually used for the summons, the parties' address is replaced by their attorneys'. It should also be noted as a *caveat* that a few times the file retrieved contained only the purchase slip or some other very limited information without any reference whatsoever to the claim or the parties. Theoretically, some of these could have been international cases. Eventually, out of the 2200 cases, 34 cross-border cases were found and subjected to further analysis.

## 2. Judgement Analysis

In addition to the evaluation of actual files, a research of all international civil judgements decided in the year 1992 in New York State and published in the LEXIS[21] legal database was conducted.[22] The year 1992 was chosen as the most recent full year during the

21     LEXIS(c) is an online service designed for American lawyers to help simplify legal research. The U.S. legal system is largely based on common law and precedent, and lawyers preparing a case need to search for prior rulings. With hundreds of thousands of cases filling up the shelves of libraries and more cases being decided daily, a cite and word search utility such as LEXIS (and WESTLAW(c), a competing company's product) provide a simple and time-saving tool for research. For many cases the expensive fees of these services have to be compared to the lawyers' hourly rates. Today LEXIS covers almost all cases published since WW II, even earlier for some jurisdictions, and also a number of cases not published elsewhere. In addition it contains statutes and regulations, all U.S. patent filings, and administrative decisions in many areas. Access is provided via telephone line and a modem from any personal computer.

22     Wagner-Döbler and Philipps have discussed the usefulness of computerized legal data bases in assisting in the compilation of a suitable data basis for legal sociological research: Roland

conduct of the study. Other than the file research, it was not necessary to include a grace period for the resolution of the litigation,
since these cases had already found a procedural resolution of the
question before the court (at least temporarily, in any event).

After several trial runs with various search words and combinations thereof, it was determined that a search by country names
would bring the most comprehensive result. In fact every judgement found by any other key words tested (for example, "international", "comity", "foreign", "convention", "*forum non
conveniens*", "recognition", "country", "AG", "GmbH", "S.A.",
"SpA", and so on) was also found by country names. On the other
hand, many more were found by country names than by all other
key words and combinations thereof. Thus a key-word search was
conducted on LEXIS using country names (including wildcards,
aliases, variations, and combinations) from the U.N. member list
and geographical atlases, for all civil judgements of New York
courts (state and federal) for the year 1992. The files thus found
were scanned in several steps for false entries (for example, "John
German" or instances of case law with foreign country names)
and for duplicates, where more than one country name appeared
within a case. The remaining 380 judgements were downloaded,
converted, and stored on disk.

*3. Interviews with Lawyers*
As part of the entire project eleven lawyers were interviewed. For
this purpose, lawyers were selected on a randomized basis from
the New York legal directory. Because the interviews aimed at a
large variety of types of legal practices, the selection was made
from the court list rather than the Martindale/Hubbell legal directory, which is organized by firms and may not contain all New
York lawyers. Whenever two attorneys were in the same firm, the
firm was only contacted once. Thus, smaller law firms received a
better chance. Further, the firms were contacted, not with the request to talk to the attorney selected, but with an attorney the firm

Wagner-Döbler and Lothar Phillips, "Argumentative Leitbegriffe:
Ein Experiment in computergestützter Analyse juristischer
Urteilstexte aus den Jahren 1950–1992", *Zeitschrift für
Rechtssoziologie* (1993): 257–79.

proposed for a conversation on "international" matters. Twenty law firms were contacted by telephone. Eight firms stated that they had no knowledge of or prior experience with international matters. With two firms, it was not possible to arrange for an interview. With the remaining ten firms, an interview was arranged and held. In one very large firm, two interviews were conducted with two different departments: "international corporate" and "litigation". Each of the interviews was conducted at the lawyer's offices for a duration of one to two hours. Leading *motifs* were utilized in aid of an open conversation. Notes were taken during most interviews; a few were recorded on tape.

Within this study results from these interviews are used where they promote the understanding of the issues discussed.

## 4. Data Evaluation and Presentation

The files and judgements were subjected to a two-fold quantitative as well as a qualitative analysis. Forms were used to create a data matrix, which was used for a computerized analysis. In the forms used, several factors, if determinable, could be marked. Additional information was consistently noted and later introduced into the data base categories. The information was sought in order to determine, in particular, the parties' countries of residence involved, the type of matter, the time needed for various procedural steps, and how the matter was resolved or disposed of. Finally, the study tried to determine which legal issues were important, and, specifically, whether conflict of law, foreign law, or public policy had any role in the proceeding.

On the other hand, the original judgements were used for an extrapolation of the courts' discussion and application of law regarding topics of interest, such as conventions, foreign law, conflict of law, or justification of jurisdiction. In addition to the quantitative data, it seemed important to note the actual argumentation of the parties and the court. Notes were taken on the situation of the case and any particulars that would not appear on the data forms and would allow further evaluation of any given case.

A note should be made on the way in which some of the categories were derived. For the attorney type, the attorneys or law firms representing the parties in each case and judgement were mentioned in all but a few cases. Using legal directories, the law firms were determined for cases in which only the attorneys were mentioned, and, using the same legal directories, the New York

law firms which appeared at least twice in the data base were categorized by size.[23]

The duration of a case was calculated in days from the date it
was filed in court to the date of decision. While the date of the
judgement was always known, the date of commencement was
only partially provided in the judgements. Some of the missing
dates were obtained from the court clerks, some were extrapo-
lated from known cases of the same court and the court's index
numbers, which were always available and which are assigned by
the clerks' offices on a continuous basis. The overall complexity
of a judgement was deduced from the overall length (in bytes) of
the judgement itself. The legal complexity was deduced from the
number of case and statutory cites in each judgement. The factual
complexity was calculated from the overall complexity reduced
by the legal complexity.[24]

For evaluation of quantitative categories (duration, case value,
complexity, and risk), quartiles were created by ranking the cases
into four groups, each consisting of 25% of the cases. In the tables, the four groups are referred to as "very low" for the lowest
quartile, "medium low" for the second quartile, "medium high"
for the third quartile and "very high" for the highest quartile. The
quartiles always refer to all cases for which the respective quantitative category was determinable even if only a selected group of
cases was analysed.

The data are represented either in descriptive or in analytical
form. A description shows the quantitative distribution of a variable. By way of statistical analysis the relationship of two (or more)
variables is tested, the most common form to do this being a cross-
tab. If not indicated otherwise the cross-tabs presented herein are
significant on the 5% level, which means that the chance of vari-

---

23    Small: under 50 attorneys; medium: over 51–99 attorneys; and
      large: 100 attorneys or more. The overall cross-border litigation
      behaviour of law firms was not the subject of this study; such
      data will be utilized in further research.

24    According to the following formula:
      $$f = o - (l \times 500)$$
      where $f$ is the factual complexity, $o$ the overall complexity, and $l$
      the legal complexity. An estimated average of 500 bytes were used
      for the discussion of each legal cite. A manual scan of a random
      sample of five cases confirmed the reliability of the calculation.

ables showing differences only by accident is smaller than 5%.[25] The validity of the data shall be discussed below.

## II. Transborder Interactions in Court

### A. Overview

#### 1. *The Court System in New York*

In the United States, two different and largely independent court systems exist.[26] On the one hand, there is a federal court system that was established by the Constitution and by acts of Congress. In civil matters, its jurisdiction and procedures are governed by the Constitution, various statutes, and the Federal Rules of Civil Procedure (F.R.C.P.). Generally, the federal courts have jurisdiction when the case is within federal jurisdiction as described by the Constitution or when the dispute is between parties of different states and a threshold value of $50,000 is met (diversity jurisdiction).[27] Where more than one party is involved on either side, complete diversity is required.

### Figure NY-1: Court Systems in New York

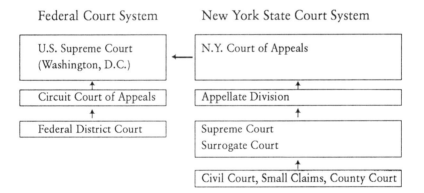

The federal courts have a three-tier system, with the district courts as general courts of first instance, "circuit" courts of ap-

---

25    See Gessner, herein.
26    For the following and further information in German, see Peter Hay, *Einführung in das amerikanische Recht,* 2nd ed. (Darmstadt: Wissenschaftliche Buchgesellschaft, 1987).
27    28 U.S.C. 1332 (a).

peal, and the United States Supreme Court as the ultimate appellate court. Some courts of special jurisdiction also exist, such as
the Bankruptcy Court or the Court of International Trade, which
deals with matters related to customs duty and trade restrictions.
Within the federal system, there are four district courts located in
New York, and the Court of Appeals for the Second Circuit, which
hears appeals from the New York district courts as well as the
district courts for the district of Connecticut and the district of
Vermont.

In the federal district courts in New York, about 20,000 civil
cases were filed, half of which were filed in the southern district.[28]
The official statistics for the federal district courts show median
time for regular civil cases in all federal district courts in New
York from filing to termination being about eight months, and
from issue to trial, if any, between 16 and 33 months. Yet between
10 and 20% of the civil cases in New York are pending for over
three years.[29] In 1992 about 2200 civil appeals were filed in the
U.S. Court of Appeals for the Second Circuit. After procedural
terminations 700 were decided on the merits. The median time
from filing to disposition was little more than six months.[30]

The federal courts' jurisdiction is of particular importance for
this investigation because matters involving foreign parties are likely
to fall under federal jurisdiction. This is true for both diversity
jurisdiction as well as for Federal Jurisdiction in Maritime and
Aviation matters and under the Foreign State Immunities Act.

Within the New York State court system,[31] which also has a
three-tier system, the state supreme court is the court of general
jurisdiction in each county, having unlimited, original jurisdiction,
and hears cases that do not fall within the special jurisdiction of
other courts. With regard to civil matters in the broadest sense,

---

28    This is second highest in the U.S. after California Central, with a
      resident population of only four million within the district (Source:
      the Statistics Division of the Administrative Office of the United
      States Courts).

29    Administrative Office of the United States Courts, *1993 Judicial
      Business of the United States Courts, Annual Report of the Di-
      rector* (Washington, D.C., 1994).

30    *1993 Judicial Business of the United States Courts.*

31    For the following, *1992 Annual Report of the Chief Administra-
      tor of the Courts*, legislative document (Albany, N.Y., 1992), 1 et
      seq.

the following courts have jurisdiction over certain defined matters.

The Court of Claims hears and determines matters against the state of New York. The Surrogate's Court hears cases involving the affairs of decedents and adoptions; the Family Courts, in addition to some criminal matters, have some jurisdiction regarding child support, adoptions, and persons in need of supervision. Outside New York City, county, district, city, town, and village courts handle a number of minor civil and criminal cases. The New York City Civil Court tries civil cases involving amounts up to $25,000. It includes a small claims part for the informal resolution (including an arbitration procedure) of matters not exceeding $2000.

Appeals from the lower courts are usually heard by the Appellate Terms of the Supreme Court. Appeals from the state supreme court and other courts of the same level are heard at the Appellate Division of the Supreme Court (which is divided into four departments by region). The Court of Appeals of the state of New York, located in Albany, is the highest court within the state court system and hears appeals from the appellate divisions.

The New York Supreme Court, therefore, is not necessarily the court where all matters involving foreign parties and arising in New York are determined. In fact, in one of the cases that are part of this study, the case was removed to the federal district court, and the distribution of international cases in the judgement analysis further confirms that the likelihood for such matters to be brought before the federal courts is higher than the likelihood of state court jurisdiction.

In 1986, according to the statistics, roughly 40,000 civil matters were filed in the New York Supreme Court for the county of New York, including appeals, matrimonial matters, tax matters, and some matters brought by or against the city of New York. There were 16,244 dispositions, and 1,612 trials commenced, approximately half of which were jury trials, the other half nonjury trials. The median time between filing and resolution was not available. Yet the official report states that, statewide, 80% of all state supreme court civil cases dispositions were achieved within the standard of fifteen months promulgated by the Chief Administrator of the Court.[32] Within all Appellate Divisions of the supreme

32   *Ninth Annual Report of the Chief Administrator of the Courts.*

court, about 10,000 records on appeal are filed every year.[33] In
1992 the Court of Appeals had to decide almost 900 civil motions
for leave to appeal, of which only 73 were granted. Together with
cases based on other jurisdictional predicates, 367 civil appeals
were filed. A large number of these were dismissed, withdrawn, or
transferred in a prescreening process. Eventually there were 173
dispositions, of which 60% led to affirmance of the lower court's
decision, the other 40% to reversal or modification. The median
disposition time was 254 days.

### 2. The Representativeness of the Data

For a full analysis of international case handling in the courts in
New York State in one year, several hundred thousand files would
need to be analysed. As mentioned only a random sample of the
state supreme court files were taken under observation, and even
this was a tedious task. An analysis of the Federal District Court's
cases could have contributed to the study. Due to construction
work, the Federal District Court for the Southern District of New
York, unfortunately, did not provide access to its files as needed
for the study. The relevance of the Federal District Court for the
Southern District of New York can be inferred from the results of
the judgement analysis showing that the district courts probably
have the highest share in international cases and the Federal District Court for the Southern District of New York the highest among
these.

### Table NY– 1: Distribution of Civil Cases in New York Courts and in New York Judgements (1992)[34]

| No. of Cases (1992) | N.Y. State Courts | Southern District | Other Federal District | Second Circuit | Total |
|---|---|---|---|---|---|
| Statistics | | | | | |
| Filed | >1,500,000 | 8806 | 7758 | 2212 | |
| Dispositions | | | | 1400 | |
| LEXIS | | | | | |
| Total | 17,997 | 2557 | 1207 | 1420 | 23,181 |
| International | 36 | 270 | 23 | 24 | 353 |
| Percent | 0.2 | 10.6 | 1.9 | 1.7 | 1.5 |

33   *Ninth Annual Report of the Chief Administrator of the Courts.*

The judgement analysis, on the other hand, while covering all
courts in the state, cannot be directly used to analyse the frequency
of international litigation, as all judgements have three prerequi-
sites that are not necessarily present in all disputes that arise: (1)
both parties must have participated to the point where the judgement or order was rendered; (2) no settlement could be reached to
the point where the judgement or order was rendered; and (3) a
disputed judgement or order was rendered by the court.

Particularly for the state courts, the information is somewhat
inconclusive. The number of annual civil filings in all state courts
throughout the state are over a million and a half, yet the official
statistics do not provide information on the number of decisions.
In addition, as noted above, the official statistics include various
items that would not be part of our analysis, domestic or international; for example, uncontested divorces (which form the major
part of divorces in New York) are resolved out of court through
lawyer-assisted negotiation.[35] Furthermore, the numbers include
cases by and against the city, tax certiorary, uncontested probate
and estate administrations, landlord-tenant cases, and some other
nongeneral civil matters.[36] Some of these would not even be resolved in a formal reasoned judgement or order. Default judgements are generally not reasoned and thus not part of the data
base either. In addition cases filed in small claims court are often
resolved in an arbitration procedure, again, without a formal reasoned judgement or order. Thus, the almost 18,000 cases reported
on LEXIS seem a somewhat large number as a basis.[37]

34    The numbers for filings, dispositions, and trials are derived, calculated, or estimated from the official court statistics. The state
court column includes state supreme courts, Appellate Divisions,
and the Court of Appeals. *1992 Annual Report of the Chief Administrator of the Courts;* Administrative Office of the United
States Courts. *1992 Federal Court Management Statistics* (Washington, D.C., 1993).

35    A year after a formal separation agreement has been negotiated,
the same may be directly filed as a divorce decree when both parties agree. Litigation is so much more expensive that most divorc-
ing couples avoid it.

36    The available New York State statistics allow the conclusion that
these cases amount to more than 1.3 million.

37    In the author's own experience in a New York law firm, all of the
cross-border court disputes that ended with an order or judgement with a reasoned opinion were published in LEXIS.

In only 34 of the 2200 cases scanned at the New York Supreme Court did a foreign party participate, which is only about 1.5%. Calculating by the total of 30,000 general civil matters handled by the court in 1986, this would amount to around 450 international matters per year for that court. The state supreme court file analysis contains not a single disputed judgement or order that would have become part of the LEXIS data base. This highly interesting result needs to be further discussed. At this point we can conclude that, out of the 450 cases, one can expect only a handful of judgements. This is indeed the case as can be seen from the above table in which only 36 international judgements were found in the entire New York State court system.

Finally, from what can be gathered from the importance of the Federal District Court for the Southern District of New York for international litigation, the state supreme court for the county of New York must have a similar role among the state courts, which is also confirmed by the New York Supreme Court share in the LEXIS international judgement analysis. A share of 1% to 2% of international matters in the sample should thus more or less reflect the actual proportion for the cases as well as the judgements, with the exception of uncontested divorces and default judgements. The importance of the latter is underlined by a result (shown in more detail below) that the state supreme court file analysis contains four default judgements and no disputed judgement, which would have been reported.

Consequently, the state supreme court file analysis, the judgement analysis, and the combination of both may provide an idea about the disputes involved. Several similarities between the (limited) supreme court file data and the (complete) judgement analysis warrant the assumption that the results can be somewhat generalized and together provide a fair picture of the structure of cross-border litigation in New York courts.

Further similarities between the two data sets can be shown, for example, in the distribution of party origin. In the state supreme court file analysis, foreign parties were about equally distributed between plaintiffs (18) and defendants (16), and a number of countries were involved, some of which appeared several times: Canada, Germany, U.K., France, Italy, Switzerland, and Australia. Liberia, Israel, Portugal, Liechtenstein, Ghana, the Dominican Republic, Honduras, Curacao, Colombia, the Bahamas, and India were involved in one case each, and one matter concerned a claim by 165 parties from all over the world against a New York investment broker.

The analysis of the judgement data, on the other hand, also shows an equal distribution between U.S. and foreign parties. The distribution of foreign parties among the various countries, as well as the types of claims involved,[38] again show similarities, which allows the conclusion that, while probably not entirely representative, the combination of the two studies provides a reliable picture of cross-border litigation in New York. Further similarities exist between the two data sets, as shall be shown.

## B. The Parties

### 1. Party Origin

As mentioned, the total distribution of plaintiffs and defendants by countries in both data bases is almost equally divided between U.S. and non-U.S. parties. The distribution by foreign countries shows an overrepresentation of developed countries in general, while most countries appear only once or twice. Corrected by the volume of trade,[39] this overrepresentation disappears. Thus adjusted, there remains, in both data bases, an overrepresentation of Great Britain, Canada, Italy, Switzerland, and Korea on the foreign plaintiffs' side and an underrepresentation of Japan. On the foreign defendants' side Great Britain, Germany, and Panama are overrepresented. The latter is related to several maritime cases in the judgement data base. The role of Great Britain in the maritime (3 cases) and in the insurance industry (6 cases) also somewhat contributes to the overrepresentation of Great Britain.

#### Table NY- 2: Country Distribution of Plaintiffs in New York Judgements (1992)

| | |
|---|---|
| Canada, Great Britain | 16 each |
| Italy, Germany | 13 each |
| France, Switzerland | 9 each |
| Korea | 7 |
| Japan, Panama, Saudi Arabia, India, Mexico, Sweden, Venezuela, Australia, Israel, Taiwan, Chile, Indonesia, Nigeria, Denmark | 3-5 each |
| BS, CAY, E, IRL, L, NL, P, RP, SF, SGP, TJ, WAL, BD, BR, BRN, CO, CY, DK, DOM, ETH. GR, GUY, H, IR, LB, NA, NL, PAK, Q, RA, RH, ROU, TR * | 1-2 each |

* Letter codes refer to international notor-vehicle country codes

38    This will be discussed in more detail below.

39    See U.S. Bureau of Statistics, *Statistical Abstract of the United States: 1992*, 1335 et seq.

## Table NY–3: Country Distribution of Defendants in New York Judgements (1992)

| | |
|---|---|
| Great Britain | 34 |
| Germany | 14 |
| Canada, Japan | 10 each |
| Korea, France, Panama, Australia, Switzerland, Italy, Israel | 5-8 each |
| Ireland, China, Cayman, Greece, Poland, Liberia, Taiwan, Chile, Venezuela, the Netherlands, Russia | 3-4 each |
| DOM, E, HK, IND, M, MEX, NA, RO, WAN, A, B, BOL, CY, DK, ET, H, IRL, IRQ, JOR, KWT, L, LIC, NZ, PY, RH, ROU, S, SA, SUD, T, VIR * | 1-2 each |

* Letter codes refer to international motor-vehicle country codes

Assuming that parties might be more likely to seek legal redress in a legal system they know suggests the hypothesis that parties from OECD countries might be more often represented than less developed countries and parties from common-law countries more often than from civil-law countries.

More than these distinctions, economic aspects seem to matter. As shall be further discussed, the party type is of particular importance. Thus, the economic structure of each of the countries involved—for example, the type of trade it is engaged in and whether export trade is predominantly in the hands of small businesses or multinationals—would play a too-important role.

Only the striking overrepresentation of British parties—and the underrepresentation of Japanese plaintiffs—with regard to available trade data could be subject to testing for legal-cultural reasons.[40] One can suppose that language aspects and, most importantly, the shared common-law tradition would lower the barriers to litigation for British parties in the U.S. On the other hand, the often-described low litigiousness within the Japanese society could have contributed to that country's underrepresentation.

Yet, again, the data are insufficient to confirm or disprove such a hypothesis on the basis of distribution alone. Too many known and unknown factors may have contributed to the disparity between Great Britain, Japan, and the other main trading partners with the U.S. who are also prominent in the court data. Japan's involvement in the U.S. economy is particularly based on activities

40    This will be further discussed below.

of large and multinational corporations[41] whose involvement in litigation is rather limited, which may partially explain the underrepresentation. As mentioned before, the prominence of Great Britain in the maritime and insurance business (Lloyd's) contributes to its overrepresentation but does not explain it entirely.

With regard to Japan, an attorney interviewed in New York[42] has in fact confirmed that in his experience, Japanese businesses seem to be particularly hesitant in commencing lawsuits. He reported as an example that it was particularly difficult to convince a Japanese client to commence litigation in a matter in which another (American) business had litigated much earlier. Yet, having learned from the success that followed, the law firm was contacted by the same Japanese firm only shortly thereafter for more litigation. This albeit single case does seem to support the inference of a role of cultural origins. More importantly, it supports hypotheses about the importance of cognitive reactions even with regard to normative reactions in transborder interactions and the role of lawyers as mediators of legal cultures therein. As a particularly interesting issue it warrants further research.

With regard to Great Britain it is striking that quite a number of U.S. law firms have close relationships with U.K. firms or have offices there. Martindale/Hubbel show a large number of affiliated firms in London, which ranks as the first in number of foreign-U.S. law firm offices. The rules for admission to the New York bar allow U.K. and other common-law countries' law school graduates to sit for the bar exam. These close ties should contribute to lowering the barriers to litigation in the United States. The common English language also eases communication between U.K. and U.S. counsel, which also warrants further research.

## 2. Type of Parties

An analysis of the type of parties involved may assist in understanding the structure of cross-border disputes. The plaintiffs are of particular interest, because it is the plaintiff who decides to take the law out of the books and put it to the test.[43] And it is the

---

41    As can be inferred from general economic data. See U.S. Bureau of Statistics, *Statistical Abstract of the United States: 1992.*

42    No. 3. The numbers refer to interviews made with ten randomly selected lawyers in New York, which will be further analysed in a planned publication on lawyers.

43    See Gessner, herein.

parties and their lawyers who decide to spend time and money in the hopes of achieving a favourable result.

It can be assumed that cross-border legal disputes in court pose significant barriers to the parties involved. In the first place, such barriers work against the plaintiffs, particularly foreign plaintiffs. With regard to the party type, one can assume that the barriers might be highest for individuals, medium for small and medium-sized corporations, and lowest for governments, banks, insurance companies, and large corporations, for whom dealing with lawyers, courts, and international transactions is generally more common. On the other hand, the "low barrier institutions" mentioned have additional nonlegal means, mainly economic and political power, to enforce their claims without court assistance. From this one would hypothesize that medium-range corporate entities are most likely to attempt to enforce their claims in court, individuals would take second place, and insurance companies and governments last. According to these hypotheses the distribution of the type of parties should be different from those purely domestic cases in the United States, where individuals played a dominant role, particularly as plaintiffs.[44] The following tables largely confirm the above assumptions.

### Table NY–4: Category Type of Defendants by Plaintiffs in New York Judgements (1992)

| Plaintiffs | Defendants | | | | | | | Total | |
| | Other | Govern-ment | Insur-ance | Multi-national | Other corp. | Bank | Private individual | (N) | % |
|---|---|---|---|---|---|---|---|---|---|
| Other | ; | | | | 3 | | 1 | 7 | 1 |
| Government | 1 | | 1 | 1 | 3 | | 1 | 7 | 2 |
| Insurance | | | 5 | 1 | 7 | | 1 | 14 | 5 |
| Multinational corp. | 1 | 3 | | 3 | 9 | 3 | | 19 | 5 |
| Other corp. | 8 | 7 | 5 | 15 | 130 | 13 | 12 | 190 | 54 |
| Banks | 1 | 1 | | | 11 | 5 | 2 | 20 | 6 |
| Private individuals | 2 | 7 | 2 | 19 | 50 | 6 | 10 | 96 | 27 |
| Total    (N) | 16 | 18 | 13 | 39 | 213 | 27 | 27 | 353 | |
| %    | 4 | 5 | 3 | 11 | 61 | 8 | 8 | | 100 |

44    David Trubek, et al, *Costs, Processes and Outcomes: Lawyers' Attitudes to Courts and Other Dispute Processing Options* (Madison, WI: University of Wisconsin Law School, 1984), 1–67 et seq.

As can be seen, ordinary corporations make up by far the largest group of plaintiffs in these cases (53.8%), followed by private individuals (27.2%). Multinationals and banks appear much more rarely as plaintiffs in the judgements, insurances and governments even less so.

Table NY–5: Type of Defendants by Plaintiffs in New York
Supreme Court File Analysis (1986)

| Plaintiffs | Defendants | | | | Total | |
| | Government | Other corp. | Banks | Private individuals | (N) | % |
|---|---|---|---|---|---|---|
| Government | | 1 | | | 1 | 3 |
| Other corp. | | 16 | 2 | 1 | 19 | 58 |
| Banks | | | | 3 | 3 | 9 |
| Private individuals | 3 | 5 | | 2 | 10 | 30 |
| Total (N) | 3 | 22 | 2 | 6 | 33 | |
| % | 9 | 67 | 6 | 18 | | 100 |

The state supreme court file analysis study can provide only limited insight, but the available data are similar to and confirm the results of the judgement analysis (57.6% ordinary corporate plaintiffs and 30.3% private individual plaintiffs). In fact the data even seem to indicate that the rate of settlements and withdrawals before a judgement or order is rendered does not depend on the type of party. In order to be able to compare the analysis of the judgement data, the following tables provide an overview of the subject matters in the state supreme court file analysis.

Table NY–6: Type of Cases in New York Supreme Court
File Analysis (1986)

| Type | No. of cases |
|---|---|
| Contract negotiated | 19 |
| Contract own form | 5 |
| Contract standard form | 5 |
| Tort | 4 |
| Total | 33 |

The table shows that the overwhelming majority of the cases in the state supreme court file analysis concerned contractual disputes.⁴⁵ Accordingly, the parties usually had a prior relationship. In only three cases did the parties have no prior relationship before the litigation. In fourteen cases the parties even had relationships continuing for more than a year. From this and the fact that most parties (70% of the plaintiffs and 82% of the defendants, Table NY–5) are corporate entities or governments, one can conclude that most of the litigating parties are not complete strangers to cross-border legal interactions. As shall be further discussed, even a number of the private individual parties are rather affluent and somewhat "globalized". The following table provides more information about the distribution of subject matters.

Table NY–7: Structure of Cases by Primary Subject
in New York Supreme Court File Analysis (1986)

| Type of Case | (N) |
| --- | --- |
| Contract of sale | 8 |
| Loan | 6 |
| Other contract | 10 |
| Tort | 10 |
| Employment | 3 |
| Trademark | 2 |
| Arbitration-related | 3 |
| Libel | 1 |
| In Rem | 1 |
| Divorce & child custody | 1 |
| Not determinable | 1 |
| Total number of cases* | 33 |

* Due to multiple entries, the total exceeds the number of cases.

The two tables show that in New York proceedings six contractual disputes also include allegations of tortious activity. This may have to do with the possibility of higher damages but probably also with the fact that a particularly tortious behaviour by one party prompted the other party to litigate rather than to negotiate. "Other contracts" include a variety of contract types, such as lease and rent, services, and transportation contracts. The larg-

45    By design, estate matters were excluded and could not appear; the same is true for matters of federal jurisdiction, particularly maritime and aviation cases, which would predominantly be brought in the federal district courts.

est single group are contracts of purchase (8), the second are loan enforcements (6).

Unless otherwise indicated, the following discussion is based solely on the judgement data, the only set with a sufficient number of distinguishable cases.

*a. Individual Parties*     Although less frequent than small and medium-sized corporations, individual plaintiffs do have a significant part in litigation (27%).[46] One could expect that, as has often been complained of in non-U.S. publications, a large number of these lawsuits are product liability suits by U.S. private individuals against foreign corporations. Surprisingly, only little more than half of these private plaintiffs are U.S. citizens (54%). The following table shows the distribution of the types of claims of U.S. private individuals.

#### Table NY–8: Type of Case (U.S. Private Individual Plaintiffs) in New York Judgements (1992)

| Type of Case | (N)* |
| --- | --- |
| Contract | 10 |
| Tort | 27 |
| Intellectual property | 3 |
| Maritime / Aviation | 13 |
| Employment-related | 9 |
| Credit-related | 5 |
| Securities (SEC) | 7 |
| Defamation / Slander | 2 |
| Family-related property | 1 |
| Others | 6 |

* The numbers amount to more than the number of cases, as there are multiple entries.

In fact, *none* of the tort cases were product liability suits. All 27 tort cases are related to and included in one of the other categories (for example, defamation/slander is by definition also a

46     Five times private parties were plaintiffs together with corporate plaintiffs. Only one case involved a deposition of the individual; in another, the individuals concerned were trustees in bankruptcy of the corporation. These cases were recoded to exclude the individual participation. In the other three cases the individuals were private investors of the corporation involved and therefore the real parties involved, thus these cases are included herein.

tort; some torts are contract-related, others securities related). The
only items falling into a category that is similar to product liability
are fifteen personal injury cases arising out of airline and ship accidents. Two of the three cases of the state supreme court file analysis by private individual plaintiffs against "governmental" parties
also fall within this category.

It seems that the widespread fears of foreign corporations of
receiving large punitive damages awards against them out of product liability cases in the U.S. are not confirmed by actual judgements. Without further information available, one can only speculate that these fears are either exaggerated or that such claims are
almost always settled before trial.

The two most important other single subjects of claim are investment-related and employment-related claims. But for employment disputes—in which the foreign corporate defendants are typically the parents of a U.S. subsidiary—and the airline accidents,
the typical U.S. individual plaintiff commencing a lawsuit against
a foreign defendant is wealthy. This is true for the credit and security investment claims, for the intellectual property claims, even
for the family property claim and the two defamation claims
brought by celebrities. Out of the seven nongovernmental cases
commenced by private individuals in the state supreme court file
analysis, three are employment-related (two of which concern accidents at work), one is a libel and defamation action, two are
investment-related, and one is a traffic accident, thus confirming
the picture that the judgement data provide.

An analysis of the foreign private individual plaintiffs shows
that their origin is distributed equally among a large number of
countries around the world. The subject matter of the disputes
may assist in understanding these further.

Table NY–9: Type of Case (Foreign Private Individual Plaintiffs)
New York Judgements (1992)

| Type of Case | No. of Occurrences* |
| --- | --- |
| Contract | 11 |
| Tort | 25 |
| Maritime / Aviation travel | 5 |
| Employment-related | 11 |
| Intellectual property | 1 |
| Credit / Investment-related | 8 |
| Trust & Estates | 2 |
| Defamation | 1 |
| Other | 4 |

* The numbers amount to more than the number of cases, as there
are multiple entries.

Surprisingly, this table is quite similar to the preceding table. Thus there is little difference in the litigation behaviour of U.S. and foreign private individual plaintiffs. In these cases, apart from the maritime and aviation cases that again are prominent, three more cases involve liability for personal injury. One is an action by a number of Irish residents for AIDS infection sustained through American blood products; a second is a medical malpractice action by a temporary trainee who has now returned to his home country; and two arise out of injuries and death, respectively, which occurred during employment in the U.S. at the place of work. The latter three, as well as the other employment-related cases, are directly related to temporary migration.

As with U.S. private individual plaintiffs, the affluent private individuals are also as highly represented as foreign individual plaintiffs (10 out of 45). Two more cases involve estate-related disputes concerning a significant value in assets in the United States claimed by various opposing foreign and domestic beneficiaries.

One result seems to be that there are a significant number of wealthy individuals willing and able to sue at home and abroad for claims related to their investments, their family assets, or their reputation or intellectual property, and that the respective disputes amount to 25 out of the 99 private individual plaintiffs and 7% of the total number of judgements. There seems to be a stratification aspect here.

Another significant number of lawsuits by private parties (17) is directly related to tourism and travelling for whatever purpose. Many of the cases are related to hijacking of the airline or vessel by terrorists; several cases are even related to the same event. As losing and winning motions are almost equally distributed, there seems to be no particular bias of the law or the judges in favour of foreign or U.S. plaintiffs. The numbers are too small to draw very specific inferences. It should only be noted that three of the thirteen foreign airlines/vessel owners were successful on their motions to dismiss for lack of jurisdiction. In the state supreme court file analysis, the two foreign airlines were immediately successful in their motion to remove their cases to the federal district court without a judgement.

As expected, on the defendants' side private individuals played a less important role, at least as primary actors. There are a number of cases (50) in which private individuals are named as co-parties, with corporate entities being the real "parties in interest". The remaining 27 cases in which private individual defendants were the real parties in interest are distributed twelve to fifteen by foreign to domestic parties, respectively. Again, the distribution of countries shows no particular weight on a certain country.

While the topics of the lawsuits against private individual defendants have an extremely wide range, a number of interesting particularities can be observed. Four cases each deal with securities or investment fraud, with bank obligations, and with attorney fee disputes. Furthermore, it is interesting, from a legal-cultural point of view, that while the areas of law and the backgrounds involved are manifold, eighteen (66%) of the cases against private individual defendants include serious allegations of fraud, conversion, or other wilful and malicious activity, and some even include racketeering under the RICO statute.[47] One case each deals with slander and defamation, with alleged child abduction, and with a tort in negligence by a former au pair host. Furthermore, most of these lawsuits either deal with strikingly obstructive parties or are, in the words of one judge, "bitterly contested". Again, it seems that the particularly "malicious" behaviour by one party prompted the litigation and hindered any settlement.

There is further evidence that these were highly conflict-ridden cases. While the median of the legal complexity is below average, five of the quartile of the longest and three of the quartile of the most factually complex judgements are contained in these cases, which would mean that these cases have less legal complexity in relation to their factual complexity.

With regard to the total duration of these proceedings, the median is about average, and so are the quartiles. Yet five of the

47    The Racketeer Influenced and Corrupt Organizations Act, 18 U.S.C. §§ 1961 et seq. (1988 & Supp. 1989) (Civil RICO) provides for damages and other remedies against organized crime and similar activities, specifically for federal offences committed in association with others and with a pattern of racketeering activity. A finding of a RICO violation provides for automatic trebling of the damages. Today, civil RICO claims are brought against numerous activities that are unrelated to traditional organized crime, mainly on the basis of federal "mail fraud" or "wire fraud" (18 U.S.C. § 1341, 1343), prohibiting the use of the U.S. mail or telecommunication facilities "in the furtherance of any scheme or artifice to defraud, or for obtaining any money or property by fraud. . .".

lawsuits of the quartile with the longest duration are in this group, having durations of over 31 months. The amounts at stake in these 27 cases are generally rather below average and not very striking.

One of the cases resulting from a security investments contract is interesting insofar as it was fought for more than eight years in only one court level for breach of contract (claim) and fraud, conversion and racketeering (counterclaim) about the relatively modest amount of $167,000. This case can probably be explained only by the counterclaim raising RICO and fraud allegations, which, in the case of a finding of such offences, would automatically result in treble damages under the RICO statute and punitive damages on fraud and, thus, a return far in excess of the $167,000 at stake in the claim itself.

*b. Governments*     It could be expected that governments would be somewhat rare in court. On the basis of literature on public international law and discussions about state immunity, one can expect that governments would rarely subject themselves to jurisdiction, particularly to a foreign jurisdiction. In the U.S., many actions against the government that would be termed "administrative" in civil-law countries are treated as civil actions. Because the study was limited to typical civil matters and to allow comparison with research conducted in other countries where such cases would be under the jurisdiction of special administrative courts, cases that were obviously of this nature were excluded.

On the other hand, within the context of this study the term "governments" also includes governmental entities such as banks, export companies, and airlines owned by governments, who participate in regular business transactions and who are subject to almost regular jurisdiction within the purview of their business activities. In this respect one can expect such governments to behave in court to a large extent as regular business actors. Furthermore, one can expect that governmental resources should make them act like large (multinational) corporations. In particular one would expect large, well-known law firms representing these clients and that the governments' success rate would be higher than usual.

Finally, there is a special issue with regard to state immunities that should have an influence on these cases. A special situation arises whenever a party to a dispute is a sovereign entity or subentity. Not only private parties but also states are reluctant to be subject to foreign jurisdictions. Yet states are not only even

more reluctant, they are also partially immune from foreign jurisdictional powers.

While being part of international law for a long time, the objective of the U.N.-Charta to prevent future wars between nations
(Art. 1 para 1 of the U.N.-Charta) consequently led to the formally postulated (Art. 21 U.N.–Charta) recognition of the sovereign equality among nations. This rule has, inter alia, the effect
that a state need not submit to another state's coercive powers,[48]
including but not limited to another state's jurisdiction.[49] This immunity is not limited to the state itself but extends to its organs, to
its diplomatic and consular missions (and their individual representatives), and to international organizations.[50]

The United States has enacted the Foreign Sovereign Immunity
Act,[51] which regulates in detail how foreign governmental entities
should be treated in U.S. courts. With regard to U.S. governmental entities, federal law is also decisive. Thus, not surprisingly, federal law was at issue in 22 of the 26 cases with governmental
parties.

While the U.S. government agencies generally used in-house
counsel, a large number of the foreign governmental parties used
large and medium-sized law firms to represent them, and these
foreign governments won the respective judgement in ten out of
fourteen cases. A few further peculiarities distinguish these cases
from other cases. While the length of the judgements shows that
their factual complexity was not significantly different from the
other cases, the average duration of the proceedings with governmental participation was only slightly higher than the overall average, and the monetary claim slightly below average, the legal
complexity is distinguishable.

48      ... *par in pares non habet imperium*; Georg J. Dahl, Jost Delbrück,
        and Rüdiger Wolfram, *Völkerrecht Vol.* I, 2nd ed. (Berlin: Duncker
        & Humblot, 1988), 453.
49      Dahl, Delbrück, and Wolfram, *Völkerrecht*, 453.
50      Vienna Conventions of 1961 and 1963, §§ 18–20 GVG, see
        Baumbach and Lauterbach-Albers, *ZPO-Commentary*, 51st ed.
        (Munich: C.H. Beck, 1993), introduction and commentary to §§
        18-20 GVG, with further references.
51      Of 1976 (FSIA), 28 U.S.C. §§ 1602–1611 (1982).

### Table NY–10: Legal Complexity Quartiles of all Cases by Government Party Cases in New York Judgements (1992)

| Complexity | Frequency | Percent |
|---|---|---|
| Very low | 4 | 15 |
| Medium low | 7 | 27 |
| Medium high | 10 | 39 |
| Very high | 5 | 19 |
| Total | 26 | 100 |

While government cases in the highest quartile are not overrepresented, there seems to be a strong overrepresentation of the medium-high complex cases. An appropriate conclusion is that, while the cases are generally somewhat of standard or even of lesser factual complexity, one single issue adds to legal complexity, particularly when foreign governments appear as defendants, because all of these cases are in the two highest quartiles.

In eight of these ten judgements concerning foreign governmental defendants, the same claimed to be protected by sovereign immunity, thus needing discussion of the topic.[52] Immunity was granted in four cases and denied in two, based on state defendant's commercial activity. In one instance, the case was dismissed for *forum non conveniens*, so the judge did not address the issue. In one case, sovereign immunity was denied for the P.L.O. but granted with respect to personal service on its New York mission to the U.N., holding that the U.N. was effectively not part of U.S. territory. The FSIA also played a role in the immediate removal of the state supreme court cases against foreign (government-owned) airlines to the federal district court. The third case involved a slip-and-fall personal injury claim against the building owner, the tenant, and, inter alia, a foreign diplomat as speaker and organizer of a meeting at which the accident occurred. The defendant diplomat claimed foreign sovereign immunity and, again based on the FSIA, the case was removed to the federal district court.

This shows that, while not too frequent, state immunity needs to be taken seriously as an obstacle to pursuing claims. In hind-

---

52  In four more judgements, one of which has been discussed above, state immunity played a minor role as it had been waived. Two more judgements involved the immunity of the U.S. itself, which need not be discussed here.

sight the results are well reasoned in each case, and an independent observer has to conclude that they were foreseeable. It can only be suggested with regard to the four cases in which immunity was granted that the plaintiffs had brought the action on the assumption that the foreign state might not raise that defence. The reason for bringing the claim might have been either a lack of knowledge and experience or, more likely, a particular risk was taken by the attorneys in these cases in light of the potential reward (the numbers involved are relatively large) and under the assumption that political considerations might have led the foreign state to waive sovereign immunity. The case against the diplomat shows a particular lack of competency by the plaintiff's attorney. Adding the diplomat to the defendants unnecessarily caused obstruction without which the claim might have succeeded.

The data further show that, of the 26 cases with government participation,[53] like multinational corporations, governments were sued more often (18 times) than they commenced lawsuits themselves (8 times). Governmental parties of U.S. nationality appear four times as plaintiffs and eight times as defendants. Four of these eight cases involved monetary claims of a penal character by the SEC, tax offices, or customs offices for the other party's criminal behaviour. In two cases the governmental agency was a statutory bankruptcy trustee under state insurance laws. One more case involved the workers' compensation board and is one of the migration-related cases described under "individual parties".

Some cases with foreign government plaintiffs were quite interesting as well. For example, they involved a claim by the Philippine Government against its former President Marcos and a claim by the provisional government of Liberia for assets that had been put in custody by a former government official in order to avoid loss during the civil war that ensued in that country.

The remaining cases mostly concerned regular business transactions. In fact all foreign government defendants were government-owned commercial entities and could be treated as such, but for issues related to foreign sovereign immunity.

---

53   One case does not appear in Table NY-4, as the respective governmental party appeared for statutory reasons only and did not participate in the proceeding.

*c. Large Enterprises*      Large commercial enterprises with a high volume of trade, multinational or large corporations, banks, and insurance companies have certain similarities and special features distinguishing them from other types of parties. While trade volume and revenue may be comparable, the particular business of these enterprises makes it necessary to distinguish and discuss each in turn. Their share in both data sets is rather low.

For completeness, it should be added that in the state supreme court file analysis there is no case involving a multinational corporation or insurance company and two cases by the State Bank of India and one by a German bank against small corporations and private individuals for recovery on defaulted loans. One case was instituted by a U.S. corporation against foreign accounting firms, banks, and their managers alleging malpractice, fraud, and breach of fiduciary duty regarding a corporate acquisition.

i. Multinational Corporations

Multinational corporations rarely have lawsuits and even more rarely commence the same. Of the latter, about half are against governments, banks, or corporations of their own size, the other half against medium- and small-sized corporations. The numbers become very small if one considers their share in trade volume. This confirms a hypothesis that these multinational corporations can utilize their economic power and other mechanisms to avoid court disputing.

Most multinationals have in-house legal counsel and, in addition, utilize large expert law firms to organize their legal relationships. All these aspects also apply to banks and insurance companies, yet both are in a special litigation risk-prone situation because risks are a major part of the business.

ii. Banks

It would not be surprising to find a large number of lawsuits by banks against small corporations and private individuals to recover on defaulted debts, and this is true for fourteen out of the twenty lawsuits commenced by banks. The other six need further attention and shall be explored. Of particular interest are the five lawsuits by banks against other banks, because trade practices such as letters of credit would suggest a worldwide relationship of trust and understanding between banks, which would hinder such lawsuits.

It turns out that, in one case, the defendant bank was not the real party in interest because it made a cross-claim against the third party responsible for the loss.

In four out of the five remaining bank against bank cases, one of the banks was from a non-OECD country. One was a claim by a Nigerian bank for the turnover of its assets on account at a New York bank, which had commenced an interpleader because the Nigerian bank itself was involved in a proceeding in Nigeria between various groups of shareholders of that bank and because there was doubt whether the Nigerian managers who instituted the claim in New York were duly representing the bank. Another case involved an Iraqi bank, directly related to the Gulf War. A third case was a claim against a Sudanese bank out of a guarantee for a defaulted Sudanese company. One case was even more interesting, in that it was a claim by a rather small French bank, which acquired approximately 20 million dollars of Paraguay's foreign debt at discounted value with the purpose of attempting to recover 100% or any other profit it might have been able to make by resale, by negotiation with the debtor country, or by suing the same.

The final case is different insofar as the lawsuit was commenced by a number of foreign banks from a variety of countries against a U.S. bank. The foreign banks had purchased debt risks of a certain company from the U.S. bank defendant and were now alleging misrepresentation and liability of the U.S. bank, as the debtor had fallen into bankruptcy. The U.S. bank successfully defended itself with a contractual clause that had shifted the burden of gathering information about the debtor to the purchasing banks. In Austria, the country of one of the banks involved, the losses in that particular investment had even become an issue in the press. While the foreign bank managers had apparently negligently underestimated the risks involved, and while the U.S. bank legally had acted correctly, the case can also be seen as one in which the U.S. bank had not acted according to the foreign banks' expectation of a trustworthy relationship. It comes as no surprise that the U.S. bank had had little success in selling the debts to U.S. banks.

Generally it seems that the worldwide relationship of trust and understanding needs to be qualified with respect to LDCs. Banks from non-OECD countries are apparently burdened with extraordinary problems of underdevelopment which undermine their ability to maintain the "standards" of the international banking community. The last case discussed appears as an example of European naïveté vs. American business shrewdness and thus shows signs of cultural conflict. The example seems somewhat strange within the banking environment and, in fact, none of the banks are known as "big" international banks. Being one example only, it is definitely not representative, and whatever conclusions need to be drawn with regard to (legal) cultural conflicts should be taken from different types of cases.

iii. Insurance Companies

As said before, it is assumed that multinational corporations have economic power and, thus, because of the large sums potentially involved in a loan or insurance loss and in future revenue by the respective bank or insurance company, it comes again as no surprise that there are no disputes between a bank or a multinational corporation against an insurance company. Furthermore, insurance companies rarely need to commence action against the insured for premiums, their best remedy being the invalidity of the coverage.

Insurance companies, on the other hand, could be expected to be found on the defendant's side, being sued by private individuals and small corporations as insurance companies may be reluctant to pay the loss where future business with that particular party does not play a role in comparison to the sum at stake. This was true in seven cases and essentially true in three more cases in which the insurer was in fact unwilling to pay, but for procedural or other legal reasons was positioned nominally on the plaintiff's side. Three more cases involved insurers who paid the loss and then commenced lawsuits as consignees against the party allegedly liable for the loss, one of which was a large corporation.

Thus, with regard to insurance companies, three lawsuits commenced by the insurance companies against parties other than insurance companies deserve further investigation as they cannot be explained outright. However, these cases are not spectacular either. One involved a claim for unpaid premiums by a building consortium, and in the other two the insurance company was involved not as insurer but as an investor having lost monies in such an investment.

Finally, insurers do dispute among each other as parties in interest between a value insurer and a liability insurer or between insurers and reinsurers. The five disputes between insurance companies are either of these two types. Clearly what is true for the banking business is not true for the insurance business. Here the disputes between insurance companies were not unusual or striking in any way except for their factual complexity, mostly due to the large number of parties (members of various insurance or reinsurance consortia) whose participation in the matter needed

to be outlined by the judge. It does seem to matter, and there seems
to exist the need for legal resolution of the question of who would
bear a particular insurance loss, particularly for transportation
risks, being the origin for eleven out of the 22 cases in which insurance companies were involved, and for all five intrainsurance matters, which seemed to pit insurance companies against each other.
It might even be true, as a maritime lawyer in New York suggested
in an interview,[54] that the international insurance business is somewhat divided into groups who are in constant battle with each
other. Insurers and reinsurers could be two, cargo and liability
insurers could be two more, battling on behalf of equally divided
groups of clients they underwrite and who, in turn, battle on who
has to insure and to pay the premiums. Notwithstanding, the
number of lawsuits is far less than the supposedly high number of,
for example, transportation accidents and losses in which value
and liability insurers stand against each other and which are resolved without resort to court disputing. Further research may be
warranted on this field of interaction.

*d. Small and Medium-sized Corporations*        Lawsuits by small
and medium-sized corporations against each other account for the
bulk of all lawsuits in both data bases. This was expected because
(1) they lack the economic power and mechanisms that enable
large corporations to avoid litigation; and (2) the barriers of access to litigation that may hinder private individuals from litigating have a lesser weight. Correspondingly, in fact, from an economic and social perspective, a large number of individual parties
involved in the data are on a comparable level to a corporation.

Due to their importance in cross-border litigation and due to
their large number, a case-by-case description seems of little use.
An overview of the types of claims and other items involved shows
that these cases are more appropriately dealt with under the specific topics.

## III. The Commencement of Action

### A. Jurisdiction and Service of Process

Regardless of the type of conflict or the parties, once the
plaintiff has made the decision to resort to litigation, there are

54    No. 4.

legal requirements and threshold questions that determine, in part, the available forum for such court action as well as the procedural steps necessary. First the conflict needs to be made "judiciable" in order to be brought before a court. Second an appropriate court needs to be found or selected, and, third, in most cases notice has to be made to the court and the opposing party, which is the required step that legally commences an action.

The first step shall be dealt with in more detail below. The second step has two peculiar aspects to it, which need to be further analysed and discussed.

On the one hand, several aspects would lead a party to select a certain forum of formal resolution to resolve a dispute. Accessibility, convenience, the expected type of proceeding, costs, duration, the applicable law, the expected outcome, and the possibilities for enforcement are the factors that should lead a rational actor to determine the preferred forum; the legal requirements the forum has for the institution of a lawsuit of the particular type that the plaintiff envisages are the barriers that effectively limit the choice. The law has defined the latter requirements under such topics as jurisdiction (and lack thereof), forum selection, and *forum non conveniens*.

The prime legal barrier to litigation in a particular forum is whether the respective forum has the legally defined power to entertain the claim, the "jurisdiction". In civil-law systems there is a clear distinction between subject matter jurisdiction, which defines the area of law and the type of cases a court deals with, and "locality" jurisdiction, which, somewhat like venue, defines whether the court with the correct subject matter jurisdiction may entertain the lawsuit or whether another court with the subject matter jurisdiction but at a different place should be the appropriate court. In many cases by design, the venue is, exclusive of all other courts, in the defendant's domicile. The divisions in common-law legal systems are somewhat different, not that clearly defined, and need to be described in their own terms.

Traditionally, in the U.S. the courts had *in personam* jurisdiction over parties who resided within the state and who could be "personally" served therein. Still, "personal" service within the state is one of the most important and traditional means to obtain jurisdiction *over a defendant*, thus giving the court the power to enforce decisions against that person. In New York, for example, personal jurisdiction over an individual can be acquired by personal service within the state or by personal service on a New York domiciliary anywhere.

The residence requirement has been extended to include persons "doing business within the state" without necessarily residing therein, by itself or through agents and representatives acting within the state.[55] In addition to the possibilities of serving individuals set forth above, personal jurisdiction may be obtained by personal service upon a nondomiciliary when C.P.L.R. § 302 applies to create a basis for long-arm jurisdiction. With regard to corporations, this is extended to all corporations doing business in New York.

In practice this means that a New York subsidiary may often suffice to obtain jurisdiction on its foreign parent who is deemed "to do business in New York through its agent",[56] the subsidiary.

---

55    The New York Civil Procedure Laws and Rules (CPLR), for example, provides in § 302:

As to a cause of action arising from any of the acts enumerated in this section, a [New York] court may exercise personal jurisdiction over any non-domiciliary . . . who in person or through an agent:

1. transacts any business within the state or contracts anywhere to supply goods or services in the state; or

2. commits a tortious act within the state . . .; or

3. commits a tortious act without the state causing injury to person or property within the state . . . if he

(i) regularly does . . . business within the state . . . or

(ii) expects or should have expected the act to have consequences in the state and derives substantial income from interstate or international commerce; or

4. owns, uses or possesses any real property situated within the state.

56    *Kreutter v. McFadden Oil Comp.*, 71 N.Y.2d 461, 527 (1988); *CutCo Industries Inc. v. McNaughton*, 806 F.2d 361 (2d Cir. 1986); *Volkswagenwerk Aktiengesellschaft v. Beech Aircraft Corp.*, 751 F.2d 117, 120 (2d Cir. 1984); *Titu-Serban Ionescu v. E.F. Hutton & Co.*, 434 F. Supp. 80 (SDNY 1977), *aff'd* 636 F.2d

In some limited cases this has even been held to include cosubsidiaries and foreign subsidiaries of New York parents.[57]

Furthermore, in other cases U.S. courts have *in rem* or *quasi in rem* jurisdiction when the subject *res* is or was (sometimes, should be) physically located in the state. The *quasi in rem* theory is an abstraction of the *in rem* jurisdiction, which serves as the theoretical basis for jurisdiction in matrimonial cases, estate matters, bankruptcy, and disputes within corporations where the subject *res* is not physical but rather a matter of concept such as the place of the marital domicile. However, jurisdiction in these cases is now generally governed by specific statutory provisions.

Today, in effect, United States courts have broad jurisdictional powers under rules favouring the plaintiff's domicile. Foreign parties from countries where exclusive jurisdiction is usually at the defendant's domicile are often surprised to be subject to the jurisdiction of U.S. courts. Subsequent to the landmark case of *International Shoe v. Washington* 326 U.S. 310 (1945), most states have enacted "long arm statutes",[58] which extend the jurisdiction of the courts to the utmost limits of "due process" as defined in that case and subsequent interpretation.

A notable exception to the general availability of jurisdiction is the requirement for any corporation that regularly transacts business in New York to obtain a license to do so and therefore to pay fees and taxes to the state. One sanction for not obtaining such license may be that the subject corporation is automatically "barred from seeking the protection of the courts" and may not sue in New York.[59] In fact, in one case of the state supreme court file

1202 (2d Cir. 1980); *Saraceno v. S.C. Johnson & Son, Inc.*, 83 F.R.D. 65 (SDNY 1979); *Liquid Carriers Corp. v. American Marine Corp.*, 375 F.2d 951 (2d Cir. 1967); *Taca Int'l Airlines, S.A. v. Rolls-Royce of England, Ltd.*, 15 N.Y.2d 97, 204 N.E.2d 329, 256 N.Y.S.2d 129 (1965).

57   See *Eddie Palmieri v. Gloria Estefan et al.*, 793 F. Supp. 1182 (SDNY 1992).

58   E.g., New York's CPLR § 302.

59   New York Business Corporation Law (B.C.L.) §§ 1301 et seq., 1312; Again when raised as a defence by the New York defendant, this can be surprising for foreign parties, particularly those from civil-law countries, who expect the courts at the defendant's domicile to take jurisdiction.

analysis, the U.S. defendant motioned for dismissal on the grounds that the foreign plaintiff had not obtained the license under the B.C.L. The foreign (civil-law) plaintiff seemed to have assumed without further doubt that the proper place of litigation was the defendant's domicile. In fact, his own courts would probably have denied jurisdiction. Fortunately for him, doing business in the context of the B.C.L. is more narrowly defined as in the C.P.L.R. so that it cannot often lead to denial of jurisdiction, and the court held accordingly. The fact that the plaintiff would have been without forum if the decision had been otherwise was of no express concern to the parties or the New York court.

In order to somewhat limit the effects of the broadness of jurisdiction, the courts have developed very specific requirements with regard to "out-of-state" service of process. The ideology strictly requires actual notice by the defendant of the pending lawsuit, whereas formal requirements are less important. Thus, even abroad, service by mail (if authorized by the court), by personal delivery through any person engaged for this purpose, by delivery to a contractually designated or statutory "agent for service of process",[60] provided that the service is successful in that it can be proven to have reached the knowledge of a responsible person, is sufficient.[61] In any event, service of process is of ultimate importance.

60     E.g., the New York Secretary of State is the statutory agent for the service of process for all corporations incorporated or licensed in New York and for all motor vehicles that use New York roads (and have an accident). See B.C.L. § 304 (a):
       The secretary of state shall be the agent of every domestic corporation and every authorized foreign corporation upon whom process against the corporation may be served.
       New York Motor Vehicle and Traffic Law § 253 provides, inter alia, that
           1. The use . . . by a non-resident of a vehicle in this state . . . shall be deemed equivalent to an appointment by such non-resident of the secretary of state to be his true and lawful attorney upon whom may be served the summons in any action against him, growing out of any accident . . . in which such non-resident may be involved while using . . . such vehicle in this state. . . .
61     A standard form provided by a New York publishing house (Blumberg) with boxes where the process server may indicate various clauses and a detailed description of the person to whom the

As can be thus expected in most cases (four out of five) of both data sets, as far as it can be determined, jurisdiction over the U.S. defendants was easily obtained by service of process in New York, either directly or through an agent for service of process (discussed below). The basis on which the New York court had (allegedly) obtained jurisdiction over the foreign defendant is illustrated by the following table. Service of process being the predicate for trial and the type of service being directly or indirectly dependent on the jurisdictional predicates, the examination of the latter will show the relevance of different types of service in practice.

Table NY–11: Basis of Jurisdiction in New York Supreme Court File Analysis (1986) and in New York Judgements (1992)[62*]

| Alleged Basis of Jurisdiction | Files | Judgements |
|---|---|---|
| Agent for service of process | 0 | 0 |
| Forum selection clause | 3 | 5 |
| In rem, quasi in rem, or place/occurrence | 2 | 11 |
| Long-arm jurisdiction or implied agency | 3 | 22 |
| Multiparty and/or multiple jurisdiction | 6 | 18 |
| Personal service in New York | 0 | 9 |
| Total | 14 | 65 |

The table shows that long-arm jurisdiction is an important yet disputed tool in obtaining jurisdiction over nondomiciliaries, especially corporations. The *in rem* cases are either maritime or estate matters. The nonoccurrence of "agent for service of process" in the judgements may be due to the fact that the alleged basis of jurisdiction is in most cases unknown in which the same remained unchallenged by the defendant. In one case an agent for service of process had in fact been contractually designated but was of no

document was delivered: estimated age, estimated size, hair and skin colour, the function and name the person held him/herself to be, etc.

62.    Unfortunately, in most cases the alleged basis of jurisdiction is known only when challenged by the defendant. All other cases have been omitted from the table. Thus the number of cases is lower than the total number of cases with foreign defendants.

significance for jurisdictional purposes in that case. It is, however,
pointed out by the parties in that case that,

> [S]uch a Service of Suit clause is a "standard" one, "often" included
> in reinsurance contracts, and is part of the custom and practice in the
> industry.[63]

The broad jurisdictional powers of New York courts and, thus,
their availability raise the question for the plaintiffs' reasons to
select the New York forum. Depending on the (more restrictive)
jurisdictions of other courts, New York may have indeed been the
only available forum. On the other hand, the plaintiffs may have
preferred New York despite the availability of other courts for
various reasons, and these need to be discussed. A glance at the
distribution of plaintiffs by country shall outline the relevance of
this question. The file analysis in the New York state supreme
court shows an equal distribution of cases between domestic and
foreign plaintiffs, if not a slight overrepresentation of foreign plaintiffs. The judgement data base again shows a slight overrepresentation of foreign plaintiffs.

### Table NY–12: Distribution of Plaintiffs by Origin in New York Supreme Court File Analysis (1986) and in New York Judgements (1992)

| Origin | Files (N) | Judgements (N) | % |
|--------|-----------|----------------|-----|
| Foreign | 18 | 172 | 49 |
| U.S. | 13 | 162 | 46 |
| Mixed cases | 2 | 19 | 5 |

The foreign plaintiffs in the state supreme court study are di-
vided among diverse countries (Australia, the Bahamas, Switzer-
land, Columbia, France, Italy, Israel, Liberia (1 each), Canada,
Germany and India (2 each), and Great Britain (3 cases). The dis-
tribution of the foreign plaintiffs in the judgements, as shown in
Table NY-2, follows the list of U.S. major trading partners with
Great Britain and Canada heading the list, followed by Germany,
Italy, France, Japan, Panama, South Korea, and Australia.

---

63    *John Hancock Property And Casualty Insurance Company et al.
      v. Reinsurance Company, Ltd.*, 1992 U.S. Dist. LEXIS 1113
      (S.D.N.Y. 1992).

In Germany, as part of the research project,[64] out of 339 civil
and commercial cases in the district courts of Hamburg and Bremen,
the plaintiff was foreign in 65% of the cases and in thirteen out of
sixteen cases with U.S. parties participating.

Comparing the German study with New York, the data seem
to indicate either, to some degree, a relative reluctance of foreign parties to litigate in New York, or a relative preference of New York
plaintiffs to litigate in New York and the fact that the jurisdictional rules are favouring the plaintiff at the New York domicile in
comparison with Germany's (and other civil-law countries') more
strict rules.

Nevertheless, on the other hand, the fact that foreign plaintiffs
appear frequently as U.S. plaintiffs indicates that foreign parties
are not generally opposed to bringing a lawsuit in New York. In
one case the judge felt need to state that:

> [p]erhaps the most glaring relevant fact is the frail connection be-
> tween plaintiffs' claims and this forum.[65]

The original hypothesis was that there should be significant
differences in the behaviour of foreign and domestic parties. Yet
the New York data disprove this proposition to a large extent; few
tables show any interesting difference between international cases
commenced by foreign or by domestic parties.

Literature provides further advice to attorneys involved in international litigation. One is the advice that, particularly in
transborder disputes, an experienced and responsible attorney
should stage several simultaneous service attempts and fully document the efforts.[66] Interviews[67] and the author's personal experience lead to the same conclusion.

A clausular solution suggested would be the naming of an agent
for service of process in contracts. This method, however, does
not appear in the cases or judgements and was not mentioned by
any of the lawyers interviewed. Of various contracts reviewed,
only one contained a clause to this effect. Thus naming of agents
of process is rarely used in practice.

64    See Gessner, herein.
65    Mary C. Doe v. Hyland Therapeutics Division, et al., 807 F. Supp.
      1117 (S.D.N.Y. 1992).
66    Born and Westin, International Civil Litigation in United States
      Courts, 168.
67    No. 3 and 6.

In order to further attempt to determine the reasons for selecting the New York forum, a particular aspect may be of help. Forum selection agreements largely allow the parties to select the
forum of their choice limiting the application of specific jurisdictional rules, thus making the choice more independent. The reasons for parties to select a forum in such agreements may assist in
determining the reasons to select New York in general.

## B. Forum Selection — Clauses and Practice

Handbooks for international business transactions advise
that, whenever possible and not of legal disadvantage, contracting
parties should negotiate the place where such litigation would eventually occur in advance, with the objective of reaching their own
jurisdiction or at least that of a neutral forum.[68] Thus, most international contracts include forum selection clauses—if not arbitration clauses.[69]

There are several reasons mentioned for the use of forum selection clauses. Procedural differences and different substantive rules
of law and choice-of-law principles may have a consequential influence on the outcome of any dispute. Even where the legal norms
do not show many differences, the legal culture may bear on the
outcome of litigation. Cost and speed of litigation differ from jurisdiction to jurisdiction, and there may even be actual or assumed
forum bias or other nonlegal influences on courts. In addition,
when transborder legal conflicts arise, litigation may occur at several different jurisdictions,[70] so that forum selection agreements
may make the forum, and thus its outcome, more predictable.

---

68    E.g., Otto Sandrock and Harald Jung, "Internationale
      Gerichtstandsvereinbarungen", in *Handbuch der Internationalen
      Vertragsgestaltung* 2, *rn.*1, ed. Otto Sandrock (Heidelberg: V.
      Recht u. Wirtschaft, 1980); Rainer Hausmann, "Gerichstands-
      und Schiedsvereinbarungen", in *Internationales Vertragsrecht, Das
      internationale Recht der Schuldverträge*, ed. Christoph Reithmann
      and Dieter Martiny (Cologne: Schmidt, 1988), *rn.* 1164 with fur-
      ther references. See also *The Bremen v. Zapata Off-Shore Co.*,
      407 U.S. 1 (1972) at 12.
69    Sandrock and Jung, "Internationale Gerichtstandsverein-
      barungen".
70    Generally and for the U.S., see Born and Westin, *International
      Civil Litigation in United States Courts*, 221 et seq.

It is commonly assumed that seeking the law in a foreign forum is a disadvantage. The expressed and implied reasons for this
assumption are the knowledge of the legal culture of that forum
by the respective party leading to predictability of expectations.
Furthermore, the ease of access to the local court and the lack of
language barriers in the same during the procedure, as well as the
avoidance of foreign (additional) counsel and the costs related
thereto, are mentioned as factors favouring one's own jurisdiction.

Apart from the signs of cultural animosity towards foreign jurisdiction and the legal insecurity implied in such statements, there
is considerable logic therein. A further result of these considerations is that the party disadvantaged by the forum selection clause
is not likely to bring suit in the foreign forum and is thus deprived
of legal rights.[71] On the other hand, there also may be jurisdictions
that are generally preferable to both parties due to their qualification and expedience.

A forum selection clause is a contractual clause that provides
for a particular court or courts to have exclusive or nonexclusive
jurisdiction in some or all conflicts that may arise between the
parties to that contract. Generally a forum selection may be made
before a conflict arises, as in contractual forum selection clauses.
A standard provision to this effect would be, for example:

> The Courts of the City of New York shall have exclusive jurisdiction
> to resolve any dispute between the parties hereto arising out of or in
> connection with the subject matter of this agreement. Both parties
> expressly submit to the jurisdiction of said courts.[72]

Another possibility is a forum selection agreement after a conflict arises. Parties may agree explicitly or, in some jurisdictions by
implication, on the adjudication of their dispute by a particular
court. In some jurisdictions arguing on the merits without dis-
claimer may be considered an implied consent to jurisdiction.

71   This aspect is widely discussed in domestic legal circles in connec-
     tion with consumer protection and standard forms, e.g., the Ger-
     man ZPO, § 38.
72   See Martin D. Fern, Timothy A. Covington, and Ronald F. Sullivan,
     *Warren's Forms of Agreements, Business Forms,* IV (New York
     and Oakland: Mathew Bender Looseleaf, 1991), 70–470.

For the legal effectiveness of a forum selection clause or agreement it is crucial that the court selected (prorogation) accepts jurisdiction delegated by such a clause and that other courts which may have jurisdiction over the matter under their procedural rules decline jurisdiction pursuant to the clause where that jurisdiction is excluded (derogation).

A legal system or a court (and particularly the individual judge) selected may find it highly inconvenient to be bothered by a dispute over which it would not usually have jurisdiction and not enforce the forum selection clause. However, but for exceptions in some special areas of law, such as family, estate, labour, and real estate, there is internationally a general acceptance of prorogation.[73] It seems that either courts feel rather honoured than bothered by their selection or the complicity between local lawyers, who gain revenue through referred cases, the legislators, and the courts, leads to the hospitable attitude. Partly for the latter reasons, New York has even enacted a statute providing for the enforcement of agreements selecting New York courts under certain circumstances.[74]

Derogation is a more difficult issue, as states and courts seem to feel deprived of their sovereign exercise of jurisdiction when another court is selected. Thus, a variety of countries and courts do not recognize derogation of their courts.[75]

The U.S. Supreme Court has, within the last twenty years, held enforceable all forum selection clauses before it, although some lower courts have held otherwise.[76] The leading modern U.S. case

---

73   For German law in particular (and generally), see Haimo Schack, *Internationales Zivilverfahrensrecht* (Munich: C.H. Beck, 1991), rn. 436.

74   New York General Obligation Law §5-1402 (Consol. 1978), McKinney's G.B.L. 1994 ed.; see Carsten-Thomas Ebenroth/ Regina Tzeschlock, *"Rechtsklauseln in internationalen Finanzierungsverträgen nach New Yorker Recht"*, I Prax 1988, 179et seq.

75   Born and Westin, *International Civil Litigation in United States Courts*, 247et seq.

76   See discussion in *John S. Roby v. Lloyd's of London*, Fed. Sec. Rep. (CCH) P96, 971 (SDNY 1992); Born and Westin, *International Civil Litigation in United States Courts*, 221 et seq.

on foreign forum selection in the international context[77] is *The Bremen.*[78]

> [S]uch clauses are prima facie valid and should be enforced unless
> enforcement is shown by the resisting party to be "unreasonable"
> under the circumstances. [...] There are compelling reasons why a
> freely negotiated private international agreement, unaffected by fraud,
> undue influence, or overweening bargaining power, such as that in-
> volved here, should not be given full effect.[79] [quotation marks by the
> Court]

While landmark cases and statutory provisions in many countries generally enforce derogations, others do not. Furthermore,
even in countries where derogation is generally enforceable, there
are always limitations that, justifiably or unjustifiably, are construed to apply, particularly by lower courts.[80]

Four[81] partially related aspects are most important in the rejection of forum selection clauses: first, where the domestic court has
special exclusive jurisdiction, as in the special areas of law mentioned, such as family, estate, labour, and real estate law or in
areas that have both civil and administrative sides, such as securities and antitrust; second, where the court is dissatisfied with the
general circumstances of the agreement, such as the overweening
bargaining power of one of the parties. The German Civil Procedures Code holds unenforceable forum selection clauses against
private parties in domestic contracts[82] but allows them among commercial parties and in international contracts.[83] Several U.S. courts

---

77    Born and Westin, *International Civil Litigation in United States
      Courts*, 232.
78    *The Bremen v. Zapata Off-Shore Co.*, 407 U.S. 1 (1972).
79    *The Bremen*, at 9 and 14.
80    A list with case descriptions from U.S. and English judgements in
      which forum selection clauses were held inapplicable can be found
      in: Ralph H. Folsom, et al, *International Business Transactions in
      a Nutshell* (St. Paul, Minn.: West, 1992), 507et seq.; Born and
      Westin, *International Civil Litigation in United States Courts*, 247;
      Schack, *Internationales Zivilverfahrensrecht*, rn. 451.
81    Born and Westin, *International Civil Litigation in United States
      Courts*, 248et seq.
82    § 38 para 1 ZPO.
83    § 38 para 1 and 2 ZPO.

have relied heavily on the fact that a forum selection clause had not been individually bargained for in refusing to enforce it.[84]

Third, another set of three examples revolve about the language of the forum selection clause, which can be found to be unclear, thus leading to the conclusion that the parties only meant to provide for an additional forum not excluding the one called in the case.[85] Courts have also made differences in the scope of application of the clause. Two frequently used formulations for forum selection clauses are "all disputes arising under this agreement" and "all disputes relating to this agreement". Although these formulations appear similar, courts have sometimes concluded that the phrase "*arising* under this agreement" is less expansive than "*relating* to this agreement".[86]

Finally, and most importantly, are various aspects of *ordre public* or public policy. Under these theories courts deny enforcement of a forum selection clause where the court feels that in the foreign forum a party will be deprived of procedural justice or of substantial rights as available in the forum. Abroad as well as in the U.S. there are various decisions to this effect.[87]

The most interesting cases for the purpose of this study are those in which the denial of enforcement of a forum selection clause is based on the allegation of the selection of a biased foreign tribunal. In the U.S. this rule was frequently invoked in recent litigation involving Iranian entities.[88]

In the non-Iran-related *Union Insurance Society of Canton v. S.S. Elikon* 642 F.2d 721 (4th Cir. 1981), the court held a forum selection clause unenforceable on several grounds. The clause had been contained on a preprinted bill of lading, and the *Carriage of Goods by Sea Act*[89] (COGSA) had been mentioned in the contract, thus apparently contradicting the forum selection clause. The

---

84    Born and Westin, *International Civil Litigation in United States Courts*, 256, with further references.

85    Schack, *Internationales Zivilverfahrensrecht*, rn. 451.

86    Born and Westin, *International Civil Litigation in United States Courts*, 227, with further references.

87    See references in Folsom, et al, *International Business Transactions in a Nutshell*, 507et seq.; Born and Westin, *International Civil Litigation in United States Courts*, 247.

88    Born and Westin, *International Civil Litigation in United States Courts*, 263, with further references.

89    46 U.S.C. §§ 1300 et seq. (1976).

court then noted that the COGSA essentially represents the American enactment of the *Hague Rules*—to which Germany, the selected forum, is also a party—but dismissed this point with a cite from a 1976 case from the Second Circuit:

> A clause making a claim triable only in a foreign court would almost certainly lessen liability if the law which the court would apply was neither the Carriage of Goods by Sea Act nor the Hague Rules. Even when the foreign court would apply one or the other of these regimes [...] *there would be no assurance that it would apply them in the same way as would an American tribunal. . . .*[90] [omissions and emphasis by the author]

It finally concludes that "[w]hile the Court of Bremen is not an unreasonable forum on its face, it becomes more suspect in view of [Defendant's] headquarters in Bremen".

These and other judgements have led to warnings in the use and wording of forum selection clauses, which Gruson formulates from the lawyer's perspective that:

> choice of law, choice of forum and choice of jurisdiction clauses are (1) fairly simple to handle; and (2) virtually 100% legal [but], if you do not do a good job on them, you are going to wind up with egg all over your face.[91]

Despite the warnings and examples and a number of cases to the contrary by various authors, all authors agree that forum selection clauses should be used wherever possible and provide examples and reasoning for their preferred clauses, which would presumably hold before the courts.

Special note should be taken of the so-called "least preferred forum selection clauses"[92] designed to force each party to sue at

90      *Indussa Corp. v. S.S. Ranborg*, 377 F.2d 200 (1967) (*en banc*); *S.S. Elikon* at 724; as contrast see, for German law, the cites by Schack, *Internationales Zivilverfahrensrecht*, rn. 452 et seq.

91      Michael Gruson, in William A. Hancock, "ABA National Institute on International Contracting", in *Laws of International Trade*, ed. William A. Hancock (Chesterland, OH: Business Law Inc., 1991), 711.19. See the discussion therein, particularly Chapter 711, 711.14et seq.

92      William A. Hancock, "Commercial Issues in International Contracts", in *Laws of International Trade*, ed. William A. Hancock (Chesterland, OH: Business Law Inc., 1991), 714.11.

the other party's domicile, thus creating barriers and promoting negotiation and amicable resolution. What is standard in most civil-law countries and under the regime of the Brussels Convention is used here as a specific remedy towards U.S. long-arm statutes.

The literature's discussion of the legal-cultural advantages of suing at home for any plaintiff should lead one to believe that disputes generally would be initiated overwhelmingly at the plaintiff's domicile rather than the defendant's. It has been discussed, on page 85, that New York law easily allows jurisdiction at both plaintiff's and defendant's domicile in New York, making the choice almost free, subject only to certain rational considerations. Neglecting for a moment these rational considerations, a legal-cultural approach would lead to the expectation that the more powerful party of a contractual relationship will enforce its own jurisdiction clause. This possibility is emphasized by an additional aspect found in the judgement study. As to the underlying reasons for the motion for dismissal on the grounds of *forum non conveniens*, in most cases (25 of 31), the foreign defendant made the motion for dismissal.[93] Therefore there seems to be a reluctance to be sued in a foreign forum. It has been shown, however, that such reluctance is not reflected in the distribution of the plaintiffs' origins, nor is it reflected by a large number of forum selection agreements. In fact forum selection agreements do not play a significant role in court at all.

It is possible that, where there is no issue, references to forum selection agreements may have been omitted in the judgements. However in most cases even nonrelevant issues of a contract were cited for background purposes and forum selection clauses were not often part of such cites. Thus the number of references should be higher if forum selection agreements were more frequent. On the other hand, the determinable bases for jurisdiction made forum selection clauses unnecessary for New York jurisdiction in those cases. Such clauses would only have served to exclude New York's broad jurisdictional powers rather than create the same. This possibly would lead to omission. However, it can be assumed that the rareness of the data of selection of law clauses, which are usually combined with forum selection clauses in handbook sample contracts, would rather point to an overall rareness of such clauses in court.

93   See further discussion below.

Having excluded forum selection agreements as a reason for selecting the place of litigation, the following reasons have to be considered for the frequent occurrence of foreign plaintiffs in both data bases.[94]

First, forum selection clauses may be generally less frequent than literature and interviews[95] with legal practitioners suggest. Either such clauses are not frequent in contracts or drafted contracts are not as frequent as previously thought. In fact forum selection clauses are rare in all analysed cases despite a large number of cases based on negotiated contracts. It must be remembered that businessmen often do not invest the necessary time and expense but hope and assume that business deals by telephone, telex, or facsimile without protracted contract negotiations and lawyer interference will suffice. There may be a large number of relationships without drafted contracts or drafted contracts without forum selection clauses contrary to the literature. Within the judgement data, forum selection clauses had been used in only five out of 224 contractual cases.

Still this theory does not provide a sufficient explanation for the reasons why plaintiffs seem to prefer defendants' domicile as place of jurisdiction. As previously discussed U.S. procedural rules allow, if not favour, jurisdiction at the plaintiff's home, which, in the absence of forum selection clauses, should lead to an overall preference of initiating a lawsuit at one's own domicile.

Second, conceivably, contracts with forum selection clauses are crafted with care and consideration and thus are rarely brought to court. The surprising lack of American-type contracts in the German file analysis seems to confirm this thought. Within the state supreme court file analysis, at least half of the disputes were contractual, yet in only three cases was the court's jurisdiction allegedly based on a forum selection clause. These three cases were among the more successful ones procedurally, as they ended with a judgement or order—alas by default as the defendant failed to appear.

Within the New York judgement data base, all five forum selection clauses were motioned in a motion to dismiss, and four of the forum selection clauses were enforced, the fifth being deferred for further argument. Of the four, two led to a dismissal in favour

94    And, in fact, in all studies of the project. See also Gessner, herein.
95    No. 1, 3, 6, and 8.

of a foreign jurisdiction. Despite warnings in literature and case law of the possibility of unenforceability of forum selection clauses, this seems to be rather exceptional as the data show no such occurrence.

At least the lawyers who were interviewed[96] themselves take pride in that their contracts are so good as to not create disputes, and, in case a dispute arises after all, they are usually able to settle amicably most disputes out of court. After all the existence of a contract with a forum selection clause is usually predicated on the involvement of lawyers. The parties' contact to these lawyers is probably utilized once a dispute arises, and early involvement of lawyers may contribute to early out-of-court settlements.

Third, whereas the stronger party in a contract will succeed with its forum selection clause, that party also has the means to enforce its rights without resorting to courts. It is the weaker party that has to sue (at the stronger party's domicile) in order to reach its goals. The data also suggest this possibility. A comparison of the party type of the state supreme court file analysis shows that there were more lawsuits of private plaintiffs against corporations than the reverse. The judgement analysis distinguishes between different sizes of corporations (see Table NY–4). The distribution of type of parties confirmed this hypothesis, as more than 80% of the cases were commenced by private parties or small and medium-sized corporations. On the defendant side the larger corporations and institutions were slightly more often represented, but it still appears as if they are usually able to avoid litigation altogether.

However if one assumes that private and small corporate parties face the highest barriers to court access,[97] private foreign parties should rather sue at their own domicile, while only bigger foreign corporate plaintiffs might sue abroad. Considering the U.S. procedural possibilities of choosing one's own domicile as forum, the numbers should be untainted by jurisdictional limitations.

96   Particularly, No. 2, 3, and 6.
97   See discussion in Joel B. Grossman, et al., "Dimensions of Institutional Participation: Who Uses the Courts, and How?", in *Civil Litigation Research Project, Final Report, Part B* (Madison, WI: 1983), III–446ff., and *The Journal of Politics* 44 (1982): 86et seq.

### Table NY–13: Distribution of Plaintiff Type by Country of Origin in New York Judgements (1992)

| Plaintiff Type | Country of Origin | | Total | |
|---|---|---|---|---|
| | Foreign | U.S. | (N) | % |
| Other | 2 | 4 | 6 | 2 |
| Government | 4 | 4 | 8 | 2 |
| Insurance | 5 | 9 | 14 | 4 |
| Multinational corp. | 16 | 3 | 19 | 5 |
| Other corp. | 91 | 96 | 187 | 53 |
| Banks | 17 | 3 | 20 | 6 |
| Private individuals | 45 | 54 | 99 | 28 |
| Total          (N) | 180 | 173 | 353 | |
| %  | 51 | 49 | | 100 |

This hypothesis is not exactly confirmed by the data in the preceding table. Rather, private individual plaintiffs are almost equally distributed between foreign (45%) and U.S. individuals (55%), and the same is true for small and medium-sized corporations (49% to 51%, foreign and U.S., respectively). Such corporations and private parties form the major part (81%) of all plaintiffs. Banks and large corporations are overwhelmingly foreign rather than of U.S. origin (approximately 85% foreign). This overrepresentation of large entities would confirm the hypothesis of lower access barriers for these types of foreign parties to U.S. courts compared to individuals and smaller corporations. However the participation of foreign individual and smaller corporate plaintiffs is so large that, even if said barriers do play a role, they are not ultimately decisive. Therefore, in the type of cases herein, other aspects than barriers to access to court have more influence on the decision of where to commence action.

Fourth and finally, it may be more favourable to sue at the defendant's domicile than is generally assumed. Potential advantages are the ease of service of process, namely, the advantage of starting the lawsuit faster, and the ease of enforcement of a judgement, once obtained. In fact in one of the New York judgements analysed, the parties had drafted an agreement that provided for a waiver of sovereign immunity but did

not affirmatively or exclusively select New York as the only proper, or preferred forum. To the contrary, the silence of this carefully worded document on this point indicates that the parties intended otherwise applicable rules to control.[98]

Thus forum selection clauses may even be wantonly avoided. However based on the insistence of literature and lawyers on the importance of forum selection clauses in one's own favour, this probably does not occur that frequently. However, it may be that, based on the importance lawyers and literature place on one's own forum, many parties cannot agree on any forum without the danger of severing their relationship. While the usage—or nonusage—of forum selection clauses has provided some idea as to the structure of international litigation, the low number of these cases has not resolved the question as to the reasons for the selection of New York courts as a forum, and even less for litigation itself.

## C. The Selection of Arbitration as Forum

The discussion of arbitration clauses, as an alternative dispute resolution to court litigation, may shed additional light on the selection of New York courts. Literature often advises the use of arbitration clauses in international contracts, because arbitration[99] awards have an easier path to recognition and enforcement than judgements. Congress has enacted legislation that governs arbitration in areas of federal law and international commerce. The Federal Arbitration Act[100] provides, in Section 2, that it ap-

98    *Proyecfin de Venezuela et al. v. Banco Venezuela*, LEXIS 7929 (SDNY 1992).

99    For further information on arbitration in the U.S., see Herbert M. Lord, "Arbitration in the United States", *The Maritime Lawyer* (1984): 227; Michael J. Mustill; "Arbitration: History and Background", *Journal of International Arbitration* 6, no. 2 (1989): 43 et seq. and, of course, Martin Domke, *The Law and Practice of Commercial Arbitration* (Mundelein, IL: Callaghan, 1968).

100   United States Arbitration Act of 12 February 1925, amended 30 July 1947, further amended in particular 13 July 1970 by incorporation of the UN Convention on Recognition and Enforcement of Arbitration Awards, and further amended on 31 May 1990 by incorporation of the Inter-American Convention on International Commercial Arbitration. Since 1954 the U.S. Arbitration Act is published under 9 U.S.C. §§ 1–14, 201–208, 301–307, cited therefrom.

plies on all maritime transactions and those that concern inter-state and international commerce. Within its purview, the Federal Arbitration Act overrules state law and has to be applied by federal courts as well as state courts. Because many procedural aspects are not covered by the act, the law of the place of arbitration remains applicable[101] to some extent and especially where the parties have specifically provided that state law should apply. State statutory and common law also remains applicable whenever any aspect is not covered by the act.[102] This item is important for the commencement of the arbitration, because the New York CPLR,[103] for example, provides for rules regarding a "demand for arbitration" or "notice of intention to arbitrate" with a twenty-day notice period in which the other party has the final chance to request a "stay of arbitration" from a court or lose most of its rights to challenge the arbitration, or even the award in court, on the grounds that there is no valid arbitration agreement, that such agreement has not been followed, or that a statute of limitation applies. For cross-border arbitration, § 202 FAA provides that all commercial arbitration is governed by the act, excluding only arbitration proceedings that have taken place within the U.S. among exclusively American parties and that have no connection to foreign property or contractual obligations or any other international connection.[104]

Yet before arbitration awards are to be enforced, the agreement itself may be subject to scrutiny. The U.S. Supreme Court has strongly argued in favour of the recognition of arbitration clauses on the basis of *The Bremen* and a definition of arbitration clauses being just another type of forum selection clause. In *Scherk v. Alberto-Culver Co.* 417 U.S. 506 (1973) the court held that:

> An agreement to arbitrate before a specified tribunal is, in effect, a specialized kind of forum-selection clause that posits not only the situs of the suit but also the procedure to be used in resolving the dispute, and the invalidation of the arbitration clause in this case would not only allow respondent to repudiate its solemn promise but would, as

101   New York Bar Association, ed., *Committee on Arbitration: An Outline of Procedure under Arbitration Law in New York, New York* (New York: New York Bar Association, 1984).

102   *Todd Shipyards Corp. v. Cunard Line Ltd.*, 1989 AMC 2866, 2869 (NDCA 1989) (*M/V Sagaford*).

103   See § 7503 (c) CPLR.

104   *Bergesen v. Joseph Muller Corp.*, 170 F.2d 928 (2d Cir. 1983).

well, reflect a parochial concept that all disputes must be resolved under our laws and in our courts.[105] [citations omitted]

Several statutory provisions extend the protection of arbitration beyond that concept of similarity to forum selection clauses. The UN Convention and the Inter-American Convention on International Commercial Arbitration have been ratified by the United States.[106]

The lawyers interviewed on this topic were rather divided. Some preferred arbitration,[107] some preferred court litigation,[108] some answered the question depending on the circumstances,[109] and the lawyers with little international experience usually had never given any thought to this question.[110] For the first two groups, the lawyer's personal experience regarding the particular client base and case structure of the firm made the difference. Maritime lawyers who often work with arbitration clearly preferred this method of dispute resolution. An experienced litigation lawyer, on the other hand, answered:

> We know our courts and how to proceed therein, we know everything there is to know about the Rules [of civil procedure] and all, we know the judges . . . . But we have little experience with arbitration, I just don't know enough about arbitration . . . . No, we do not advise our clients to arbitrate. I even believe we can get a case resolved much faster and cheaper in court.[111]

The third group answered that they generally used forum selection and choice of law clauses. In some circumstances, however, arbitration was preferred. Such circumstances mentioned were cases

---

105   *Bergesen*, at 507.
106   For the Convention on the Recognition and the Enforcement of Foreign Arbitration Awards of 10 June 1958, in force since 7 July 1959, 330 UNTS 1959; United States Arbitration Act of 12 February 1925, as amended 30 July 1947, the incorporation the convention by amendment of 13 July 1970, and of the Inter-American Convention by amendment of 31 May 1990, since 1954 as 9 U.S.C. §§ 1–14, 201–208, 301–307; below cited as §§ of the FAA.
107   No. 2 and 4.
108   No. 3 and 6.
109   No. 5 and 8.
110   No. 1, 5, 7, and 8.
111   No. 3.

in which enforcement seemed necessary in a jurisdiction that would rather enforce arbitration clauses than judgements and cases in which a certain procedure was preferred that could be defined in advance, such as a procedure in which oral testimony would be excluded as far as legally possible. These cases involved patterns where the travel of witnesses to remote jurisdictions was to be avoided. The law on arbitration gives the possibility of selecting and regulating the procedure to a certain extent. In a contract, a clause was found in which the parties had provided that for all purposes, sworn affidavits should suffice and, whenever a party would demand oral testimony, it would have to bear the costs, including travel and reasonable living expenses, regardless of the outcome of the proceeding.

A final category in which the "divided" attorneys preferred arbitration involved matters with "political intricacies", particularly with regard to the reputation of the parties involved. The lawyers reasoned that arbitration would allow for more secrecy than court litigation. Thus, in the bylaws of an association with a client referral system in the area of financial services, disputes between the members regarding the referral fees were referred to arbitration within the association.

In general recognition and enforcement is awarded to most written international commercial arbitration agreements and awards thereunder under certain limiting circumstances. It is the limiting circumstances and exceptions that are interesting for our purposes.[112]

In the New York state supreme court file analysis, four cases involved arbitration, which is quite a large number of this small set (see, Table NY-7). In two cases an arbitration award had been obtained by the U.S. petitioner: in one the petitioner requested and received recognition of the award; in the other, the petitioner motioned and received an order vacating the arbitration award on the grounds that the arbitrators had erred and exceeded their authority (*ultra vires*). One case involved a motion to compel arbitration, which was denied on the grounds that the arbitration would prolong the proceedings.

---

112    It would be too much to discuss all legal aspects of arbitration agreement under the FAA, New York CPLR § 7501, et seq., and common law.

The judgement analysis is similar. In 32 of the judgements (approximately 8%), arbitration clauses played a role, distributed as follows:

### Table NY-14: Judgements Relating to Arbitration in New York Judgements (1992)

| Type of motion | Judgement/Order for plaintiff | Judgement/Order for defendant | No result |
|---|---|---|---|
| To compel | 11 | 2 | 1 |
| Recognition | 7 | 1 | 0 |
| Third-party | 5 | 0 | 0 |
| Other | 0 | 0 | 5 |
| Total | 23 | 3 | 6 |

The "other" proceedings involved one in which the parties had an arbitration agreement, but apparently—and for unknown reasons—neither of the parties motioned to enforce it. Another case involved a liability claim against the American Arbitration Association for allegedly misadministering a proceeding, a third case involved a liability suit for costs against the other party for breach of an arbitration agreement, and two were cases in which an arbitration agreement had been made but had not been pursued due to the plaintiff's bankruptcy.

The high number of occurrences of arbitration agreements *in court* is quite surprising indeed, the idea of arbitration allegedly being the avoidance of court litigation. Lacking information as to the occurrence and duration of arbitration proceedings in general and the arbitration matters in the data bases in particular, final conclusions are not possible. The following table shows the duration quartiles for the cases involving arbitration agreements.

### Table NY-15: Duration of Cases Involving Arbitration Agreements in New York Judgements (1992)

| Duration | Frequency | Percent |
|---|---|---|
| Very low | 6 | 19 |
| Medium low | 12 | 38 |
| Medium high | 10 | 31 |
| Very high | 4 | 13 |
| Total | 32 | 100 |

Table NY-15 shows that the medium-low (37.5%) and medium-high (31.3%) duration cases are overrepresented among these cases, and those of very short (18.8%) and very long duration

(12.5%) are underrepresented. This would mean that most of these cases cannot be determined in a summary proceeding in lieu of the arbitration agreement and do take a considerable amount of time. For the arbitrating parties the high number of proceedings in which arbitration has to be compelled or recognized in court means an additional proceeding involving loss of time and additional expenses, particularly where, as in two of the cases, an appeal is involved.

From the legal summary it is not surprising that (eventually) most arbitration agreements are honoured and enforced by the courts. Thus it is the three cases in which motions to compel or recognitions were denied that require further attention.

In two cases the motion to compel arbitration or motion to dismiss or stay pending arbitration was denied as the proceeding involved parties who had not submitted to the original arbitration agreement. The subsequent incorporation of the arbitration clause of one agreement into another agreement was held to be faulty. It is customary in maritime trade and in the insurance business to incorporate an arbitration clause of a master contract, for example, the charter party between owner and charterer, into a third-party contract, such as a bill of lading between the charterer and the owner or shipper of the goods. Here, however, the court held in one of the cases that the charter party had been formulated to refer "all disputes between owner and charterer" to arbitration. The incorporation by mere reference into the bill of lading had thus not automatically included the shipper of the goods, who had not been named. In the other case a battle of forms had led to an unclear situation as to whether the incorporation of a clause from an insurance contract into the reinsurance contract had been effective.

A third case, *Iran Aircraft Industries v. AVCO*, 980 F.2d 141 (2nd Cir. 1992) was an Iranian case under the Algiers Accord,[113]

113    "The [arbitration] Tribunal was created by the Algiers Accords (the 'Accords'), an agreement between the United States and Iran, through the mediation of Algeria, which provided for the release of the 52 hostages seized at the American Embassy in Tehran on November 4, 1979. In addition to providing conditions for the release of the hostages, the Accords established the Tribunal to serve as a forum for the binding arbitration of all existing disputes between the governments of each country and the nationals of the other." *Iran Aircraft Industries*, at 143.

in which the court denied enforcement of the arbitration award of $3.5 million on the grounds that the procedure had been unfair. The arbitration tribunal had initially advised the U.S. respondent, who was now requesting to vacate the award, that certain documents perhaps did not need to be produced. However, in its award the tribunal based its decision in part on the absence of these documents. The court held by majority that recognition of the award should be denied pursuant to Article V(1)(b) of the New York convention, which provides for nonenforcement where:

> The party against whom the award is invoked was not given proper notice of the appointment of the arbitrator or of the arbitration proceedings or was otherwise unable to present his case . . . .

However, a dissenting opinion[114] by Chief Justice Cardamone argued on the fact that the tribunal had not clearly indicated that the documents need not be produced and that the tribunal had later specifically asked for the same. Thus the respondent had voluntarily chosen a risky course of action for which he should be held responsible. Cardamone argued further:

> One of the reasons for this dissent is because until today no federal or foreign case appears to have used article V(1)(b)'s narrow exception as a reason to refuse to enforce an arbitral award due to the arbitration panel's failure to consider certain evidence. Moreover, some decisions have rejected the article V(1)(b) defence under other, somewhat analogous circumstances. [citation omitted]

Quite interestingly in five of the cases the plaintiff had obtained a favourable arbitration award but the debtor had dissolved before enforcement. The plaintiffs were trying to obtain remedy from alleged alter egos,[115] owners or successor companies of the original debtor claiming fraud. All these proceedings were in preliminary stages and survived the motion for summary judgement to dismiss. Of the other successful cases two are noteworthy. In one of the cases the defendant had unsuccessfully motioned to vacate the award on the grounds of "manifest disregard of the law". In the other case both parties had motioned for recognition of the award, but were in disagreement as to the reading of the award, which provided a formula for the calculation of damages rather

114   *Iran Aircraft Industries*, at 155 et seq.
115   I.e., names that are only an alias for another person or company, being actually identical when looking below the surface.

than a sum. The court confirmed and recognized the award in part and remanded to the arbitrators to solve the remaining questions. This result is surprising insofar as the law does not usually allow this procedure. The general rule provides that once the arbitrators have rendered their award, their power ends.

In summary, in most of the cases and against all motions to the contrary, arbitration agreements are enforced, even when the debtor attempts to avoid payment by restructuring the company. Yet the warnings in the literature are not to be discarded. In fact careful wording of arbitration agreements as well as incorporation clauses might help, but it seems a certain insecurity always remains with regard to court interpretation.

Furthermore, it is inherent in the arbitration system and in governmental monopoly of force that for any compulsory measure the parties or the tribunal must seek the assistance of the state through the courts. When this happens, though, the original intention to save costs in the resolution of disputes in alternative forums is defeated. In effect, where arbitration is met by uncooperative opponents, time and cost effectiveness is lost. Thus it is a dispute resolution technique that works for cooperating parties rather than for adversarial disputing.[116] On the other hand, there may be circumstances in which arbitration is reasonable and favourable for both parties and in which such clauses should be and are employed.

## D. *Forum Non Conveniens*

A particular legal aspect of cross-border litigation in New York courts may assist in resolving the question of the reasons for selecting New York as one's forum for litigation. A potential way to limit the effects of overly broad jurisdictional rules is the legal doctrine of *forum non conveniens*.[117] According to this doctrine, a court that otherwise has jurisdiction may decline to entertain a

---

116  This is confirmed by a study by Ayse Özel, *Schiedsgerichtsbarkeit als alternative Streiterledigung—eine empirische Untersuchung der Vor- und Nachteile am Beispiel der New Yorker Seeschiedsgerichtsbarkeit* (unpublished paper, Bremen: University of Bremen, 1991).

117  A detailed discussion can be found in Lesley Jane Smith, "Antisuit Injunctions, Forum non Conveniens and International Comity", *Recht der Internationalen Wirtschaft* (1993): 802.

claim if it feels that it is the inappropriate court for the case. A court may decline a case on the grounds of *forum non conveniens* if another "appropriate"[118] court exists that would have jurisdiction and would entertain the case. Upon motion, or *sua sponte*,[119] the court has to weigh the facts that point to itself or to another forum to determine the most appropriate forum for the dispute, considering, inter alia, the selection of the plaintiff, the inconveniences of either party and the witnesses, the availability of evidence, and the docket of the court. Motions to dismiss on the grounds of *forum non conveniens* are frequently employed in transborder and interstate disputes, thus showing that the defendant often may prefer a different forum than the plaintiff.

The foreign defendants in the state supreme court file analysis rarely participated. The relevance of *forum non conveniens* for the judgement set is illustrated in the following table.

### Table NY-16: The Role of *Forum Non Conveniens* in New York Judgements (1992)

| | Forum non conveniens discussed | Application denied | Case dismissed | Case dismissed on other grounds |
|---|---|---|---|---|
| No. of cases* | 31 | 12 | 14 | 7[†] |

\* This is 8% of the data base.
† In two of the cases dismissed on other grounds, *forum non conveniens* was explicitly denied, and one case was referred to a magistrate to decide.

While the numbers are not overwhelming, it shows that there is at least some significance to this aspect and that the argument of *forum non conveniens* directly leads to dismissal in more cases than it is denied.

Within the judgements motions for dismissal on the grounds of *forum non conveniens* were frequently employed—31 times. In 25 cases the foreign defendant asked for dismissal on this basis, while the U.S. defendant did in six cases, the latter apparently on the grounds that the law would be more favourable abroad than at home. The success of these motions is almost evenly divided.

118   This does not mean that a different legal system or different chances for the parties in that court disqualifies that court.

119   I.e., on its own decision. The civil-law equivalent would be the concept of *ex officio*.

Considering the factors that play a role in the result, it could be suggested that it may make a difference which countries are involved. However, while the U.K. and Australia (both of which are common-law countries) are somewhat overrepresented, this is true for the denied as well as the dismissed cases. Both also include Ireland, Germany, Canada, Poland, China, Japan, and several Latin American countries.

Upon further review it seems that the most relevant factor leading to a denial of the respective motion or dismissal of the case was the personality and discretion of the judge involved. This fact reduces the explanatory power, if any, of the results of motions on *forum non conveniens* for the litigants' behaviour.

In half of the cases in which *forum non conveniens* was held inapplicable, the same judge was involved, and that judge dismissed no case on that ground. On the other hand, three judges dismissed all of their cases in favour of a foreign jurisdiction either on the ground of *forum non conveniens* or on another ground (8 on the grounds of *forum non conveniens*). Other judges were involved only once, so it is difficult to ascertain their position. The importance of personal preferences is further underlined after secondhand review of the reasons for the decisions, distinguishing between relatively clear-cut and apparently doubtful cases.[120] Further personal preferences involved conditioning of the dismissal on the defendant's submission to the foreign court's jurisdiction and waiver of defences with regard to statutes of limitation by express declaration to the court. In four cases such conditions were imposed—three by the same judge, while the judge in the fourth case was involved only once so her personal preference cannot be determined.

Interestingly, despite a completely randomized assignment of judges to matters in New York, there is some disparity—too much to be random—in the number of decisions in international matters by each of the 40 judges. The court's clerk office for the southern district explained that, in fact, there were a number of senior judges with a reduced caseload. Considering this, and further taking into account the judges beginning or ending office in mid-year,

---

120  This secondhand review is problematic and should be used with caution, especially from a legal standpoint, considering that the facts are only summarily available. Nevertheless it can be useful in some cases.

the disparity becomes less. Thus, while the assignment system seems randomized after all, the practice with regard to *forum non conveniens* is not. It should be noted at this point that in all other respects the judge assigned did not have a significant or explanatory influence on the cases.

Consequently it appears that in any event *forum non conveniens* is an important question, yet, due to the wide discretion of the individual judges, there is only limited assurance as to the outcome of a respective motion. Thus, (1) the legal area of *forum non conveniens* is an area of insecurity with regard to the law as it is applied, and (2) *forum non conveniens* is not a secure protection for foreign defendants against being brought before U.S. courts against their will.

Nevertheless, the fact that in 25 out of 173 cases (14.5%) against foreign defendants motions regarding *forum non conveniens* were employed at least confirms some considerable degree of reluctance by foreign parties to be sued in New York as well as the fact that, without *forum non conveniens*, New York's jurisdictional rules are relatively broad. For several reasons the number of motions for *forum non conveniens* cannot be used as a precise measure for the reluctance of foreign defendants. In particular, it is unknown how many foreign defendants did not move for dismissal despite their disregard for the New York forum because such a motion would have been futile for legal reasons. Nor is it known how many of the foreign defendants moving for dismissal on *forum non conveniens* employed this means simply in order to delay and defeat the plaintiff's claim in the first place, rather than opposing the forum alone.

## E. Dispute Resolution in Litigation

### 1. Introduction

Apparently foreigners usually do not have nonrational and legal-cultural reasons for avoiding New York courts as the forum for dispute resolution. Of the rational reasons, one should assume that the anticipated ratio of success would be the most decisive. In order to examine the successfulness of transborder litigation, one must define "success". As viewed from different sides of a lawsuit—the attorneys, the court, or the general public—success probably has different meanings. In addition a party may even consider losing a lawsuit as success, when the time lost by the opponent is an advantage, and a winning party may have even preferred an amicable resolution. And not all proceedings are commenced in order to obtain an enforceable judgement. Internal accounting and taxation may sometimes be a reason for commencing a lawsuit as a corporation or a department within a corporation may have to prove that it has made reasonable efforts to offset the losses, and a landlord-tenant judgement for past rent due may be necessary for the landlord in order to rerent the apartment even when the past rent judgement cannot be enforced against the defendant.

Despite these limitations, the following analysis shall focus on the plaintiffs' monetary or formal success rate in relation to the claim for the following reasons. First, as mentioned, this formal "success rate" may be a factor in the decision of whether a lawsuit would be commenced in the forum studied. Second, despite the fact that other results may be the intended success for either party, it is a valid assumption that in most cases winning the case is still the goal. After all, even for attorneys on an hourly fee schedule it is of long-term advantage to win their cases in order to maintain their reputation.[121] Third, using this formal monetary success rate also allows a comparison of different factors leading to the court's determination.

One further *caveat* needs to be mentioned as it forms the basis for the following discussion. In most cases judgements that cannot be enforced are without any effect and are but a Pyrrhic victory. This is likely the case in judgements in which the defendant was never properly served with a summons and complaint. The right to be heard is generally considered essential to a fair trial, and the latter is usually a prerequisite for the recognition and enforcement of foreign judgements.[122] Default judgements or quasi-default judgements bear the likelihood of lack of actual service and shall be examined further in each case for the probability of enforcement against the defendant. The judgement set is insofar limited but

121    Herbert Kritzer, et al, *The Impact of Fee Arrangement on Lawyer Effort,* (Working Paper, Madison, WI: University of Wisconsin Law School, 1984); Earl Jr. Johnson, "Lawyers' Choice: A Theoretical Appraisal of Litigation Investment Decisions", in *Civil Litigation Research Project, Final Report, Part B* (Madison, WI: University of Wisconsin Law School, 1983), III–175 et seq., and *Law & Society Review* 15, no. 3–4 (1980–81): 567 et seq.

122    See discussion below.

also particularly interesting, because therein there are only cases in which both sides participated at least to the point where the respective decision was rendered. Default judgements are generally not publicized. The official statistics for the federal courts in New York[123] show that only about a third of all civil cases are terminated on their merits.[124]

Furthermore, whenever a settlement agreement was reached during the proceeding, for the purpose of this chapter, this is not termed "success in court", although the court proceeding may have been the catalyst for the settlement; there are not enough data on such cases. Therefore, the question is limited to whether a plaintiff has a chance to succeed in court.

Finally lawyers would argue that the most important factor to the outcome of a lawsuit are the merits of the case. However, this study assumes that there may be other, nonlegal factors that have an effect on the outcome.

Apart from the availability of courts as such, and the courts of New York in particular, the questions arise as to when and why a plaintiff decides to utilize and pursue litigation in the first place. One could assume that litigation is sought when negotiations prove of no avail and where the plaintiff expects to succeed (which, for the time being, leaves open the question of why the other party, the potential defendant, would not settle a claim in advance where the plaintiff can be expected to succeed).

## 2. Analysis

In per cent of the value or, where inapplicable, in per cent of the counts of the brief or motion, the plaintiffs formally reached the following results:

### Table NY-17: Success in Court in New York Supreme Court File Analysis (1986)

| Plaintiff's success | Cases |
|---|---|
| Yes | 8 |
| Mixed | 1 |
| None | 24 |
| Total | 33 |

123  Administrative Office of the United States Courts, *1992 Federal Court Management Statistics* (Washington, D.C., 1993), calculated from pp. 6 and 45 et seq.

124  Excluding prisoner petitions, which are treated as civil cases in some statistical reports.

In further examining the successful cases, the most remarkable result is that only one of the cases from the state supreme court file analysis ended with a final judgement after controversy. In this case a construction worker had brought suit against his employer, the contractor and the building owner, and a foreign bank, which was the building owner's creditor. The plaintiff succeeded in two out of eight counts and received 11% of the amount requested in his complaint (termed "mixed" in the table). Out of the remaining successful cases, the following list gives an idea of what happened with these cases.

### Table NY–18: Description of Successful Cases by Origin of Plaintiff (Foreign/U.S.) in New York Supreme Court File Analysis (1986)

*Foreign country plaintiffs*
Settlement out of court and subsequent joint motion to dismiss without prejudice
Declaratory judgement upon settlement between the parties
Judgement on promissory note, probably enforceable

*U.S. plaintiffs*
Default recognition of a default arbitration award
Default judgement vacating a default arbitration award
Default order (defendant alleges in correspondence that it would not be enforceable in Italy, where a parallel proceeding is pending)
Judgement on promissory note, probably unenforceable
Default judgement (defendant tenant now presumably in Ghana)

The table allows the conclusion that three of the foreign plaintiffs were successful, two of whom reached a settlement. Of the U.S. plaintiffs, five were formally successful in court, in addition to the partially successful case described above, which must be considered special because the U.S. plaintiff stood against a mixed U.S.-non-U.S. set of defendants in which the U.S. defendants were the more important ones.

However, a closer look at these five cases in which the U.S. plaintiffs were apparently fully successful reveals that none of these judgements has any chance of being actually enforced against the defendant. In one case this is even expressed by the defendant, who declined to answer specifically. In the other cases it is apparent that the defendants never actually received notice of the proceedings. As shall be discussed more specifically, lack of notice is a legal bar to recognition and enforcement in most jurisdictions and legal systems.

In comparison to these initial results of the state supreme court file analysis, the judgement set has certain disadvantages. It has to be noted again that cases in which service on the foreign defendant failed, that have been procedurally given up by the plaintiff, or were settled after filing are not generally contained in this set. On the other hand, the judgement set has the advantage of excluding certain nonlegal aspects and focusing the attention on the law.

Of the following tables, Table NY–19 refers to the success rate of the respective parties in all decisions, including interim decisions not concluding the case. Table NY–20 refers only to those 174 decisions (49%) that finally concluded the case.

### Table NY–19: Overall Success Rate by Country of Plaintiff in New York Judgements (1992)

| Country of Plaintiff | Winner | | | | | | | |
|---|---|---|---|---|---|---|---|---|
| | Plaintiff | | Defendant | | Mixed | | Total | |
| | % | (N) | % | (N) | % | (N) | % | (N) |
| Foreign | 53 | (40) | 48 | (127) | 46 | ( 5) | 49 | (172) |
| U.S. & Foreign | 7 | ( 5) | 5 | ( 14) | | | 5 | (19) |
| U.S. | 40 | (30) | 47 | (126) | 55 | ( 6) | 46 | (162) |
| Total    % | 21 | | 76 | | 3 | | 100 | |
|          (N) | | (75) | | (267) | | (11) | | (353) |

### Table NY–20: Success Rate by Country of Plaintiff for Final Decisions in New York Judgements (1992)

| Country of Plaintiff | Winner | | | | | | | |
|---|---|---|---|---|---|---|---|---|
| | Plaintiff | | Defendant | | Mixed | | Total | |
| | % | (N) | % | (N) | % | (N) | % | (N) |
| Foreign | 57 | (24) | 47 | ( 59) | 50 | (3) | 49 | ( 86) |
| U.S. & Foreign | 7 | ( 3) | 2 | ( 3) | | | 3 | (6) |
| U.S. | 36 | (15) | 51 | ( 64) | 50 | (3) | 47 | ( 82) |
| Total    % | 24 | | 72 | | 3 | | 100 | |
|          (N) | | (42) | | (126) | | (6) | | (174) |

The results of the tables rather seem to disprove the above hypothesis that assumes the probable success ratio as a rational incentive to commence a lawsuit. In fact only about a quarter of the plaintiffs in the New York Supreme Court file study reached success at least formally (8 out of 33) and, again, only a quarter of the plaintiffs were successful in the New York judgement analysis (23.3%). For the latter it makes little difference whether the judgement finally settled the case (27.9% success rate) or whether it was an interim judgement that only decided a particular motion (23.3% overall success rate), although in the interim decisions the plaintiffs were slightly less successful. It further seems that foreigners are even slightly more successful than U.S. litigants in both groups (23% vs. 19% overall and 28% vs. 18% final decisions). This may have to do with the potentially greater barriers that would dissuade foreigners from commencing a claim, or it may simply have to do with the cases against foreigners dismissed for lack of service or jurisdiction or similar reasons that would account for the small difference. The little differences, if any, that could be found with regard to the parties' behaviour in court rather points to the latter. On the other hand, the state supreme court file analysis indicates that U.S. plaintiffs more frequently obtain default judgements against foreign defendants. In the event of a response by the defendants, many of these cases of default judgements would probably have been dismissed for jurisdictional or similar reasons.

One wonders why plaintiffs would litigate when the average success rate is less than 25%.[125] One could imagine that the plaintiffs commence the lawsuits with an eye on the amounts at stake, taking a risk for the chances of gaining more than they have to invest. If this were true one should observe a relationship between (1) the legal costs invested and the value of the case and (2) the success rate, the legal costs invested, and the value of the case (risk/chance). The duration of the proceeding would have some influence on the legal costs, as would the length of the judgement indicate the extensiveness of counsels' presentation of facts, legal argument, and disputing. For the following tables the overall complexity multiplied by the duration were used as indicators for the lawyers' time and legal costs invested (investment). The risk was calculated as the ratio of the "investment" divided by the value of

125    Trubek, et al. come to a much better ratio for domestic cases; in fact, they resume that litigation does pay off for the parties involved. David Trubek, et al., "Civil Litigation as the Investment of Lawyer Time", in *Civil Litigation Research Project, Final Report, Part B* (Madison, WI: University of Wisconsin Law School, 1983), II–173 et seq.

the case. Thus, the higher the fees in relation to the value, the higher the risk the party is willing to take.

### Table NY–21: Investment by Value in New York Judgements (1992)

| Value | Investment | | | | | | | | | |
|---|---|---|---|---|---|---|---|---|---|---|
| | Very low | | Medium low | | Medium high | | Very high | | Total | |
| | % | (N) | % | (N) | % | (N) | % | (N) | % | (N) |
| Less than 200,000 | 44 | (14) | 20 | (9) | 26 | (12) | 13 | (7) | 24 | (42) |
| 200,000 to 650,000 | 16 | (5) | 28 | (13) | 28 | (13) | 30 | (16) | 27 | (47) |
| 651,000 to 2.5 million | 22 | (7) | 28 | (13) | 22 | (10) | 26 | (14) | 25 | (44) |
| More than 2.5 million | 19 | (6) | 24 | (11) | 24 | (11) | 30 | (16) | 25 | (44) |
| Total        % | 18 | | 26 | | 26 | | 30 | | 100 | |
| (N) | | (32) | | (46) | | (46) | | (53) | | (177) |

### Table NY–22: Success of Plaintiff by Risk in New York Judgements (1992)

| Success of Plaintiff | Risk | | | | | | | | | |
|---|---|---|---|---|---|---|---|---|---|---|
| | Very low | | Medium low | | Medium high | | Very high | | Total | |
| | % | (N) | % | (N) | % | (N) | % | (N) | % | (N) |
| Lost | 75 | (33) | 68 | (30) | 69 | (31) | 71 | (31) | 71 | (125) |
| Mixed | 5 | (2) | | | 4 | (2) | | | 2 | (4) |
| Won | 21 | (9) | 32 | (14) | 27 | (12) | 30 | (13) | 27* | (48) |
| Total        % | 25 | | 25 | | 25 | | 25 | | 100 | |
| (N) | | (44) | | (44) | | (45) | | (44) | | (177) |

* At about 27% the plaintiffs' success rate in this table appears slightly higher than the 23.3% found in the preceding tables, which is due to the fact that in about half of the cases the value of the case was not determinable or the case was of a nonmonetary nature. Chances are that in a dismissal the value is more likely to be omitted in the judgement (and was thus not determinable) than where the judgement is in favour of plaintiff and the amount needs to be stated.

The tables show that, for the cases in which the value of the case is known, there is no relationship between either the fees and the value or the risk and the success.[126] Thus, "risks and chances" do not seem to determine the plaintiffs' decision to litigate. It should be noted that none of the other possibly related factors such as the duration, the overall or legal complexity, or the investment indicate a strong relationship to the success rate.

126   Note that, accordingly, the preceding tables are not significant at the required 5% level.

As the state supreme court file analysis indicates, and other studies have often observed,[127] most cases never reach a decision but are settled out of court before or even during litigation ("litigotiation"). Upholding the theory of rational actors, the only possible explanation for the low success rate of the plaintiffs found in the New York judgement analysis is that probably most plaintiffs commence a lawsuit either to win or to reach an agreeable settlement. Whenever the plaintiffs' chances are favourable, it seems, defendants will rather settle than wait for a decision. Only when the defendants believe themselves to be sued without proper cause, will they refuse to settle and rather continue litigation; these are the cases that are litigated to the very end of a judgement. Thus, it may probably be the defendants' behaviour, rather than the plaintiffs', that decides the length and the outcome of a proceeding. Furthermore, this reasoning confirms the initial thought that a judgement analysis by its concept has little value in estimating the plaintiffs' success rate in relation to all lawsuits commenced in court.

Nevertheless, the judgement analysis still allows conclusions with regard to those parties litigating to the very end. For these, when estimating globally the plaintiffs' attorneys' fees for each case with relation to the success rate, it is clear that overall the exercise of litigation made little sense for the plaintiffs in these cases.[128]

## F. Duration of Proceeding

Returning to the other rational reasons for the selection of New York courts as the forum for dispute resolution, the duration seems to be important. Particularly from the rational and normal plaintiff's point of view, and the consideration of whether and where to commence a claim, the success rate of court proceedings has to be viewed in relation to the time of proceedings. Assuming that transborder disputes generally have a rather complex legal and factual pattern, it should come as no surprise that the procedures

127　Herbert M. Kritzer, *The Form of Negotiation in Ordinary Litigation,* (Working Paper, Madison, WI: University of Wisconsin Law School, 1985), 1.

128　Which is a quite different result than has been obtained by Trubek, et al. for domestic disputes: Trubek, et al., "Civil Litigation as the Investment of Lawyer Time", II–173 et seq.

are unusually time-consuming. In fact, several times the judges in the judgements data base made a statement similar to this one:

> As this Court has previously observed, this action, which has been pending for the better part of a decade, has "consumed more legal, financial and judicial resources in the litigation of essentially threshold issues than scores of cases that have been filed, resolved and forgotten in this Court during the same time period". *Walpex Trading v. Yacimientos Petrolíferos Fiscales Bolivianos*, 789 F. Supp. 1268 (SDNY 1992), ("Walpex IV") *citing*, here, *idem*, 712 F. Supp. 383, 385 (SDNY 1989) ("Walpex II"), *idem*, 756 F. Supp. 136 (SDNY 1991) ("Walpex III"), and *idem*, 109 F.R.D. 692 (SDNY 1986) ("Walpex I").

The New York Supreme Court file analysis is of very limited value in considering the duration of proceedings. First, as has often been mentioned, the number of cases is too small. Second, the number of cases disposed of by the court is even smaller and, as described, there are no cases in which the plaintiffs were actually successful in their pursuit. Yet, as can be shown, some conclusions can be made.

### Table NY–23: Distribution of Duration in New York Supreme Court File Analysis (1986)

| | |
|---|---|
| Less than 6 months | 10 |
| 6 months - 1 year | 4 |
| 1 - 3 years | 5 |
| More than 3 years | 13 |
| Total | 32 |

The duration of proceedings in the state supreme court file analysis shows an unequal distribution. Generally cases seem to take either less than six months or more than three years. Considering the frustration of the plaintiffs litigating over three years, few of them ever reaching any success in those proceedings, one wonders why lawsuits are commenced:

### Table NY–24: Duration of Cases from Filing to Close by Success Rate in New York Supreme Court File Analysis (1986)

| | No Success | Success | Total |
|---|---|---|---|
| Less than 6 months | 7 | 3 | 10 |
| 6 months - 1 year | 3 | 1 | 4 |
| 1 - 3 years | 2 | 3 | 5 |
| More than 3 years | 11 | 2 | 13 |
| Total | 23 | 9 | 32 |

Table NY–25: Duration of Procedure from Filing to Close by
Type of Conclusion of Case in New York Supreme Court File
Analysis (1986)

| | Judgement or order | Failure to appear | Settlement out of court | Voluntary withdrawal | Not concluded | Removal to other courts | Total |
|---|---|---|---|---|---|---|---|
| Less than 6 months | 3 | 1 | 4 | 1 | | 1 | 10 |
| 6 months - 1 year | | 1 | 2 | | 1 | | 4 |
| 1 - 3 years | 1 | 2 | 2 | | | | 5 |
| More than 3 years | 1 | 1 | 4 | 1 | 6 | | 13 |
| Total | 5 | 5 | 12 | 2 | 7 | 1 | 32 |

The success rate and duration seem to have little influence on one another. Contrary to a theory on the domestic level,[129] litigating longer does not necessarily increase the plaintiff's chances for success; rather, the success rate seems to diminish slightly with a longer duration. Six cases have not been concluded in any particular way even after several years.

It is interesting to consider various aspects in order to determine, as far as possible with this limited number of cases, which aspect of a case would usually lead to a longer duration. The following table shows the relevance of various aspects that could potentially add to litigation time.

Table NY–26: Duration of Procedure from Filing to Close by
Number of Hearings, by Time Needed to Serve on Defendant,
and by Special Activity: were there discovery, deposition, jury, or
expert witnesses? New York Supreme Court File Analysis (1986)

| | Hearings | | | Service in Months | | | Specials | | Total |
|---|---|---|---|---|---|---|---|---|---|
| | None | 1-3 | More | Less than 1 | 1 | More than 1 | No | Yes | |
| Less than 6 months | 9 | 1 | | 9 | | 1 | 9 | 1 | 10 |
| 6 months - 1 year | 3 | 1 | | 3 | | 1 | 4 | | 4 |
| 1 - 3 years | 4 | 1 | | 3 | 1 | 1 | 5 | | 5 |
| More than 3 years | 9 | 1 | 3 | 9 | 3 | 1 | 10 | 3 | 13 |
| Total | 25 | 4 | 3 | 24 | 4 | 4 | 28 | 4 | 32 |

129    Trubek, et al., "Civil Litigation as the Investment of Lawyer Time",
       II–1et seq.; Kritzer, et al., "The Impact of Fee Arrangement on
       Lawyer Effort"; Johnson, "Lawyers' Choice: A Theoretical Appraisal
       of Litigation Investment Decisions", III–175 et seq. / 567 et seq.

As expected it seems to take somewhat longer for a case when more hearings are necessary. Surprisingly it makes little difference how long it took to serve the other party. This, however, can be easily explained. As discussed most foreign parties were never properly served in the first place, and service on domestic parties poses few difficulties.

Battles over jurisdiction had no effect on the distribution. Combining all other potential special procedural activities, which could contribute to a longer case it seems that these cases probably do take longer. In addition the four cases in which a translation was necessary all took longer than a year.

There seemed to be an advantage for non-U.S. plaintiffs over U.S. plaintiffs, their procedures being slightly shorter than vice versa. Considering the above discussion of success rates, which also work in favour of foreign plaintiffs, this result is most interesting. It can be easily explained by lesser problems with regard to service of process on a domestic party vis à vis service of process abroad.

The judgement analysis may further explain the factors leading to longer procedures. Not surprisingly the following aspects all lead to a difference in the duration of a proceeding: appeals took longer (counted from the commencement of the action); bench decisions with dissenting opinions took longer than unanimous decisions; and temporary restraining orders and injunctions took less time than other proceedings. Interestingly, and as should be, proceedings involving motions to dismiss for lack of jurisdiction, *forum non conveniens*, lack of personal service, or requests for *comity* to a foreign proceeding took less time; here, the cases in which the court granted the motion to dismiss influenced the median. While not always successful such motions have a statistical chance of ridding the defendant of the proceeding at an early stage—of course, the chances for the plaintiff to win on a motion for summary judgement are rather low at any early stage. Again, not surprisingly, cases in which either foreign law or treaty law was applied took much longer than other cases. The complexity of the factual pattern played a role in the duration; the legal complexity did not.

However, two aspects that influence the duration are quite interesting indeed. Firstly, the duration of the proceeding seemed to depend on the origin of the foreign party. While the countries as such do not make a difference, a distinction between common-law countries and other, or civil-law, countries showed an unequal distribution. While unimportant for most other aspects, here the legal-cultural difference does play a role as can be seen from the following table.

### Table NY–27: Duration by Parties' Country of Origin (Common Law or Not) in New York Judgements (1992)

| | Duration | | | | | | | | | |
|---|---|---|---|---|---|---|---|---|---|---|
| | Very low | | Medium low | | Medium high | | Very high | | Total | |
| | % | (N) | % | (N) | % | (N) | % | (N) | % | (N) |
| Common law | 39 | (27) | 46 | (35) | 36 | (26) | 19 | (14) | 35 | (102) |
| Other | 61 | (42) | 55 | (42) | 64 | (47) | 81 | (58) | 65 | (189) |
| Total % | 24 | | 27 | | 25 | | 25 | | 100 | |
| (N) | | (69) | | (77) | | (73) | | (72) | | (291) |

Clearly it seems that the very lengthy proceedings particularly involved parties who are not from common-law countries (80% compared to a total of 65% of noncommon-law foreign parties), whereas foreign parties of common-law origin are overrepresented in the second quartile (46% compared to a total of 35% of common-law foreign parties). Thus the legal-cultural difference and potential sources for misunderstanding, inadequate expectations, or difficulties in the interpretation of law and facts between common-law and noncommon-law legal cultures add to the duration of some cases. The results further underline concepts relating to the present importance of the joint background of common-law legal cultures.

The second interesting aspect is that the defendant's law firm seems to have had a particular influence on the duration of the proceeding, as can be seen from the following table. (The plaintiff's law firm or the party type of any of the parties involved did not seem to have much influence on the outcome or the duration.)

### Table NY–28: Duration by Defendant's Attorney in New York Judgements (1992)

| | Firm Type* | | | | | | | | |
|---|---|---|---|---|---|---|---|---|---|
| | Large | | Medium | | Small | | Total | | |
| | % | (N) | % | (N) | % | (N) | % | (N) | |
| Very low | 21 | (13) | 27 | (10) | 31 | (10) | 25 | ( 33) | |
| Medium low | 34 | (21) | 16 | ( 6) | 16 | ( 5) | 25 | ( 32) | |
| Medium high | 18 | (11) | 11 | ( 4) | 38 | (12) | 21 | ( 27) | |
| Very high | 26 | (16) | 50 | (17) | 16 | ( 5) | 29 | ( 38) | |
| Total % | 47 | | 29 | | 25 | | 100 | | |
| (N) | | (61) | | (37) | | (32) | | (130) | |

* The table is limited to those cases in which New York law firms appeared for the primary defendant and in which the same appeared at least twice in the data base. This method excludes the relevance of the difference between one-shot and multiple players and draws attention to the size of the law firm as a decisive factor.

As mentioned before the attorneys' role in international litigation warrants further research. This research is preliminary, considering that (1) defence work is almost exclusively billed by the hour, which usually increases with the duration of the litigation, and (2) the defendant's success rate is high and, not seeming to depend on the law firm, a shorter duration should be beneficial to the client. The table shows that boutique speciality firms[130] seem to have more of the proceedings with the shortest duration (31.3%) and less of the proceedings with the longest duration (15.6%) than other types of firms. If divided in half, the large law firms have the highest share (56%) of proceedings that take less than the median duration. Thus there apparently is an advantage in having oneself defended either by a specialized boutique or by a large firm. It is disadvantageous to select a medium-sized firm. The boutique has the special knowledge and the large firm enough specialists of all kinds to work effectively. The experience these firms often advertise about themselves has some truth in it, after all.

## G. Political Cases

Apart from the other issues and categories discussed, there seems to be a special category of cases related to and arising out of political conflicts in foreign countries that somehow find their way into civil disputes before courts in the United States. While most of these cases involve governments or governmental entities, they may even appear in other categories. It is in any event surprising to find at least eleven cases of this kind in the data base. There is the claim by the Philippine Government against the former President Marcos, the claim by the provisional government of Liberia for funds secured in the U.S. by former government officials, the liability claim against the P.L.O. for an alleged terrorist act, several claims by and against institutions from Iraq, Kuwait, and Iran that have become an issue due to the conflicts in that region, and so forth. Another type of case that can be brought into this category are cases that derive from problems of underdevelopment, as can be found in some of the cases in which foreign banks were involved.

## IV. The Proceeding

Having failed to sufficiently explain the plaintiff's reasons to litigate, the discussion nevertheless has provided somewhat of a

---

130   One should recall that only repeat players are included in this table.

picture of international litigation in New York courts. To complete and further illustrate this picture, additional aspects of cross-border litigation shall be analysed.

## A. Conflicts of Law

### 1. Domestic v. Foreign Law

Of particular prominence in legal literature on international matters is the subject called conflict of law or private international law. The role of this legal area is to decide which legal system to apply in cases with international connections. While theoretical reasonings may vary,[131] each forum will first apply its own forum state laws. Yet for a long time the courts and legislators of most countries have realized that in some transborder disputes the application of forum law leads to inadequate results. Today most countries have a sophisticated set of rules to decide in which cases a law that is foreign to the forum should be applied rather than the "home" law. Each country, subject to its own sovereignty, has developed rules to be applied in its courts. Conflicts should be distinguished from international procedural rules, which determine jurisdictional questions, although they may overlap—not in theory but in the results.

In determining the applicable law in cases with foreign connections, conflicts of law follow connection criteria, which are classified by the areas of law to which they apply. Thus different connection criteria apply to contracts than to family relationships. Scholarly distinctions are made between **strict** connection criteria, which call for the application of a specific law either directly or in a rule-exception relationship, and **relative** connection criteria, under which various aspects of the case and the parties are gathered and weighed in order to determine the legal system with "the most significant relationship" to the case. The development of conflict of law with regard to torts may best illustrate the topic, because in torts the parties usually have little influence on the applicable law.

### 2. Special Issue: The "Proper Law of the Tort"

The rise of the nation-state has brought up the universally accepted theory that every nation-state would have the **sovereign** right to

131 Kegel takes the position that all cases are governed by private international law, leading to the application of domestic law in domestic disputes. Gerhard Kegel, *Internationales Privatrecht*, 5th ed. (Munich: C.H. Beck, 1985).

rule the conduct of all persons on its **territory**, for the mutual welfare of all its inhabitants. Consequently it has been almost universally accepted that torts should be governed by the law of the place
where they have been committed, the *lex loci delicti commissi*.[132]
The principle is founded in theories of sovereignty and territoriality and in common sense, for example, that traffic rules should
apply equally to all who participate in traffic of a given place.

Courts and scholars have found, however, that there are cases
in which the locality of the tort is mere coincidence while the relationship of the parties is not. Slander among a tourist group in a
bus that has just crossed a border is often used as an example.[133]

Other arguments point out that the financial situation of
tortfeasor and victim are determined by their social environment
rather than the place of the tort and that sociological considerations should be added to dogmatic ruling.[134] It may not be just to
compensate an accident victim living in a developed country by
the standards of a less developed country, nor may it be just to
have a person living in a low-wage country pay U.S. punitive damages. Regarding contract-related torts it is argued that in such cases
the law governing the tort should follow the law governing the
contract. Several attempts by courts and legislators can be found,
linking the law of the tort to the parties' nationality,[135] domicile,
or usual place of residence,[136] rather than to the place of the tort.

---

132   A special problem is involved in cases in which the actual tortious
      act and the damages occur at different places. Courts and schol-
      ars have dealt with this issue, which would be too far beyond our
      topic to discuss here. See, e.g., European Court of Justice, judge-
      ment of 6 October 1976, Case 16/76 ECR 1976 p. 1473.

133   Heinz Binder, "Zur Auflockerung des Deliktstatuts", *RabelsZ* 20
      (1955): 401, 464, with further references.

134   See discussion at Mummenhoff, "Ausnahmen von der lex loci
      delicti im internationalen Privatrecht", *Neue Juristische
      Wochenschrift* (1975): 476 with further references.

135   E.g., German *Reichsverordnung über die Rechtsanwendung bei
      Schädigungen deutscher Staatsangehöriger außerhalb des
      Reichsgebiets* of 7 December 1942, RGBl. I 706. Its continuing
      applicability was confirmed by BGH NJW 1961, 731; as distin-
      guished in BGH NJW 1992, 3091, there is some doubt whether
      the *Reichsverordnung* is still applicable to all cases to which its
      wording applies.

136   BGH NJW 1992, 3091.

In the U.S., where conflict of law applies not only in international but also in interstate matters, the discussion differs from state to state. In effect the result is mostly oriented at the state interests that its laws apply to the case,

> that the law of the jurisdiction having the greatest interest . . . will be applied and that the facts or contacts which obtain significance in defining state interests are those which relate to the purpose of the particular law *Miller v. Miller*, 237 N.E.2d 877 (N.Y.C.A. 1968) at 879. "that the application of Michigan law would defeat a legitimate interest of the forum state without serving a legitimate interest of any other state". *Tooker v. Lopez*, 249 N.E.2d 394 (N.Y.C.A. 1969) at 398.

Critics have identified its randomness as the most important problem with all the changes to the *lex loci delicti commissi*. Lord Wilberforce has formulated as follows:

If one lesson emerges from the United States decisions it is that case to case decisions do not add up to a system of justice.[137]

### 3. Choice of Law Clauses

Whatever is suggested with regard to forum selection clauses, literature militates more strongly for the specific selection of applicable law in international contracts.[138] It is argued that, regardless of the forum, the contracting parties should state the legal system under which a contract should be interpreted. In connection with arbitration clauses some authors even suggest that it is possible to proclaim that no state's law should be used, but rather the contract itself and usances of the trade.[139]

Again, against the background of problems that have arisen in court with rather restrictive interpretation of choice of law clauses, there are various attempts to give advice on the choice of law clause that is most likely to be successful. For example, the simple "law and forum New York" is held to be entirely insufficient, as it may not be clear, for example, whether this includes federal law.

---

137   *Chaplin v. Boys*, [1971] AC 356, [1969] 2 All ER 1085, [1969] 3 WLR 322, [1969] 2 Lloyd's Rep 487, 47 MLR 650, (House of Lords 1969); Similarly, the German BGH in: NJW 85, 1286.

138   Christoph Graf von Bernstorff, *Management im Auslandsgeschäft* (Frankfurt/Main: Fritz Knapp Verlag, 1991), 70, speaks of minimizing risks by choice of law.

139   Trade practices.

Some authors suggest that the clause should specifically exclude the application of the selected law's conflict of law rules so that a *renvoi* cannot take place.[140] They argue that the selection of a jurisdiction's law that does not exclude that jurisdiction's conflict of law rules may lead to the application of another jurisdiction's law *via* that loophole, thus creating a solution the parties wished to avoid by using the contractual clause on the applicable law. Others argue that this would be a mistake.[141] The issues seem somewhat similar to forum selection clauses in that case law has created many differentiations leading to a certain insecurity in the use of such clauses.

## B. The Practice: Foreign and Uniform Law

### 1. Conflicts of Law and Application of Foreign Law

Contrary to its theoretical prominence conflict of law, as a topic by itself, played a rather limited role in both analyses. The state supreme court file analysis, by its content and design, would have little discussion of such questions because most files did not contain a lengthy discussion in the first place. Yet even in the New York judgement analysis, conflict of law as such was discussed only in eleven out of 352 judgements. In three of these eleven judgements, the conflict issue did not concern non-U.S. law but rather a conflict of law between the law of different states of the U.S. In two more of the eleven cases, the conflict issue did not directly lead to the discussion of the content of foreign law, but rather the applicability of foreign law served as an additional argument for a dismissal of the case on the grounds of *forum non conveniens*. In six cases conflict of law was discussed and led to the application of foreign law. In two of these cases the issue of foreign law concerned a very limited aspect of the case, such as the interpretation of a specific contractual subissue or the admissibility of evidence

---

140    In conflicts of law, in some cases, the laws of the first jurisdiction (where the case is actually before court) demand the application of the laws of a second jurisdiction. If the laws of this second jurisdiction, in turn, demand the laws of a third (or even the first) jurisdiction to apply, this redirection is termed *renvoi*.

141    See the discussion in Hancock, "ABA National Institute on International Contracting", Chapter 711, particularly Gruson, 711.17et seq., therein.

protected by a foreign statute on confidentiality of attorney-client correspondence. All other cases concerned the application of foreign law in a tort case. In all cases the most significant relationship doctrine was applied and led to the application of foreign law.

Nevertheless the discussion and application of foreign law was slightly more prominent than these numbers suggest. Again in none of the state supreme court cases did the application of foreign law play any role, particularly because there were no disputed final judgements. In the judgement analysis, the (potential) application of foreign law was rather limited as well. Yet in 22 (6%) out of the 352 judgements, foreign law was discussed. Thus, in eighteen cases in addition to the four mentioned, the discussion of foreign law followed without further discussion of the issues of conflict of law.

The German data, herein, seemed to suggest a specific lack of knowledge on the part of the legal personnel leading to the avoidance or nonuse of conflicts issues. For the New York analysis, this seems rather unlikely because conflicts play a role for domestic cases within the U.S. as well (as the three cases described would also confirm). Rather, it seems that in most cases this question is undisputed by the parties. Either a contract provided for foreign law or the case apparently seemed clear enough for all parties concerned. Of course the same would apply to many cases in which U.S. law was applied.

Following the German discussion it appears to be beneficial to analyse the depth of analysis and discussion in which the New York courts awarded the foreign law. The following table shows the basis upon which the courts refer to, discussed, and applied foreign law.

### Table NY–29: Basis of Discussion of Foreign Law in New York Judgements (1992)*

| Type of Law | Total no. | Case law | State law | Expert opinion | General statement | Ext. disc. | Mentioned | Applied | Discarded |
|---|---|---|---|---|---|---|---|---|---|
| Common | 9 | 5 | 4 | 7 | 0 | 9 | 0 | 8 | 1 |
| Civil | 13 | 0 | 4 | 4 | 4 | 6 | 4 | 4 | 3 |
| Total | 22 | 5 | 8 | 11 | 4 | 15 | 4 | 12 | 4 |

* Multiple entries add up to more than the number of cases.

The numbers do seem to indicate a preference for the application of common law, rather than civil law, by U.S. courts. It is striking how often the content of civil law is merely mentioned in the form of a general statement before it is applied or discarded, whereas common law, particularly U.K. law, is discussed extensively. The picture becomes even clearer when the language and reasoning of some cases is compared. An extreme example of a general statement found in the judgements was as follows:

> [T]he law of Venezuela applies . . . . [Plaintiff] does not dispute that Venezuela has no law of unfair competition (statutory or otherwise) . . . . Therefore, [Plaintiff's] unfair competition claim must be dismissed . . . for failure to state a claim upon which relief can be granted.[142]

In another case, in which a contractual provision on costs was to be construed under Mexican law, the efforts made by the court to resolve the legal question were even less:

> In such a situation, the Restatement (Second) of Conflict of Laws calls for the application of the law of the forum: "Where either no information, or else insufficient information, has been obtained about the foreign law, the forum will usually decide the case in accordance with its own local law except when to do so would not meet the needs of the case or would not be in the interest of justice". Restatement (Second) of Conflicts of Laws § 136 cmt h at 378–9 (1971), cited with approval in *Scientific Holding Co. v. Plessey Inc.*, 510 F.2d 15, 23 n. 5 (2d Cir. 1974). Accordingly, "costs" will be interpreted under New York law.[143]

On the other hand, in a case in which Bahamian law was to be applied, after extensively discussing a statute and expert opinion, a certain aspect in the application of the statute remained unclear and both parties' expert witnesses agreed that there was no Bahamian decision on that point. The court turned to U.K. law and found a 1953 decision that in turn had relied heavily on a New York decision by Chief Justice Cardozo of 1928, which was still a leading case in that area of law. From there on New York law was discussed for the conclusion of the question. A similar reasoning was employed to decide a question under Australian law by turning to U.K. and U.S. law alternatively on the argument that Australian law would refer to U.S. decisions in that area of law. In several cases particularly involving U.K. and Australian law, the

142    *Westel v. AT&T*, LEXIS 12301 (SDNY 1992).
143    *Nacional Financiera v. Americom Airlease* 803 F. Supp. 886 (SDNY 1992).

experts had provided the court with copies of decisions from those countries, on which the court then relied without further reference to the experts themselves.

With regard to civil-law countries, particularly with regard to Japan and Switzerland, the courts based their decisions three times mainly on cites from U.S. literature on the respective country's law. A third strategy, employed with regard to Switzerland and Finland, was to refer to prior U.S. case law, which had interpreted the same foreign statute. While it is common practice for federal courts to refer to other federal courts' decisions in the interpretation of state law (notwithstanding the supremacy of state courts in interpretation of state law) it is unique to follow the same course with regard to foreign law.

Unfortunately the numbers are too small and the examples too rare for final conclusions on the practice in cases in which foreign law is actually applied. Yet the numbers do show a certain willingness by U.S. courts to consider foreign law—albeit not as large as commonly cited decisions would suggest—in which, for example, the Second Circuit has warned of the need to

> guard against an excessive reluctance to undertake the task of deciding foreign law, a chore federal courts must often perform.[144] [T]he need to apply foreign law is not itself a reason to apply the doctrine of *forum non conveniens*.[145]

On the contrary, not by itself but as a leading argument, several dismissals on *forum non conveniens* mentioned the necessity of applying foreign law.

Despite the rather superficial reference to the foreign law in a number of cases, the remaining fifteen cases in which foreign law was actually discussed extensively display, as far as can be determined in hindsight, a considerable degree of competence by the New York courts in the discussion of the matter. In a case in which German law[146] was concerned, the discussion involved not only the statute itself but the understanding of the principles behind the

144   *Manu Int'l, S.A. v. Avon Prods., Inc.,* 641 F.2d 62, 68 (2d Cir. 1981); accord *Volkswagen de Mexico, S.A. v. Germanischer Lloyd,* No. 90 Civ. 1248, 1991 U.S. Dist. LEXIS 15572 (SDNY 28 October 1991).

145   *Olympic Corp.,* 462 F.2d at 379.

146   This case was selected as this author, a German-trained lawyer, could easily determine the correctness of the decision.

statute, which were quite different from New York principles. Both the law and reasoning were correctly applied.

## 2. Conventions

This display of knowledge is substantiated by the discussion of treaty law. In the judgement analysis approximately 50 cases involved the application of a convention or bilateral treaty. The court had to discuss the respective convention or treaty and its articles and apply the same to the case. Table NY–30 shows the distribution among the treaties:

### Table NY–30: Application of Treaties and Conventions in Judgements in New York Judgements (1992)

| | Number of Cases | | |
|---|---|---|---|
| Treaty | Number of references | Applied | Not applied |
| Hague Rules (COGSA)* | 17 | 17 | 0 |
| Other maritime (w/o COGSA) | 6 | 5 | 1 |
| Warsaw Convention** | 15 | 15 | 0 |
| Hague Arbitration | 10 | 10 | 0 |
| Hague Service*** | 9 | 7 | 2 |
| InterAmerican Letters Rogatory† | 2 | 1 | 1 |
| Universal Copyright†† | 2 | 2 | 0 |
| Paris Convention††† | 1 | 1 | 0 |
| Vienna Convention‡ | 1 | 1 | 0 |
| Brussels Convention‡‡ | 1 | 0 | 1 |
| Child Abduction‡‡‡ | 1 | 0 | 1 |
| Treaties of Friendship*† | 3 | 3 | 0 |

\*    46 U.S.C. §§ 1300 et seq.
\*\*   Convention for Unification of Certain Rules Relating to International Transportation by Air, 12 October 1929, 49 Stat. 3000, T.S. No. 876, entered into force 29 October 1934, reprinted at 49 U.S.C. App. § 1502 note (1976).
\*\*\*  658 U.N.T.S. 163; for the U.S. effective since 10 February 1969, 20 U.S.T. 361 et seq., TIAS 6638, (Germany: BGBl. 1980 II, 907) supplemented for the U.S. by the 1977 Department of Justice Instructions for Service American Judicial Documents abroad. In one case the convention was applied analogous on Switzerland which is not a party to the convention.
†    Inter-American Convention on Letters Rogatory of 1975, ratified by the United States in 1988.
††   Berne Copyright Convention, Berne Convention Implementation Act, Pub Law 100–568, 102 Stat. 2883 (1988), amending 17 U.S.C. § 401 et seq.
†††  International Convention for the Protection of Industrial Property, the "Paris Convention".
‡    Vienna Convention on Diplomatic Relations, 23 U.S.T. 3227, Apr. 18, 1961, T.I.A.S. No. 7502.
‡‡   European Convention on Jurisdiction and the Enforcement of Judgements in Civil and Commercial Matters (the "Brussels Convention").
‡‡‡  Hague Convention on the Civil Aspects of International Child Abduction, 51 Fed. Reg. 10490, implemented by the International Child Abduction Remedies Act (ICARA), 42 U.S.C. § 11601 et seq.
\*†   Treaty of Friendship, Commerce and Navigation of 1950 between the United States and the Republic of Ireland, 1 U.S.T. 785, T.I.A.S. No. 2155; Treaty of Friendship, Commerce and Navigation of 1953 between the United States and Japan, 4 U.S.T 2065; Treaty of Friendship, Commerce and Navigation of 1946 between the United States and the Republic of China (Taiwan), 63 Stat. 1299 (1946).

Particularly the Hague Rules, which have become part of U.S. law as the Carriage of Goods by Sea Act (COGSA), and other maritime conventions are prominent. The courts not only had knowledge of the conventions but discussed the law, based on U.S. and even foreign decisions (twice), in detail. Even in those cases, in which the respective convention was not applied, the decision was reasoned and based on articles of the convention, except in the case of the Brussels Convention where the court simply held that it would not be considered as the U.S. was not a signatory. Where the convention has become incorporated into the federal "United States Codes" series, the discussion and application was probably not too difficult because the text as well as commentaries and case law are easily available. Nevertheless even the original text was referred to, once, with a comparison between the foreign language (French) and the English language text in order to interpret an ambiguity:

> Even were we free to disregard this overwhelming precedent, we would not do so here, because even a cursory review of the original French text and its translation exposes the ambiguity recognized by Exim and the foreign courts. We turn first to the original French version of the Convention which, as the only authentic version, must guide any analysis. Subsection (h), in the original French, states that the waybill shall contain "le nombre, le mode d'emballage, les marques particulieres ou les numeros des colis". [..] Notable in a comparison of the two [language versions] is the American version's addition of the word "and" after the word "packing".....[147]

In other cases, the convention or treaty was only available as such.

Being quite contrary to the results in the German study,[148] this display of competence does seem to underline the importance of New York as an international market for legal services. Particularly, but not exclusively, in the field of maritime law, this aspect can also be confirmed by the prominence of a limited number of law firms that appear in these matters and who are apparently well versed in the application of international conventions that apply in their field of practice.

## C. Recognition and Enforcement

Probably the final stage of successful litigation is the enforcement of the judgement. Within the United States the "full

---

147    *Distribuidora Dimsa v. Linea Aerea Del Cobre S.A.*, 976 F.2d 90 (2nd Cir. 1992), citations omitted.

148    See Gessner, herein.

faith and credit" clause of the Constitution[149] provides for a not-
too-difficult means of recognition and enforcement of "foreign"[150]
judgements. Foreign judgements are simply registered in the country where the judgement creditor wishes to enforce the same. Unless the judgement debtor raises objections, no proceeding takes
place.

"True" foreign judgements, though, face severe difficulties in
recognition and enforcement. With regard to civil money awards,
the situation is still quite simple in New York and a few other
states that have adopted the Uniform Foreign Country Money-
Judgements Recognition Act.

New York has adopted the act as §§ 5301 et seq. CPLR. The
requirements for recognition are that the foreign judgement is final and enforceable. An appeal in the foreign jurisdiction shall not
hinder enforcement, but in that event the court may stay the enforcement temporarily. Further requirements are that the judgement is from a jurisdiction that provides for fair trial and that the
foreign court had personal jurisdiction over the defendant according to New York law. The latter requirement is construed liberally
with New York's long-arm statutes in mind.

Recognition *may* further be denied,
- if the foreign court lacked subject-matter jurisdiction,
- if the defendant was not afforded sufficient time to prepare
  the defence,
- if the foreign judgement was obtained through fraud,
- if the basis for the judgement violates New York's *ordre public*,
- if the judgement contradicts another final judgement,
- if the procedure was held in contradiction to a jurisdiction or
  arbitration clause, or
- in the event that the foreign jurisdiction was based only on
  the fact that the defendant was personally served within that
  jurisdiction because the foreign court was seriously inconvenient.

149    Article IV, U.S. Constitution:
       Full faith and credit shall be given in each State to the public Acts,
       Records, and judicial Proceedings of every other State. And the
       Congress may by general Laws prescribe the Manner in which
       such Acts, Records and Proceedings shall be proved; and the ef-
       fects thereof.
150    Foreign in the sense that the judgement is from a different state.

As authorized by § 5303 CPLR the plaintiff who seeks to enforce a foreign judgement commences an action with a motion for summary judgement in lieu of a complaint. Entry of the summary judgement may then be opposed by the judgement debtor on one of the grounds for nonrecognition of foreign judgements under § 5304 CPLR. The party objecting to enforcement bears the burden of evidence for either of these requirements. Unless a party objects New York will deem the requirements fulfilled.[151] Finally, § 5307 CPLR specifically provides that the courts may allow enforcement in other cases not provided for by the act.

In other areas of law[152] and in many other states, a last resort must be taken to the institution of an entirely new lawsuit on the basis of the prior foreign judgement as prima facie evidence[153] and the argument and hope that the court should give comity to the same.

In the U.S. conflicts of law, jurisdiction,[154] and the rules on enforcement of foreign judgements are a matter of state law, so that each state has its own set of statutes and case law. Nevertheless, being of a joint origin in common law, there are universal doctrines accepted throughout the United States. In this description New York state law will be the basis, because New York is the main subject of this study, together with an overview of the general doctrines as necessary.

Since the landmark case of *Erie R.R.*,[155] in diversity cases, subject to special rules for "true" federal jurisdiction, federal district courts are bound by the laws of the state in which they are located with regard to questions within state jurisdiction. Thus the conflict of law rules, as well as the rules of jurisdiction of the state are applied by the federal courts, so that, for the limited purposes of this discussion, no separate discussion is necessary.

---

151   David Siegel, *Practice Commentaries to CPLR 5303* in 7B MacKinney (New York: MacKinney, 1994), 490.

152   § 5301 (b) CPLR limits the scope of the following sections to foreign money judgements exclusive of family-law disputes.

153   Against which the opposing party has to argue and present evidence to the contrary.

154   Jurisdiction has various separate meanings, i.e., subject matter jurisdiction and jurisdiction over the case. It is not necessary to discuss these items further.

155   *Erie Railroad Co. v. Tompkins*, 304 U.S. 64 (1938).

This means that jurisdictional issues with regard to foreign problems, conflicts of law, and all other related aspects do not only arise in "international" matters but in domestic matters as well, and the law is generally well developed. In legal theory there is little difference made in the treatment of these cases, except for aspects of the "full faith and credit" clause. As this study assumes that cross-border disputes are somehow different from domestic disputes, regardless whether intra- or interstate, it is interesting to analyse whether this difference is actually treated and the effect of such treatment.

### 1. New York Practice

Most importantly recognition and enforcement of a foreign judgement is intertwined with the very first legal aspect discussed herein, namely, jurisdiction and service of process. All judiciary systems agree that an important aspect of a fair trial is the right to be heard. They further agree that actual notice of a lawsuit, accomplished by proper service of process, is the minimum requirement for the right to be heard. Yet there are important differences in the way in which service is accomplished in various jurisdictions. Generally in the U.S. it is the plaintiff's obligation to privately secure service and prove its effectiveness in court.[156] While within the U.S. personal service by an unrelated agent by hand is the standard, service by mail, "nail and mail", service on a statutory, contractual, or legal "agent for service of process", personally, or through a sheriff may also suffice. In case of any doubt, the most important question is, whether the defendant actually received notice or could have received notice.

The example of a divorce and custody case between New York and Switzerland that was not part of either data sample (as it had been decided a year earlier) illustrates certain complexities with regard to service of process that have an effect on the recognition and enforcement of the judgement obtained.

Originally, the family had married and was residing in New York. When the child was about four months old, they went for a family visit to Switzerland. There, the Swiss wife used the opportunity to leave her oppressive husband with the child and to return to her family. In a meeting at her Swiss lawyer's office, she advised her husband that she wanted to divorce him and had filed

---

156    See the above discussion on service of process.

a divorce and custody suit in the local court that day, jurisdiction being available in the Swiss court due to her Swiss nationality.[157] The husband left the country before the court officer could serve him.

In New York, the husband commenced a divorce and custody proceeding, jurisdiction being available as the place of marriage and the family's last common domicile.[158] A summons and complaint was served by certified mail directly to the wife in Switzerland. Within a few weeks, judgement in default was rendered against the wife. In the Swiss proceeding, the court arranged for service of process through diplomatic channels. When the return receipt of the certified mail was not received by the Swiss Consulate General, upon motion, the court ordered service by publication and eventually entered judgement for the wife. Both judgements were served on the respondents, respectively, both successfully received the judgements and both appealed against the decision as far as the custody was involved (naturally, there was no dispute about the divorce).

On appeal, the Swiss court held that its proceeding had commenced prior to the other proceeding with the filing of the complaint and that it therefore had to take preference. The argument that the respondent husband had not received notice of the proceeding and had thus been denied the right to be heard was rejected by the Swiss court holding that, since the appeal was a *de novo* proceeding,[159] he had the full possibility to argue his position. The husband failed to do so and the judgement became final and unappealable in Switzerland.

Upon motion for reargument in New York, the court held that service had been properly effected, that the Swiss court, by serving through publication had not given the respondent his right to be heard and that in any event, the Swiss court proceeding had commenced later than its own as service had been effected at a later point in time. Thus, the court held that the Swiss court proceeding should be disregarded and dismissed the motion for reargument.

157   Art. 59 lit. b. IPRG (Swiss Private International Law Statute).
158   New York Domestic Relations Law (D.L.R.) § 230 subd. 1 and 2 (Required residence of parties in divorce action), C.P.L.R § 314 subd. 1 (*in rem* jurisdiction over "marital *res*").
159   In which a full hearing takes place on the evidence; as opposed to an appeal on the merits of the lower court's decision only.

On appeal, the Appellate Division also rejected the request to dismiss the complaint in favour of the Swiss judgement. Yet, realizing the impasse that had occurred, the New York court decided to give the parties a chance. It reversed the lower court's judgement and ordered a new trial to give both parties a chance to argue their position on the merits. Respondent wife's attorneys on appeal had cleverly argued and successfully convinced the Appellate Division that the wife had the better position on the merits and there was a true chance that in a full hearing the result in New York would be the same as in Switzerland and the impasse would end. Eventually, the parties settled out of court as they had run short of funds to continue the legal battle.

### 2. Discussion

In this exemplary case the differences in the concepts of service of process, jurisdiction, and the date of the effectiveness of the commencement of action led to disparate decisions and a denial of recognition. Service of process is described as one of the most problematic aspects of international civil litigation, and the cases in the state supreme court file study show that service abroad is often unsuccessful.

The judgement analysis is not very useful for this question, as the existence of a published judgement is dependent on a participating defendant who, accordingly, must have received notice. Nevertheless, the mode of service is problematicized in 62 cases, which is almost 40% of the cases in which the defendant was foreign. Yet few of these defences were of any help, as only five judgements led to dismissal for deficiencies in the mode of service, all of which were cases in which the jurisdiction was predicated on personal service in the forum state.

The sample case exemplifies another aspect. It is generally accepted that

> under international law, a state may determine the conditions for service of process in its territory in aid of litigation in another state, but the state in which the litigation is pending may determine the effect of such service.[160]

160   Restatement (Third) Foreign Relations Law of the United States §471 (i) (St. Paul, Minn.: West, 1987). See also, for further discussion on the underlying principles of international (public) law, Dieter Leipold, *Lex fori, Souveränität, Discovery; Grundfragen des Internationalen Zivilprozeßrechts* (Heidelberg: Müller Jurist. Verlag, 1989), 40.

In civil-law countries service of process is usually within the courts' purview, is arranged for directly or indirectly through the court's marshal, and is considered a sovereign act.[161] The formalities must be strictly observed. For example, service by special mail[162] to the officially registered address of the defendant is the standard means of service in Germany. Little can be objected by a party so served.[163]

When service is to be obtained abroad, theoretically, little changes for the parties. A U.S. plaintiff may still obtain valid service of process through personal service, mail, or service by an agent. Courts in civil-law countries will generally attempt to obtain service of process through an official, either by requesting assistance from the foreign state or through a consular official.[164] Problems arise for civil-law courts because U.S. or other common law courts and judicial administrations may not be willing or able to provide an official for the purpose of service. On the other hand, civil-law countries often consider the "informal" U.S. ways of service of process as infringement on their sovereignty and demand that service be officially requested from a court to be arranged for by the local court. Real difficulties arise whenever service of process that would be considered valid by the court where the lawsuit is pending becomes impractical or when recognition of that procedure is sought in a different legal system that may have objections against the way service was obtained.

It follows that service of process is a legal area in which different legal cultures often conflict with each other.

If the Swiss attorney in the case described had handed over the Swiss complaint at the meeting in the office, this would probably have been accepted as proper and timely service not by the Swiss court, but by the New York court. Under all circumstances services by publication should not have been applied for, as U.S. courts generally react allergically to this kind of service of process. The example shows that in transborder legal disputes, it is particularly

---

161    Rolf A. Schütze, *"Zur Zustellung nach § 176 ZPO im einstweiligen Verfügungsverfahren"*, BB 78, 589.

162    Which is arranged by the court marshal for whom the Postal Service acts as delivery agent: §§ 193 et seq. ZPO.

163    See Baumbach/Lauterbach-Hartmann, *Kommentar zur Zivilprozeßordnung,* commentary to §§ 166 et seq. 181 et seq. ZPO.

164    E.g., § 199 ZPO.

important to consider the effects of an action in a proceeding in the place where the judgement needs to be enforced. Furthermore, the example shows the difference between the formal position of continental civil-law procedure and the discretionary flexibility and pragmatic, results-oriented position of U.S. procedural law.

Considering the legal intricacies, not surprisingly, neither the file analysis nor the judgements contained any case of actual recognition of a foreign judgement. The issue was discussed from a different angle in a few judgements, all of which concerned the request for comity to foreign pending bankruptcy proceedings. All of these requests but one were granted.

Only one judgement actually dealt with the recognition of a foreign money judgement. Plaintiff sought to enforce a U.K. award of £40,000 against a publisher for libel. Entry of the judgement was opposed on the ground that it was imposed without the safeguards for freedom of speech and the press required by the First Amendment to the United States Constitution and Article I, Section 8 of the Constitution of the state of New York. Defendant successfully asked the New York court to reject the judgement as repugnant to public policy, a ground for nonrecognition of foreign judgements under § 5304(b)(4) CPLR. The court held that

> [i]t is true that England and the United States share many common law principles of law. Nevertheless, a significant difference between the two jurisdictions lies in England's lack of an equivalent to the First Amendment to the United States Constitution. The protection to free speech and the press embodied in that amendment would be seriously jeopardized by the entry of foreign libel judgements granted pursuant to standards deemed appropriate in England but considered antithetical to the protections afforded the press by the U.S. Constitution.[165]

This was also the only case in which a public policy argument against foreign law or a foreign jurisdiction was successful. In all other cases comity was awarded to the foreign court or proceeding, following the leading case on international comity, *Hilton v. Guyot*, 159 U.S. 113 (1895), in which the Supreme Court described the doctrine as:

> the recognition which one nation allows within its territory to the legislative, executive, or judicial acts of another nation, having due

165    *Ajitabh Bachchan v. India Abroad Publications Inc.* 154 Misc. 2d 228; 585 N.Y.S.2d 661 (N.Y. Supr. Ct. 1992).

regard both to international duty and convenience, and to the rights of its own citizens or of other persons who are under the protection of its laws. 159 U.S. at 164.[166]

### 3. Treaties and Other Solutions

In order to somewhat provide for a solution, several bilateral and multilateral treaties and model laws have been drafted. The most important multilateral treaty is the Hague Convention on the Service Abroad of Judicial and Extra Judicial Documents in Civil and Commercial Matters of 1965[167] (Hague Service Convention), which is in effect for about 30 countries. One should note that the convention applies to most civil and commercial matters but, for example, specifically excludes family and matrimonial matters so that it would have been of little help in the case mentioned.

Furthermore, the U.S. and Switzerland do not have a treaty on service of process.[168] In 1961, the Swiss Embassy delivered an *aide memoire* to the U.S. Department of State protesting the service of judicial process on Swiss citizens by mail. For practical purposes a note by the Swiss Department of State[169] exists that describes a practical procedure somewhat similar to that under the Hague Service Convention. Consequently, in one of the cases from the judgement set, in which a Swiss party was concerned, the court applied the convention analogous to that case. The court further explained:

---

166   *New Line International Releasing, Inc. v. IVEX*, 140 Bankr. 342 (SDNY 1992).

167   658 U.N.T.S. 163; for the U.S. effective since 10 February 1969, 20 U.S.T. 361 et seq., TIAS 6638, (BGBl. 1980 II, 907) supplemented for the U.S. by the 1977 Department of Justice Instructions for Service American Judicial Documents abroad; Haager Übereinkommen über die Zustellung gerichtlicher und außergerichtlicher Schriftstücke im Ausland in Zivil- und Handelssachen vom 15.11.1965 (BGBl. 1977 II, 1452), for Germany in force since 26 June 1979 (BGBl. II 1979, 779 and BGBl II 1980, 907).

168   Most recently, Switzerland has acceded to the Hague Service Convention.

169   Contemporary Practice of the United States Relating to International Law 56 AMJ International Law 793, 794 (1962).

Parenthetically, *as guidance for the unwary*, it appears that the proper method of service upon a Swiss resident is by letters rogatory. It has also been suggested by the Department of State that such process should be translated into the language of the Swiss canton where the defendant resides. This also might be required to satisfy due process in New York. *East Continental Gems, Inc. v. Eli Yakutiel, Ben Mellen and Co., and Chayto, S.A.*, 153 Misc. 2d 883; 582 N.Y.S.2d 594 (Supr. Ct. N.Y. County 1992) [emphasis supplied, citations omitted]

Apparently the court realized that many litigating parties in New York could be unaware of this practice with regard to Switzerland. In application of the convention principles, it held that service by registered mail to the Swiss party was insufficient and the complaint was dismissed.

In addition to this case, in which the Hague Service Convention was applied analogously, the Hague Service Convention was applied eight times. In six cases, upon protest of the foreign defendant, the U.S. plaintiff was held to have served improperly. Yet none of the cases was dismissed. Instead the courts allowed for new service. In the other two cases the convention was held to be inapplicable. In one case it was inapplicable because the foreign state was not a signatory and in the other because personal service had been made on the N.Y. subsidiary, as agent, which was held to be sufficient.

Thus, even where the Hague Service Convention applies, problems may occur due to different interpretations in its applicability and effect. In civil-law countries, the Hague Service Convention is usually held exclusive, where applicable. In the U.S. the Supreme Court has also held service in accordance with the Hague Service Convention as exclusive means of service, where applicable.[170]

The Convention on Service Abroad of Judicial and Extrajudicial Documents in Civil or Commercial Matters applies to all cases "where there is occasion to transmit a judicial or extrajudicial document for service abroad" [hereinafter "Convention"]. Compliance with its terms is mandatory in all cases to which it applies.[171]

Yet other U.S. courts have always deemed service in accordance with the Hague Service Convention as an additional nonex-

170    *Volkswagenwerk AG v. Schlunk*, 108 S.Ct. 2104 (1988).
171    *Seymour Charas et al., v. Sand Technology Systems Int'l, Inc. et al.*, 1992 U.S. Dist. LEXIS 15227 (SDNY 1992), citations omitted.

clusive means to serve a foreign party.[172] Naturally this position can cause problems when enforcement is sought in a civil-law country. The position of some U.S. courts that the Hague Service Convention is regarded as nonexclusive has been highly criticized in civil-law countries.[173]

## V. Normative and Cognitive Reaction

Conflicts arise when the frustrated expectation is met with an economic loss. In these cases the actors often experience an additional legal frustration when their expectations in the foreign law are not met.

Although in a number of cases of the state supreme court file analysis it could not be determined whether, when, or how the matter had been concluded in any form, it is appalling how much time most cases took to reach any form of conclusion. Many times service was never effected on defendant; very often the action was withdrawn or discontinued. The judgement analysis shows a strikingly low success rate for the plaintiffs.

Many of the particular problems of international legal transactions cannot be adequately resolved, even where adequate assistance is available. Thus, the actors need to take losses, making international legal transactions a higher risk than domestic legal transactions.

Of particular significance are the higher legal costs necessarily involved in international legal transactions or disputes. Necessary use of counsel in more than one jurisdiction adds costs, as do translations and communication and travel expenses. Additional expenses are incurred enforcing judgements in a foreign jurisdiction, due to an additional proceeding not usually required in domestic disputes.

This study assumes that, due to a (likely correct) perception by the actors that their rights will not be enforceable by normative action, the predominant reaction to conflicts in international interaction is cognitive, rather than normative. More often than not, conflicts are simply resolved by abandonment of the perceived right.

---

172  See discussion in Born and Westin, *International Civil Litigation in United States Courts*, 153 et seq.

173  See Rolf Stürner, "Der Justizkonflikt zwischen U.S.A. und Europa", in *Der Justizkonflikt mit den Vereinigten Staaten von Amerika*, eds. Rolf Stürner, Dieter G. Lange, and Yasuhei Taniguchi (Bielefeld: Gieseking, 1986), 5–32, with references.

Such reaction may even be anticipated in the actor's risk calculation in advance of the international interaction by calculating different prices, by taking insurance, or by an attitude to the transaction that is somewhat similar to an expectation of winning a lot-
tery, rather than a calculated assumption of success.

It seems that, despite scholarly approaches to conflict of law,
comity, and international treaties providing for the recognition of
foreign court proceedings and judgements, it is unlikely that a claim
involving a foreign party will be brought to and positively concluded in court. With regard to the judgements it appears that,
where the plaintiff was successful, these judgements will in practice only be enforceable against assets in New York itself. As mentioned recognitions of foreign judgements appear only once in the
data base. On the other hand, the county registries for 1992 of all
New York counties contain, out of more than two million filings
of judgements, only eight against parties having their address outside of the U.S. (four in Canada and one each in Korea, Italy, the
Philippines, and the U.K., for amounts between $250 and $276,000).

The reasons for such failure of the courts are not clear. A possible reason for the many withdrawals and stipulations of discon-
tinuance in the file analysis may be a settlement by the parties. It is
clear, however, that in many cases the difficulties and costs involved in perfecting service of process on foreign parties and anticipated further difficulties in proceeding and enforcing a judgement—if any is to be had—drives the parties to abandon the lawsuit altogether. Thus it can also be assumed that many parties will
not even institute a lawsuit involving foreign parties in an otherwise probable cause.

Considering the inadequacies of approaches employed in domestic transactions and their institutions, the question arises
whether the actors in international transactions have found alternative means to secure the success of their international legal transactions and turn the negative cognitive reaction of abandonment
to a positive cognitive reaction of adjustment that would serve the
goal.

A specific cultural behaviour by the parties could not be found.
The plaintiffs' cultural "litigiousness" could best be determined in
comparison to the amounts at stake or the duration of the case.
Yet there was no strong relationship between either domestic and
foreign plaintiffs with regard to such value of the case. Rather it
seems that the behaviour of the parties in court is filtered through
so many legal rules and by so many professionals that the differ-

ent origin plays little if any role in the litigants' behaviour. Differences, where they exist, would rather manifest themselves out of court in prelitigation activities.

Other institutions—including, foremost, lawyers—probably provide assistance in resolving the particular problems of international legal transactions. However, even these institutions are, in part, helpless, as they often lack the necessary skills to resolve these problems. This theory can be indirectly inferred from the low success rate in the court study. Often enough, when a party is involved in an international legal transaction it turns to its local legal counsel and is met with a lack of knowledge by that counsel of foreign law and of the particularities of international matters. Furthermore, in addition to a missing knowledge of particular laws, there is mostly a deficit of understanding of foreign legal culture by counsel and thus a prejudice against foreign legal systems and their lawyers. In fact the lawyers' lack of knowledge and misconceptions can be outright dangerous for the clients.

A few lawyers have developed a special experience and knowledge in international matters. Even these lawyers' efforts are frequently hampered by communication difficulties, particularly with foreign correspondent counsel or with their own clients, and by the inadequacies of the legal systems.

Institutions other than lawyers aiding parties in international legal transactions include banks, insurance companies, investment advisors, and government and government-aided instrumentalities, such as consulates, trade commissions, and offices in the home countries promoting export as well as offices in host countries promoting job-creating investments. Finally, in many countries trades have (more or less) private organizations assisting their members. While providing invaluable assistance for initial contact and for access to lawyers and other specialized institutions, these institutions either lack the knowledge or skills for resolving the problems themselves or are restricted by the limits of their self-interest and budget to bear the expenses necessary for such aid or to provide truly reliable partisan assistance.

In addition international legal transactions are subject to communications problems. The communication problems start with language difficulties. Such language difficulties are present even where one of the parties has a general knowledge of the foreign language, because often such general knowledge is insufficient for contract negotiation, for understanding foreign "legalese", and for other detailed communications.

Cultural and legal-cultural communication barricades also add to the obstacles of international legal transactions. The actors frequently experience cultural frustration due to frustrated expectations in the other side's behaviour. These frustrations, once experienced or anticipated, lead to the actors' cultural insecurity for a perceived lack of knowledge of the foreign culture. In addition there is the actors' legal insecurity for perceived lack of knowledge of the foreign laws.

Finally, the geographical distance itself and the time zones that may lie between the parties can slow down communications or, at least, make such communication more strenuous on the parties. As one interviewed attorney put it, "When I last had a major case involving litigation with an Australian and a European client, I did not sleep enough for weeks, as I had to be up early for Europe, and late for Australia."[174] As another example the German reduction of weekly working hours has made it very difficult to make direct telephone calls to German lawyers, companies, banks, insurance companies and government offices from the United States.

At this point particular attention has to be drawn to the legal-cultural aspects of transborder legal disputes. One important reason for the difficulties in reaching clear standards in the administration of such cases may be the differing views by the parties, and ultimately, by the courts, of different jurisdictions about procedural and material justice. In the event of a conflict, all parties have to find that the law in the respective countries is not adequately suited for international legal transactions.

The difficulties begin with a more complex fact pattern in international cases than usually present in domestic cases. Usually, the law is not even adequately suited to the more complex fact pattern present in international cases. In addition, a matter becomes even more complex where the laws of more than one jurisdiction need to be applied. Added to the complexities are language problems, as documents, witness testimony, laws, and sometimes entire proceedings need to be translated for understanding by the court or by the parties involved.

Also, when it comes to litigation, the parties may find out that procedural rules are not adequately suited for parties residing in different jurisdictions. Where the procedural rules treat the foreign party as domestic, the rules do not even recognize the difference. Where the procedural rules treat the foreign party differ-

174   No. 8.

ently, such differentiation adds to the complexity of an international litigation. Additional difficulties in litigating or defending claims arise when the law is different from the parties' expectations.

Either way, as a result of inadequate procedural rules, the parties either have additional, sometimes insurmountable obstacles in litigating their claim or alternatively the parties, usually the defendants, may find themselves subject to a jurisdiction where they did not expect to litigate.

Even after litigation has been completed, the judgement may not be enforceable for lack of adequate legal provisions facilitating the enforcement of foreign judgements. The ill-adjustment of the procedural rules of one jurisdiction to parties residing in another is often mirrored by the enforcement rules of that other jurisdiction, and the foreign party's feeling of unjust treatment by the foreign jurisdiction is mirrored by a prejudice of the procedural rules and the courts of that party's home, creating obstacles against enforcement of judgements against that party.

International conventions and model laws have done little or nothing to resolve the mentioned problems associated with international legal transactions. Very few conventions and model laws are adopted by more than a handful of countries, even if a few notable, highly successful examples can be mentioned. Furthermore, the conventions and model laws generally deal with very limited areas and provide, at most, a patchwork of solutions to problems that encompass broad areas, leaving the gaps to be filled by domestic law.

It seems that legal theories, statutory law, and supreme court decisions do attempt "final" and adequate solutions for resolution of international legal matters by categorizing such cases as to their proper forum—proper law with the implied effect of security of administration of justice. The general assumption is that, based on the various facts of a case, the proper, just, and most adequate forum can be found, thus, the law. Once these two aspects have been defined at the very beginning of the proceeding, the case may proceed as any other case and find its resolution.

In practice, however, the results in the definition of proper law and forum are manifold. One likely possibility is that the lower courts are not willing to follow the rules prescribed, which may lead to different results than in domestic cases, particularly where the domestic party may lose in comparison. The other likely possibility is that the complexities of international matters are such that the standard solutions are not entirely helpful for the court, which has to apply the law in an actual situation. The developments in the area of *lex loci delicti commissi* described above are an example.

In conclusion, the structural problem is that there are basically two different approaches to legally and procedurally solve cross-border disputes in courts. The first is that they may be resolved by rules made for domestic disputes, which may not be adequate for every case. The other possibility is to create special law, which adds to the complexity. Neither of the two solutions seems to be the best for all cases.

## Abstract

New York, as a major marketplace for international legal interactions, is a most important field for research on cross-border legal interactions. New York may well be one of the places in which the future of international legal practice is decided. With regard to the courts two opposite directions may be found as trends of that development leading into state law—and courts—on the one hand, and out of the same, on the other hand. This study attempts to outline aspects of cross-border court litigation as a basis for the answer to these questions. The empirical study is based on a court file analysis of matters filed in 1986 and on court judgements rendered by 1992. The files and judgements were subjected to an analysis of factors regarding the parties, the dispute matters, and the procedure itself. The court dispute process is considered as a means of achievement and preservation of economical interests as well as a battlefield for legal interests. In comparison the results confirm the lead that New York has taken in the international arena in actual numbers and in the openness of the law to certain cultural and foreign legal elements, even though the latter is still rather underdeveloped even in New York. All in all litigation in New York appears to be a rather uneconomical forum—in terms of time and money—for the resolution of cross-border disputes while the legal framework itself seems well adapted and adequate.

## The Author

Hanno von Freyhold. Lawyer. Research Assistant at the Centre for European Law and Policy at the University of Bremen (ZERP). From 1992 to 1993 Attorney at Law licensed in Berlin and practising on international matters in a law firm in New York. Currently conducts research on cross-border civil litigation as well as policy research for the European Commission. *Address*: ZERP, Universitätsallee GW 1, 28359 Bremen, Germany. *e-mail*: HVF@ZERP.uni-bremen.de.

# 3 International Cases in German First Instance Courts

VOLKMAR GESSNER

## I. Project Design

### A. The Courts

In spite of its federal structure, Germany has a highly unified court system with three tiers in civil matters. The lowest level is split into two types of courts of first instance, namely the *Amtsgericht* (county court), which in 1988 had jurisdiction over cases of a value up to 5000 DM, and the *Landgericht* (district court) with jurisdiction exceeding this limit. Apart from the (limited) jurisdiction in general civil matters, the *Amtsgericht* decides all family matters as court of first instance.

At the county court, civil matters as well as family matters (in a special section) are decided by a single career judge, at the district court by a bench of three career judges (chamber for civil matters) or, on request of the plaintiff, by a commercial chamber (*Kammer für Handelssachen*) that has one career judge and (on request of the parties) two lay judges from the local business community.

Career judges in Germany have to pass two state examinations and share the same legal education as those jurists who enter private practice, become a civil servant, or seek employment in industry. This unified legal education does not prevent judges from becoming socialized—due to very little regional mobility—in a quite stable local legal culture. Because those parts of the German population who are or descend from immigrants have so far not been able to become members of the judiciary, a German judge typically has no experience outside his/her local environment. This background may become relevant if international cases must be decided.

### B. The Sample

*1. Selection of Files*
Because German official statistics do not contain any information about international cases, we had to evaluate court files ourselves.

This could be done only by way of a sample because the total number of civil cases in Germany (West) amounts to more than three million annually. We decided to evaluate basically all (civil) cases that entered the *Landgerichte* (district courts) in Bremen and Hamburg in 1988 and all family cases that were filed at the *Amtsgericht* Bremerhaven in 1988 and 1989. To ensure that the cases were terminated by the time we went into the archives (fall 1992 until summer 1993) we had to go back a few years and chose 1988 and 1988-89 respectively (after four years a civil case is definitely terminated—even running through several appeals; if a case is taken to the supreme court, it may take one more year).

Bremen (500,000 inhabitants) and Hamburg (1.6 million inhabitants) are large commercial cities in northern Germany. Because both have important seaports and are centres of export trade, international cases will be overrepresented compared to the German average. Without a similar study in other parts of Germany, the degree of overrepresentation (which may be substantial) cannot be estimated. Because in Bremerhaven (136,000 inhabitants) only family cases were evaluated, the commercial structure is irrelevant for our purposes. Yet our data are biased for a different reason, namely the existence of a major U.S. army base. A substantial part of the international family cases in our sample reflects this specific circumstance. By filtering out these U.S. cases (as frequently shown in the tables in this report) the data should be fairly representative for a middle-sized German town.

The Hamburg sample has a unique characteristic in that it has one (in 1988) international chamber, in other words, a chamber (with a panel of three judges) specialized in international matters.[1] Unfortunately this special jurisdiction did not facilitate our search for international cases as much as we had expected because (1) the court's definition of "international" was different from ours, and (2) the "international" jurisdiction is subordinate to the jurisdiction of other chambers for special subject matters, for example, to that of the chambers for road traffic cases, for press cases, for guardianship, for landlord-tenant disputes, for state liability, and, if chosen by one of the litigants, to the chambers for commercial claims. With the exception of road traffic cases these specializations virtually exclude international cases. We decided therefore not to

---

[1]     Cf. Kurt Siehr, "Special Courts for Conflicts Cases: A German Experiment", *American Journal of Comparative Law* 25 (1977): 663–80.

go through the files of the chambers for special subject matters and to confine ourselves to a sample—in addition to the international chamber—of the chambers for commercial claims.

From the Bremen sample we learned that international road traffic cases have a certain quantitative relevance and that by not evaluating this special chamber in Hamburg we missed eight cases. Wherever this could be done without additional information about the characteristics of these cases the tables were corrected correspondingly. Summing up this sampling report we evaluated:

• in Bremen: all civil cases (decided either by the chambers for civil matters or commercial chambers) that were initiated in 1988;

• in Hamburg: all cases of the "international chamber" plus all of the cases of six commercial chambers that were initiated in 1988;

• in Bremerhaven: all cases of the family court (*Familiengericht*, which is a section of the *Amtsgericht*) that were initiated in 1988 or 1989.

## 2. Selection of International Cases
In the archives our first step was to look in the files (7591 in Bremen, 4438 in Hamburg, and 3193 in Bremerhaven) in order to find out whether the case was international. Our definition of this term— one party in the case has its domicile outside Germany—was easy to handle because the first page of the file always contains information on the addresses of the parties. International cases were set aside for evaluation, while national cases were set back on the shelves.

## 3. Evaluation of International Cases
International cases were evaluated by filling in an evaluation sheet for every single international file. In order to do this the file had to be read, if not completely, at least in large part (German civil procedure makes sure that all relevant information appears in the file). This evaluation sheet only complemented the information already collected as a matter of routine for each file by the court staff and then evaluated by the National Office of Statistics (*Statistisches Bundesamt*).

## 4. Coupling of Research Data with Official Statistical Data
After obtaining the necessary authorizations from the Ministries of Justice in Hamburg and Bremen and after a difficult search through the data archives in both states (Bremen and Hamburg have the status of federal states), we were able to couple our re-

search data with the corresponding statistical data of each case. In many of the following tables these international data sets are compared with the data of national cases taken exclusively from the official statistics.

## 5. Quality of the Sample

Apart from the above-mentioned overrepresentation of international cases in all three courts, we do not see any restrictions on generalizing the data for Germany as a whole. Regional differences may arise concerning the distribution of specific foreign parties in international cases (more Italian parties in Munich, more French parties in Cologne) or concerning sector-specific types of conflict resolution (more arbitration in maritime trade than in the textile sector) but we did not expect regional differences in procedural aspects. In order to check the quality of the sample, we selected some significant indicators for a comparison between the sample (Hamburg and Bremen) and the data given for the Federal Republic as a whole (Table D–1).

### Table D–1: Comparison of Indicators of the Survey Sample (Hamburg and Bremen) and the Aggregated Data for the Federal Republic (Official Records for 1988)

|                                   | Federal Republic | Hamburg | Bremen | Hamburg and Bremen |
|-----------------------------------|-----------------|---------|--------|--------------------|
| Parties / Plaintiffs              |                 |         |        |                    |
| State agencies                    | 2%              | 1%      | 2%     | 1%                 |
| Insurance companies               | 1%              | 1%      | 1%     | 1%                 |
| Incorporated firms                | 36%             | 43%     | 39%    | 42%                |
| Unincorporated firms              | 9%              | 7%      | 8%     | 7%                 |
| Private individuals               | 52%             | 49%     | 51%    | 50%                |
| Parties / Defendants              |                 |         |        |                    |
| State agencies                    | 3%              | 3%      | 3%     | 2%                 |
| Insurance companies               | 6%              | 6%      | 6%     | 6%                 |
| Incorporated firms                | 26%             | 38%     | 32%    | 37%                |
| Unincorporated firms              | 9%              | 7%      | 8%     | 7%                 |
| Private individuals               | 56%             | 47%     | 52%    | 48%                |
| Outcome of Proceedings            |                 |         |        |                    |
| Judgement                         | 31%             | 28%     | 22%    | 27%                |
| Settlement                        | 16%             | 15%     | 22%    | 16%                |
| Judgement in default              | 18%             | 19%     | 19%    | 19%                |
| Withdrawal of claim               | 13%             | 13%     | 16%    | 14%                |
| Amount of claim                   | 18914 DM        | 20748 DM | 18281 DM | 20208 DM         |
| Duration of proceedings (months)  | 6               | 6       | 7      | 6                  |

Table D–1 indeed shows very little difference between the sample and the totals as regards procedural aspects of civil cases. Even the comparison of party characteristics shows the good quality of the sample, the only important exception being the more frequent appearance of incorporated firms as plaintiffs as well as defendants in the Hamburg and Bremen courts. This leads to the mentioned overrepresentation of international cases—which are, as we shall see, mostly commercial claims—in the sample.

## 6. Validity of the Data

The sample is very large (more than 15,000 cases), which means that even small quantities in our tables may have explanatory power.

As regards the correct data collection, our own data went through various checks and now seem "clean". The statistical data are probably less trustworthy (the court staff does not have the reputation of taking this task too seriously) but are in general not in doubt and are widely used in Germany—and for more important purposes than this research report.

## 7. Presentation of Data

This report presents data either in descriptive or in analytical form. A description shows the quantitative distribution of all characteristics of a variable (for example, a party to a lawsuit may be plaintiff, defendant, plaintiff intervenor, or defendant intervenor). By way of statistical analysis the relationship of two (or more) variables is tested (for example, the nationality of a party and success in lawsuits), a cross-tab being the most common form of doing this. If not otherwise indicated the cross-tabs presented in this report are significant on the 5% level, which means that the chance of the variables showing differences only by accident is smaller than 5% (Pearson Chi-Square test).

The total number of cases varies between the tables due to the fact that not every case contains the information needed for the respective tables.

# II. International Civil Proceedings
## (Except Family Cases)

## A. Frequency of International Cases

The relevance of professional knowledge in private international law, foreign law, and international civil procedure is questioned because thus far quantitative approaches are nearly absent in these fields of legal science.[2] Monographs, textbooks, and articles either go straight into the presentation of the (extremely sophisticated) normative order elaborated for conflicts of law cases or point in a few words to the increase of international (commercial, family, and tourist) interactions.[3] Those who mention globalization processes assert direct effects on international caseload in national courts[4]—a position harshly criticized by others who point to the unsuitability of national courts for international cases and the universal preference for arbitration procedures,[5] or even to the unsuitability of private international law in gen-

2    Siehr ("Special Courts for Conflict Cases", 664) offers numbers of *published* cases but every attempt to draw conclusions regarding the occurrence of international cases in German courts from these numbers would obviously be misleading. The publication policy of courts and law reviews is highly selective.

3    E.g., Council of Europe, *The Practical Guide to the Recognition and Enforcement of Foreign Judicial Decisions in Civil and Commercial Law* (Strasbourg: Morgan Grampian, 1975), 3; David McClean, *International Judicial Assistance* (Oxford: Clarendon Press, 1992), 1; Haimo Schack, *Internationales Zivilverfahrensrecht* (Munich: Beck, 1991), 5; Rolf A. Schütze, *Deutsches Internationales Zivilprozeßrecht* (Berlin and New York: Walter de Gruyter, 1985), 12. An exceptionally detailed description of quantitative aspects in the area of recognition and enforcement of foreign judgements is to be found in Dieter Martiny, *Handbuch des Internationalen Zivilprozeßrechts,* Vol.III/1 (Tübingen: Mohr, 1984), 34.

4    E.g., Murad Ferid, *Internationales Privatrecht*, 3rd ed. (Frankfurt/Main: Metzner, 1986), 54, who writes about an unexpected number of international cases in all jurisdictions. See also Dagmar Coester-Waltjen, *Internationales Beweisrecht* (Ebelsbach: Rolf Gremer, 1983), 2, who wrongly deduces the frequency of cases where evidence in foreign countries has to be taken from the frequency of cases where foreign law has to be applied. Neither situation has anything to do with the other.

5    E.g., Michael D. Medwig, "The New Law Merchant: Legal Rhetoric and Commercial Reality, Law and Policy", *International Business* 24 (1993): 589–616.

eral.[6] We will not be able to render sufficient information to answer such basic questions because private international law has a wider area of application than international civil procedure. To a certain and, due to a reform of German private international law in 1986, small degree, it also applies in cases between German residents of foreign nationality (such as in divorce cases) and even in exceptional cases between residents of German nationality. But in order to overcome unhelpful speculations as regards the role of national courts in resolving *disputes between parties residing in different countries,* it may be worthwhile to study the following results from our file analysis in two district courts.

### Table D–2: Relative Share of International Cases in the District Courts of Bremen and Hamburg (1988)

|  | Bremen | | | Hamburg (sample) | | | Bremen and Hamburg | | |
|---|---|---|---|---|---|---|---|---|---|
|  | All cases | International | | All cases | International | | All cases | International | |
|  | (N) | (N) | % | (N) | (N) | % | (N) | (N) | % |
| General | 3605 | 45 | 1 | 6661 | 110 | 2 | 10,266 | 155 | 2 |
| Commercial | 833 | 91 | 11 | 930 | 99 | 11 | 1763 | 190 | 11 |
| Total | 4438 | 136 | 3 | 7591 | 209 | 3 | 12,029 | 345 | 3 |

Table D–2 shows the proportion of international cases in the caseload of the Bremen and Hamburg courts. Out of 12,029 civil cases we found 345 international cases (2.8%). It seems adequate to mention that 23 of these international cases concerned the recognition and enforcement of foreign decisions and other claims within enforcement procedures, which is, legally and sociologically seen, a conception quite different from a normal lawsuit. The corrected proportion of international lawsuits within the total number of lawsuits in Bremen and Hamburg would then be 2.6%.

Depending on one's expectations this overall proportion may seem high or low, but there is no doubt that the proportion of international cases in the caseload of commercial chambers of the *Landgerichte* Bremen and Hamburg is quite a surprise. Even tak-

---

6    Cf. René David, "The International Unification of Private Law", in *International Encyclopedia of Comparative Law* II, Ch. 5, 7; Coester-Waltjen Internationales Beweisrecht, quotes Herbert F. Goodrich (*Vanderbilt Law Review* 6 (1953), 444), who maintains that conflict of law is "an entertaining dialectic for law professors".

ing into account that both cities are export oriented and are the commercial centres of northern Germany, a share of more than 10% in commercial lawsuits is striking. This result is a clear refutation of the above-mentioned position of the law merchant literature, which says that national courts play no role in the resolution of international business disputes. The two district courts of Bremen and Hamburg had the same international caseload as the ICC International Court of Arbitration, which received 333 cases in 1991.[7] Of course we cannot tell anything about the proportion of lawsuits within the totality of commercial controversies; this proportion may be very low—and will be analysed in other parts of our empirical research. But however frequent international arbitration procedures may be, the number of plaintiffs who decide to go to court in a commercial cross-border dispute is quite substantial.

Our data refer only to the situation in 1988 and hence cannot confirm or refute the argument of an increase of international cases in court due to globalization processes in recent years or decades, nor would we dare to speculate about such a tendency. What is certainly more frequent is the occurrence of cross-border interaction. Whether this results in more frequent disputes is an open question, because at the same time internalization and rationalization processes can also be observed, which aim at reducing the conflict potential. On the other hand, the courts may have become more attractive due to various national measures, such as the reform of private international law, as well as due to international conventions, such as those referring to international judicial assistance.

Of particular interest is whether these international cases are initiated by German or by foreign parties. Reading legal publications and information material for practitioners and businesspeople, we find a constant warning against suing abroad. It is said to be difficult to understand court organizations and procedures in a foreign country and to predict the decision of a foreign judge. Other arguments concern the language problem, the duration, and the costs of a foreign lawsuit.[8] The German Supreme Court talks about

7    Cf. Michael T. Medwig, "The New Law Merchant", 597.
8    Cf. Rolf A. Schütze, *Rechtsverfolgung im Ausland* (Heidelberg: Verlag Recht und Wirtschaft, 1986), 24; Gerhard Kegel, *Internationales Privatrecht*, 6th ed. (Munich: Beck, 1987), 684; Schack, *Internationales Zivilverfahrensrecht*, 77; Joachim Quittnat, *Das Recht der Außenhandelskaufverträge* (Heidelberg: Decker, 1988), 170.

"a natural interest of a citizen to sue in his own country where he knows best the state structure and the language and where he is culturally and socially deeply rooted".[9] It follows from these warnings that all businessmen who use standard contracts introduce a jurisdiction clause and derogate foreign jurisdictions—and, if they have accepted a jurisdiction clause leading to a foreign court, that they rather give up their claims than sue abroad.[10] Finally, there may be even an explicit discrimination against foreign plaintiffs: on request of the defendant they may have to make a security deposit for legal costs of the lawsuit (in Germany § 110 ZPO). The only aspect in favour of suing abroad seems to be the easier enforcement of the judgement if the defendant is sued in his/her own country. One would therefore expect most international cases to be initiated by domestic parties and only occasionally the reverse. Surprisingly enough rather the opposite is true: 209 (65%) of 320 international cases in Bremen and Hamburg were initiated by foreigners. We do not yet know whether German parties also mostly sue in the country of the foreign defendant or whether German courts are particularly attractive to foreign plaintiffs, but we at least can tell that German parties are not taken to court more often abroad than in Germany. This information is inferred from data we got from the international judicial assistance department of the Bremen district court: in 1988 this department registered 94 incoming requests for service of process.[11] If one takes into account that these requests concern only in part initial summonses it follows that an unknown quantity of less than 94 Bremen residents was sued in a foreign country in 1988.[12] Compared to 88

9    BGH 44, 46. Similarly in BGH 60, 85 (90), BGH NJW 81, 2642 (2643).

10   Christoph Graf von Bernstorff, *Vertragsgestaltung im Auslandsgeschäft* (Frankfurt/Main: Fritz Knapp, 1991), 158.

11   The most frequent requests came from Italy (25), France (14), Belgium (10), the U.S. (9), and Turkey (8).

12   We must admit that this method of ascertaining the number of Bremen residents sued in another country is not 100% waterproof. Because Germany has objected to the "freedom to send judicial documents, by postal channels, directly to persons abroad" of the Hague Convention of 15 November 1965, official involvement cannot be avoided for service in Germany. But German residents, while travelling in the common-law countries, can be served according to informal traditions of the common law—situations which might be more prominent in textbooks than in legal practice.

Bremen residents who were sued in Bremen during the same year,
this is an equal or very probably lower number. It is either legally
necessary, or for other reasons attractive, for foreigners to sue a
German resident in Germany and not in their own country of residence. We will try to explain this later.

As regards the country of residence of both foreign plaintiffs
and foreign defendants, Tables D–3 and D–4 give more details.

### Table D–3: Country of Residence of Foreign Plaintiffs in the District Courts of Bremen and Hamburg (1988)

| Country of residence | Number of cases |
|---|---|
| Italy | 27 |
| The Netherlands | 24 |
| United Kingdom | 22 |
| Switzerland | 16 |
| France, U.S.A. | 13 each |
| Austria, Belgium | 9 each |
| Denmark, Luxembourg | 8 each |
| Spain | 7 |
| Sweden | 6 |
| Hong Kong | 5 |
| Turkey | 4 |
| Norway | 3 |
| Iran, Monaco, Lebanon, Yugoslavia, Australia | 2 each |
| Sri Lanka, Cyprus, Egypt, Greece, Hungary, Honduras, Israel, Ireland, Iceland, Japan, Malta, Mexico, Poland, Puerto Rico, Argentina, Cameroon, Indonesia, Rumania, Finland, Syria, China, Tonga, South Africa | 1 each |
| Total | 207 |

These frequencies obviously have to be interpreted against the
background of trade relations between Germany and these countries. But there is also a legal aspect. By the time these lawsuits
were initiated (1988), Belgium, Denmark, France, Greece, Italy,
Ireland, Luxembourg, the Netherlands, and the United Kingdom
had ratified the Convention on Jurisdiction and the Enforcement
of Judgements in Civil and Commercial Matters (Brussels Convention 1968) which requires, on the one hand, suing the defendant in the courts of his/her country (Art. 2) but also permits (except in consumer and some other cases) derogation of this jurisdiction either by a jurisdiction clause (which is the rule in standard contracts) or by an agreement on the place of performance.[13]

13    Cf. decision of the European Court of Justice (12/76) of 6 Octo-
      ber 1976.

It stipulates in Articles 31 and 32 that a judgement given in a contracting state shall be enforced in another contracting state after submission of an application to the local courts at the place of domicile of the party against whom enforcement is sought. Notwithstanding this simple enforcement procedure, which was intended to allow plaintiffs to bring their disputes to their national courts, plaintiffs in many situations have to sue or seem to prefer suing in the defendant's country. Fifty-three percent of international cases with foreign plaintiffs were brought by citizens of countries of the Brussels Convention. If one adds lawsuits with plaintiffs from countries that have signed bilateral agreements on jurisdiction and enforcement with Germany (such as Austria, Switzerland, and Norway) more than 70% of the foreign plaintiffs use the German courts and not their national courts in spite of unproblematic enforcement of their national judgements in Germany. The facilities offered by the Brussels Convention and other bilateral agreements do not seem to be attractive for plaintiffs. They prefer to bring the lawsuit where they want to enforce it.

If we consider another result to be discussed below, namely that enforcement of foreign judgements is extremely rare (only 23 such applications were found in our two district courts), there is also little doubt that residents of Germany are not sued frequently in other countries (as long as they do not have a subsidiary there).

#### Table D-4: Country of Residence of Foreign Defendants in the District Courts of Bremen and Hamburg (1988)

| Country of residence | Number of cases |
| --- | --- |
| Switzerland | 13 |
| France, United Kingdom | 11 each |
| The Netherlands | 8 |
| Belgium | 7 |
| Austria, Turkey | 6 each |
| Spain, Sweden | 5 each |
| Denmark, Hong Kong, Italy | 4 each |
| Cyprus, Finland, U.S.A. | 3 each |
| Israel, Norway | 2 each |
| Sri Lanka, Ecuador, El Salvador, Egypt, Greece, Iran, Luxembourg, Mozambique, Taiwan, South Korea, Soviet Union, Thailand, Nigeria, South Africa | 1 each |
| Total | 111 |

The data presented in Table D-4 also suggest that German residents seem to prefer suing the defendants in their home countries even if this conclusion cannot be verified by a comparison to the number of enforcement applications or requests for international service of process (both being unnecessary if the defendant is sued in his/her country of residence). If one imagines the number of commercial activities within the European Union, our 47 lawsuits against defendants from the EEC countries (42% of all German claims against foreign defendants) are certainly a very small quantity and simply cannot represent the bulk of lawsuits between Bremen and Hamburg residents and the rest of the European Union.

Hence it must be concluded that, contrary to our expectations and to widespread opinions in legal literature, most plaintiffs either are confronted with jurisdiction clauses against their home jurisdiction, are forced by the domicile principle of their domestic private international law to make their legal claims in foreign courts, or are taking on the burden of suing in foreign courts instead of at home for other reasons. Among these various possible reasons the jurisdiction clauses do not play—as one would have expected—the decisive role. Only 26 (20%) out of 130 foreign plaintiffs about whom we have sufficient information are obliged by jurisdiction clauses to bring their contract claims to German courts.[14] On the other hand, it follows from the legal situation that German residents are to a considerably higher degree, namely 32 (39%) out of 83 plaintiffs residing in Germany, supported by jurisdiction clauses when they sue foreigners in Germany.[15]

## B. Characteristics of Parties

Parties to a civil lawsuit are plaintiff, defendant, and third-party intervenors. Of these it is the plaintiff who deserves most interest because he/she decides to mobilize the law and to make use of the judicial system in order to resolve disputes. The plaintiff brings law out of the books and into action. The "access to law" literature tries to find out about his/her characteristics compared to the entire population in order to look for eventual social barriers in the use of the legal system. If, for example, in 1988 44% of those who initiated lawsuits in the German *Landgerichte* were firms and 50% were private persons, one concludes that firms are overrepresented and hence have easier access to judicial enforce-

14    Forty-nine files with foreign plaintiffs did not contain any information about eventual jurisdiction clauses; in 30 cases the foreign plaintiff brought a claim not based on contract. For more detailed information cf. the chapter on international jurisdiction, herein.

15    Again 22 files did not contain relevant information. Seven cases did not concern a contract claim.

ment. This conclusion is made on the assumption (not empirically verified but plausible) that even if firms do enter more frequently into legal relationships than private persons, their appearance in court exceeds by far their share of legally relevant social interactions. This test was also done for stratificatory characteristics of the individual and led to similar results (overrepresentation of the wealthier strata as plaintiffs in court). As a consequence legal-aid schemes were developed in order to facilitate the use of law by those (lower class) persons underrepresented in court statistics.

Because our knowledge of stratificatory aspects of the world society is limited, it is much more difficult to carry out similar comparisons between distributions of variables in international lawsuits and statistical descriptions of the (global) society. First of all, these descriptions are not available. Second, the reference cannot be made with mankind as a whole but only with the totality of actors participating in global legal interaction. Hence we have to ask whether the characteristics of parties we have found in our international lawsuits mirror what is known or is assumed about the characteristics of these international actors. As a first approximation Table D–5 shows the characteristics of plaintiffs in our sample of international cases in civil matters.

Table D–5: Plaintiffs in International Cases in the District Courts in Bremen and Hamburg (1988)

| Type of Plaintiff | % | (N) |
|---|---|---|
| Corporations | 46 | (162) |
| Unincorporated firms | 23 | ( 79) |
| Private individuals | 31 | ( 76) |
| Total | 100 | (317) |

The data demonstrate a strong dominance of business actors as plaintiffs in German courts. Nearly 70% of plaintiffs are firms, most of them bigger firms, and only 30% are private individuals. In order to test the hypothesis that this distribution reflects the structure of the social field of international interaction rather than the easier access of business to court proceedings, we also counted the defendants' characteristics in our international cases.

Table D–6: Defendants in International Cases in the District Courts in Bremen and Hamburg (1988)

| Type of Defendant | % | (N) |
|---|---|---|
| Corporations | 53 | (165) |
| Unincorporated firms | 18 | ( 56) |
| Private individuals | 31 | ( 98) |
| Total | 100 | (319) |

The comparison of the data in Tables D–5 and D–6 indeed shows no "access–to-justice discrimination" effect against private individuals; they appear in about the same proportion as plaintiffs and as defendants. Whereas the domestic caseload of courts is characterized by a vast amount of debt enforcement against private persons (as consumers), this situation is rare in a cross-border context. Consumers do not buy goods or services frequently in other countries, and, if they do, they have to pay in cash.

From a legal point of view, there would be no additional burden for private individuals not to initiate a lawsuit in Germany. According to German law (§ 114 ZPO) poor parties may claim legal aid and foreigners have the same right to legal aid as German parties insofar as they are private individuals. Corporations only get legal aid if a bilateral agreement with their country of residence (§ 116 ZPO)[16] exists. In our data of international cases, legal aid plays a marginal role. There are only eleven petitions, five of which were rejected. Five foreign plaintiffs and one foreign defendant successfully claimed legal aid.

Globally seen the data confirm the hypothesis of the dominance of business actors in the international arena in general; business actors—and among them particularly bigger firms organized in some form of legal structure—strongly dominate as either party to international lawsuits. Private actors appear only in every third international lawsuit. Due to many well-known filter effects, these results may not mirror the distribution of characteristics of parties to cross-border disputes in general. Most commercial disputes are resolved out of court by arbitration and many other forms of autonomous procedures. Hence the data have to be interpreted as minimum numbers of international commercial disputes. The conclusion that the social field of international actors mainly consists of business actors, and among them of relatively big firms, seems valid on the basis of the German court sample. This question will of course be taken up in other parts of our research.

In conclusion to this chapter on characteristics of parties in court proceedings, we compare in Table D–7 the sample of international cases with data from national cases taken from the official court statistics.

---

16    Cf. Adolf Baumbach, Wolfgang Lauterbach, Peter Hartmann, *Zivilprozeßordnung,* (Munich: Beck, 1994), Anh. nach § 114.

Table D-7: Characteristics of Parties (Plaintiff and Defendant) in National Cases Compared to International Cases at the District Courts of Bremen and Hamburg (1988)

| | National | | International | |
|---|---|---|---|---|
| | % | (N) | % | (N) |
| International corporations | 43 | (17,778) | 51 | (327) |
| Unincorporated firms | 7 | ( 2,876) | 21 | (135) |
| Private individuals | 50 | (20,662) | 28 | (182) |
| Total | 100 | (41,316) | 100 | (644) |

Table D-7 shows the different composition of parties in national and international court proceedings and indicates differences in the national and the international social fields of action. Taking all conflicts together (except those family conflicts that go to the family court) private individuals are important legal actors nationally but are far less important internationally.

A striking difference also can be noticed as regards the role of unincorporated firms. Contrary to our expectations, which were based on the assumption that they are less active in the international arena, they are more visible in international than in national court proceedings. A tentative explanation would be that those small firms who go into the global market have fewer remedies to resolve their conflicts than bigger firms who use either their power, their informal networks, or their experienced lawyers or arbitrators to handle their legal controversies or, rather, prevent such problems by elaborating complex international contracts. This explanation also holds true for those parties labelled as corporations by the official court statistics. As far as we can see from the data we collected, these firms, mostly in the legal form of limited companies, are small or at best middle-sized, whereas important firms or multinationals never appeared in the court files. Firms— be they incorporated or unincorporated—are visible in the sample of international cases because they dominate the arena of international legal interaction, and they are relatively more visible the less other resources of conflict prevention and conflict resolution are at hand.

## C. Characteristics of Cases

### 1. Subject Matters

The subject matters of cases are of interest from a legal as well as from a sociological point of view. The legal interest lies in the relevance of specific areas of substantive law for international cases. Sociological curiosity is directed to patterns of cross-border activities (which may be only partially and selectively reflected in court files) and to differences that might be discernible between national and international cases taken to court.

In a first approximation the data tell us that 74% of claims in international cases are based on contract, 5% on antitrust law, 5% on family[17] and succession law, 4% on tort law, and 7% on other legal areas. It is interesting to note how unimportant torts are in cross-border legal interactions in spite of so many possible sources of disputes over accidents and environmental damages.[18] This in part explains the underdevelopment of tort rules in private international law. More specific information is contained in Table D–8.

#### Table D–8: Subject Matters of International Cases in the District Courts in Bremen and Hamburg (1988)

| Subject Matter | % | (N) |
|---|---|---|
| Contract of sale | 41 | ( 83) |
| Sea/land transport | 25 | ( 51) |
| Contract for work | 12 | ( 24) |
| Commission of agents | 6 | ( 13) |
| Credit | 5 | ( 11) |
| Family affairs | 5 | ( 10) |
| Unfair competition | 5 | ( 10) |
| Road accident | 5 | ( 10) |
| Tort | 4 | ( 9) |
| Real estate | 4 | ( 8) |
| Suretyship | 4 | ( 8) |
| Maritime accidents | 3 | ( 6) |
| Agency | 3 | ( 6) |
| Corporation affairs | 2 | ( 5) |
| Insurance | 2 | ( 4) |
| Travel business | 1 | ( 2) |
| Total | 100 | (209) |

The distribution of subject matters shown in Table D–8 excludes those matters that are only defined in terms of the legal procedure chosen for the dispute: execution of judgement (32 cases), attachment (14 cases), documentary procedure, such as letters of

17   Remember that most family cases go to the family court (cf. the chapter on international family cases, herein).

18   The infrequency of traffic accident cases is explained by an agreement between insurance companies that "internalizes" cross-border cases into domestic ones—another example of creative *lex mercatoria* regulation.

credit or cheques (12 cases), and arbitration awards (5 cases). As far as cases of execution of judgements are concerned, all motions within the execution proceedings are considered. Out of 32 cases, 23 dealt with the execution of a foreign judgement in Germany (only eleven among them were judgements from countries that had in 1988 ratified the Brussels Convention on Recognition and the Enforcement of Foreign Judgements).

Unfortunately we cannot compare the subject matters of international cases with those of national cases, because information in the official court statistics (on which we have to rely in national cases) grouping 80% (!) of cases into an unspecified category "others" is very poor.[19] Except for the high number of claims stemming from sea/land transport contracts, the subject matters of our international cases look quite unspectacular and probably close to the common caseload of a national court in Germany. One looks in vain in our sample of international lawsuits for the "complexities of international trade"[20] or the peculiarities that René David claims for international relationships.[21] Nor did we find a single contract that resembles one of those highly sophisticated contracts U.S. law firms are famous for producing for cross-border affairs.[22] Our cases are simple from a legal and quite common from a sociological point of view, and none of them mirrors what is called the new quality of the international economy represented by multinational actors moving enormous quantities of goods all over the world.

Because we do not want to question the correct description of the characteristics of international trade by so many authors, we draw the conclusion that only a specific (ordinary) type of case is taken to municipal courts whereas (legally and/or economically) complex controversies indeed are resolved otherwise. Notwithstanding the picture of legal patterns of the world society drawn by national courts being only partial and selective, it is certainly

19 In addition court data collection regarding subject matters proved to be wrong to a considerable degree: whereas the statistics categorized only 11 of our international cases as dealing with "contract of sale", we put 85 cases in this category.

20 Medwig, "The New Law Merchant", 598.

21 David, "The International Unification of Private Law", 11.

22 Cf. John H. Langbein, "Zivilprozeßrechtsvergleichung und der Stil komplexer Vertragswerke", *Zeitschrift für vergleichende Rechtswissenschaft* 86 (1987): 141–57.

complementary to more spectacular descriptions. The international arena also knows daily legal problems, which are resolved as a matter of routine by ordinary legal institutions.

Among these daily legal problems of the international arena are, to a certain degree, consumer problems—but they play hardly any role in the files analysed in the district courts of Bremen and Hamburg.[23] In this respect the picture of a normal caseload has to be clearly qualified. In order to learn more about consumer sale of goods, hotel and travel, and insurance matters were selected out of the total of nine subject matters (Table D–9). The table shows that only four cases in our sample of 320 international lawsuits can be defined as consumer cases (private individuals whose claims against firms were based on a purchase of goods contract, a hotel and travel contract, or an insurance contract).

Table D–9: Type of Defendant by Type of Plaintiff in the International Sale of Goods, Hotel and Travel, and Insurance Cases in the District Courts in Bremen and Hamburg (1988)

| Plaintiffs | Defendants | | | | | | | |
|---|---|---|---|---|---|---|---|---|
| | Incorporated firms | | Unincorporated firms | | Private individuals | | Total | |
| | % | (N) | % | (N) | % | (N) | % | (N) |
| Incorporated firms | 64 | (29) | 29 | ( 5) | 32 | ( 6) | 49 | (40) |
| Unincorporated firms | 29 | (13) | 65 | (11) | 37 | ( 7) | 38 | (31) |
| Private individuals | 7 | ( 3) | 6 | ( 1) | 32 | ( 6) | 12 | (10) |
| Total        % | 56 | | 21 | | 24 | | 100 | |
| (N) | | (45) | | (17) | | (19) | | (81) |

We doubt that cross-border consumer cases are more frequent among the international cases in the *Amtsgerichte*. On the one hand, these courts are, with their jurisdiction up to a value of 5000 DM (in 1988), more prone to deal with consumer problems. On the other hand, smaller amounts of claims make the cases so unattractive for lawyers that they will normally refrain from bringing an international consumer case to a court of petty jurisdiction.

23    Insofar as our study offers answers to the recent Green Paper of the Commission of the European Communities (Kom 93, 576), where serious concern about cross-border consumer problems is articulated.

A case may also be brought to an *Amtsgericht* without being represented by a lawyer—but a private individual would be extremely courageous to do this in an international matter.

If our international cases did not show a particular high complexity they still could be relatively more important as regards the value of the claim taken to court.

## 2. Amount of the Claim

As regards the amount of the claim, international cases can be compared with national cases because official court statistics offer reliable information (attorney and court fees are calculated on this basis).[24]

Table D–10: Amount of Claim in National and International Cases in the District Courts of Bremen and Hamburg (1988)

| Value | National % | National (N) | International % | International (N) | Total % | Total (N) |
|---|---|---|---|---|---|---|
| Less than 5000 | 8 | ( 959) | 2 | ( 6) | 8 | ( 965) |
| 5000 - 10,000 | 37 | ( 4280) | 21 | ( 66) | 36 | ( 4346) |
| 10,000 - 20,000 | 24 | ( 2792) | 20 | ( 65) | 24 | ( 2857) |
| 20,000 - 50,000 | 19 | ( 2177) | 23 | ( 72) | 19 | ( 2249) |
| 50,000 - 100,000 | 7 | ( 797) | 16 | ( 51) | 7 | ( 848) |
| More than 100,000 | 6 | ( 704) | 19 | ( 60) | 6 | ( 764) |
| Total % | 97 | | 3 | | 100 | |
| (N) | | (11,709) | | (320) | | (12,029) |

Table D–10 is highly significant and contains a clear message: in international cases more money is at stake than in national cases. Forty–five per cent of national cases, but only 22% of international cases, deal with less than 10,000 DM.[25] On the lower end of the columns we find the reverse picture: in only 13% of national cases but in 35% of international cases claims are higher than 50,000 DM.

24    If an amount of money is claimed, this amount is taken as the amount of claim. If the lawsuit does not deal with payment of money, an "amount of claim at stake" is calculated by the judge in order to enable the court clerks and the attorneys to calculate their fees.

25    It may be confusing that the amount of claim in some cases is below 5000 DM, which is the threshold value of the competence of the district court (in 1988). In these cases the claim has been reduced during the proceedings.

If the subject matters of international lawsuits did not show a particular "global" aspect, one can at least confirm assumptions as to the relative importance of international legal disputes in terms of the money involved. For small amounts of money parties to an international dispute rarely go to court and will rather give up their claim. Parties seem to conceive an international lawsuit as something difficult and arduous that should be initiated only in serious situations.

### 3. Relationship between Parties
Although legal abstraction allows little insight into the complexities of social relationships and consequently court files contain hardly any data in this respect, we learned at least something about the existence and duration of contractual relations. Seventy-four per cent of our international cases were based on a contractual relationship, which is, in view of the above distribution of subject matters, no surprise at all. Most of these contracts (55%) were negotiated for a single purpose, 26% were based on a standard form elaborated and imposed by one of the parties, and 18% were based on a standard form offered by the respective business associations. In 38% of the cases we estimated the contractual relationship to be isolated and short-term, whereas the great majority of contracts (62%) seemed to be an expression of a relatively (in our definition more than a year) long-term relationship. A frequent example for this latter type of cross-border interaction was the supply of goods from foreign producers, whereas the typical one-shot contract was the contract for work or service.

### D. Procedural Aspects of International Cases
The data presented lead to hypotheses that go in opposite directions. On the one hand, the characteristics of parties in international cases differ considerably from national cases; on the other hand, the subject matters seem to be quite similar. The civil procedure[26] might in some aspects be more influenced by the first, in

---

26    For a general introduction to German Civil Procedure written in English, see John Langbein, "The German Advantage in Civil Procedure", *The University of Chicago Law Review* 52 (1985): 823–66; John Ratliff, "Civil Procedure in Germany", *Civil Justice Quarterly* (1983): 257–67.

other cases by the second variable. It might also be assumed that most more or less "exotic" inputs into the legal procedure are filtered out by the fact that foreign parties are necessarily represented by domestic attorneys,[27] leading to a levelling off of all or most differences between national and international cases. The following data will show that there are indeed many answers to our question.

Apart from a comparison between national and international cases, it is of interest to know more about the handling of international cases in particular. We will therefore deal with questions of German jurisdiction in cases with foreign parties, with questions of judicial assistance for service of process and the taking of evidence, and with the problem of the application of foreign law and international conventions.

## 1. International Jurisdiction

Germany is generous in granting international jurisdiction: apart from the universally known jurisdiction based on factors like domicile (of the defendant and in exceptional cases of the plaintiff) or *Rei Sitae,* it accepts jurisdiction by choice of forum clauses or voluntary appearance in the proceedings even if both contesting parties are nonresidents. The mere presence of any assets belonging to a nonresident defendant can also serve as a basis of unlimited jurisdiction in personam (§ 23 ZPO)[28]—a much-criticized "exorbitant jurisdiction" that nevertheless seems to be of practical importance (except within the area of the Brussels Convention, which in its Art. 5 excludes assets jurisdiction).[29]

This generosity in granting jurisdiction is clearly visible in our data. Out of a total of 337 international cases, German jurisdiction was denied to only three foreign plaintiffs (residents of

---

27  According to § 78 Zivilprozeßordnung parties need a local attorney to represent them in district courts.

28  Only recently (i.e., after the time our cases were decided) the German Federal Supreme Court introduced a "minimum contact" doctrine in the interpretation of § 23 ZPO (BGH NJW 1991, 3092).

29  Dieter Martiny ("Recognition and Enforcement of Foreign Money Judgements in the Federal Republic of Germany", *American Journal of Comparative Law* 35 (1987): 721–59) gives more details about restrictions of assets jurisdiction in various bilateral conventions.

Cameroon, the Netherlands, and Switzerland) and two German plaintiffs (suing defendants from the Netherlands and Belgium). In four of these five cases, jurisdiction clauses in favour of German jurisdiction were not accepted or the foreign defendant successfully claimed the recognition of jurisdiction clauses in favour of his home jurisdiction. A dismissal rate of 1.4% on jurisdiction problems seems to be very low indeed. It is also low if one takes into consideration that in 29 cases defendants (21 of them residents of different European countries) tried to question German jurisdiction.

Jurisdiction based on jurisdiction clauses appears much more rarely in our data than expected. Fifty-eight such clauses seem to be a low number. In 236 disputes based on contracts, jurisdiction clauses appeared in only 25% of the cases.[30] As mentioned before this surprising result certainly gives a wrong picture of international contracts on the whole (where jurisdiction clauses are said to be the rule), but it might be valid for those (few and less complex) contracts being taken to court. These low numbers indicate that parties using courts for dispute settlement are mostly unexperienced actors in the international arena; experienced businessmen have jurisdiction clauses in their contracts (which in no way means that they litigate if a dispute arises).

Our 58 jurisdiction clauses were found in contracts involving parties from France and Switzerland (eight cases), the U.K. (six), Belgium, the Netherlands (five), Denmark, Italy, Luxembourg, Sweden (three), Austria, Cyprus, Hong Kong, the U.S. (two) and Spain, Greece, Monaco, Indonesia, Cameroon, and Nigeria (one).

In general our international files did not confirm those opinions in the legal literature (mostly of common-law provenance) which emphasize the importance of choice of forum, recommend "forum shopping", and elaborate arguments for attacking jurisdiction. The issue of the correct choice of jurisdiction was raised only in 8% of the cases, and in those cases the judges dealt with it quite briefly. This might be a peculiarity for Germany (or continental law in general) where, in sharp contrast to the U.S. *forum non conveniens* doctrine and the reasonableness doctrine, there is hardly any discretion left to the court in accepting or rejecting its

---

30    As mentioned within the area of the Brussels Convention the agreement on a place of performance may be used as an alternative to jurisdiction clauses. The quantitative occurrence of these clauses cannot be ascertained in our data.

jurisdiction.[31] This conflict-avoiding function of codified law is impressively illustrated by Table D–11.

### Table D–11: Controversy on Questions of Jurisdiction by Forum Selection Clauses in International Cases in the District Courts of Bremen and Hamburg (1988)

|  | Existence of Forum Select Clause | | | | | |
|---|---|---|---|---|---|---|
|  | No | | Yes | | Total | |
| Jurisdiction Dispute | % | (N) | % | (N) | % | (N) |
| No | 95 | (146) | 71 | (41) | 89 | (187) |
| Yes | 5 | ( 7) | 29 | (17) | 11 | ( 24) |
| Total    % | 72 | | 28 | | 100 | |
|          (N) | | (153) | | (58) | | (211) |

The data in Table D–11 are interpreted in the following way: if the contract contains a forum selection clause, the defendant tries in nearly every third case to challenge the chosen jurisdiction. If no such clause has been contracted, jurisdiction is clearly defined by the German Code of Civil Procedure so that only every twentieth defendant raises legal arguments against the forum.

### 2. Service of Process

In order to better understand our research data on the modes and success of service of process in the observed international cases, a short introduction into this very special and complicated legal field,[32] where each country has its own law and practice, seems necessary.

In many common-law jurisdictions the responsibility for service rests in principle with the plaintiff or his/her attorney who leaves a copy of the document with the person to be served. There are a number of exceptions, so that in England a county court summons will normally be served by an officer of the court sending it by post; in the United States federal courts, summonses in civil actions may be served out of state by a United States Marshal. What is the exception in common-law countries is the rule in civil-law countries. Originating summonses will be served by an officer of the court who has to deliver the document either in person or by using a formal delivery provided by the Postal Service. The

31    Heimo Schack, "Die Versagung der deutschen internationalen Zuständigkeit wegen forum non conveniens und lis alibi pendens", *RabelsZ* 58 (1994): 40–58.

32    For more detailed information cf. McClean, "International Judicial Assistance", 6–55.

formal civil-law tradition requires international service to be initiated by specified officials and (because service of process is considered an act of state, an expression of sovereignty) the strict observation of all formalities in the state of destination. The mode of communication originally required by this doctrine is the diplomatic or consular channel, but this has been considered inadequate since the beginning of this century. A number of international (bilateral or multilateral) conventions tried to ease international service procedures, the most recent one being the Convention on the Service Abroad of Judicial and Extrajudicial Documents in Civil or Commercial Matters (The Hague Service Convention, 1965). According to this convention each contracting state designates a central authority, which undertakes to receive requests for service coming from competent authorities or judicial officers in other contracting states and arranges to have the documents served by a method prescribed by its internal law.

The Hague Service Convention was in force at the time the observed international cases were initiated (1988) between Germany and 24 other contracting states. Direct communication between German courts and foreign central authorities facilitates service of original summons, whereas subsequent service of documents during the proceedings in Germany are facilitated through the nomination of a representative authorized by the nonresident party (§ 174 para 2 ZPO). Service of process of parties resident in other countries is effected either on the basis of bilateral conventions or by traditional diplomatic or consular channels.

International service of process had to be expected in those 121 cases of our sample where the defendant was not resident in Germany, but only 79 files contained the corresponding information. It has to be assumed that 42 defendants had already authorized a local representative beforehand in order to avoid costs of service abroad or for other reasons. The modes used for service in those 79 files without local representatives are listed in Table D–12.

### Table D–12:Modes for International Service of Process in Civil Actions of German Residents Against Nonresidents (79 cases in the District Courts of Bremen and Hamburg in 1988)

| Convention | % | (N) |
|---|---|---|
| Hague Convention 1965 | 60 | (48) |
| Diplomatic channels | 22 | (17) |
| Others | 18 | (14) |
| Total          % | 100 | |
|                (N) | | (79) |

We were interested to know more about the efficiency of these various modes of service of process but the files did not contain sufficient information. All we could find out unambiguously (and this seems already to be an important result) is that ten attempts (8%) of international service of process remained unsuccessful— mostly not, as one might expect, in remote countries but in European countries. In seven of these ten cases the service was eventually effected by public notice (*öffentliche Zustellung*).

In order to learn more about the practical experiences in general, we interviewed a clerk (*Rechtspfleger*) in the international legal assistance department of the Hamburg district court. This is a summary of what she told us:

The service of process centralized in her department for the district court concerns not only original summons but also judgements and all other kinds of judicial decisions, but rarely summons of witnesses. In 1988, 349 such requests were sent out to foreign authorities, the number remaining quite stable over the past ten years. Whereas a complete failure is rather the exception, the experience as to the duration of service of process varies from country to country. Within three months documents are normally served in Austria, Switzerland, and the Netherlands. Three to six months are needed for service in Denmark, France, Great Britain, Portugal, Sweden, Norway, Poland, and Hungary. Service takes normally more than six months (quite often more than twelve months) in Brazil, Argentina, India, Libya, and Spain. The frequently addressed central authority of this last country is particularly slow and cooperates only with the assistance of local attorneys who seem to use everything from personal relations to bribes in order to accelerate service. The German Ministry of Justice recommends in this particular case proceeding without delivery of the document according to German internal law (*öffentliche Zustellung*, § 203 ZPO) if a period of nine months has elapsed without the request being successful. Service in Turkey is also slow but reliable. In Italy problems result from the fact that the central authority refuses to certify service of process.

In view of these experiences with international service of process (confirmed by the corresponding department in the district court of Bremen), it is quite understandable that plaintiffs prefer to avoid the problems with judicial assistance by suing in the country of residence of the defendant. Our data show clearly that proceedings with foreign defendants (who have to be served abroad) take considerably longer than the opposite situation where a foreign plaintiff sues a defendant resident in Germany: the mean duration of a proceeding with service abroad amounts to 284 days, whereas the mean duration without service abroad is 190 days.

The advantage of getting the lawsuit started more quickly may in many situations be the decisive argument in favour of suing abroad (where the defendant lives), more than the easier enforcement of the judgement.

### 3. Summary Collection Proceedings

German civil procedure offers a judicial debt collection (*Mahnverfahren*, §§ 688 ss. ZPO), which only leads to a normal lawsuit if the debtor rejects the claim within a stipulated period. Whereas in national lawsuits tried in Bremen and Hamburg a previous judicial debt collection attempt was quite frequent (30%), this procedure was rarely found in international cases (10%). Although this simple form of debt collection is also accessible for nonresidents (§ 689 para 2 ZPO), it can only be used *against* debtors if they are residents of the European Community, Norway, or Israel.[33] One must also take into account that this procedure is unknown in most foreign legal orders and that the claims in international cases are relatively high (in which case the judicial debt collection is much less frequent also in domestic disputes).

### 4. Single Judge or Chamber

The civil chambers in German district courts consist of three professional judges, while the commercial chambers consist of one professional and two lay judges. In both chambers the case may be decided by a single professional judge: in civil matters if there are no particular legal or factual problems or questions of legal policy involved (§ 348 ZPO), in commercial matters the only requisite being that both parties agree (§ 349 ZPO). According to a recent study about the selection of cases for single judge decision-making,[34] some district courts never opt for the single judge and

---

33  This follows from international conventions, in particular the Brussels Convention, cf. § 688 para. 3 ZPO with § 34 AVAVG (Gesetz zur Ausführung zwischenstaatlicher Anerkennungs- und Vollstreckungsverträge in Zivil- und Handelssachen).

34  Hubert Rottleuthner, Ellen Böhm, and Daniel Gasterstädt, *Rechtstatsächliche Untersuchung zum Einsatz des Einzelrichters* (Cologne: Bundesanzeiger, 1992).

some do so in 80% of the cases, which means that the statutory provision of reserving complex and important cases for the bench is in practice a poor guideline. The criteria in favour of the bench (better quality of the decision) compete with the criteria in favour of the single judge (speed and lower costs of decision-making). The interviewed attorneys generally did not have a strong feeling for or against one or the other type of proceedings.

As regards international cases the arguments in favour of the bench seem to prevail slightly. Whereas in 82% of the national civil cases the district courts of Bremen and Hamburg took the matters to the bench, they did so in 93% of the international cases. One explanation is that international cases are more important as regards the amount of the claim, as previously discussed. Within our sample of international cases, the decision to proceed either to the bench or with a single judge was clearly made on the basis of this criteria: the mean value of proceedings before the single judge was 22,000 DM, before the bench it was 157,000 DM.[35]

Another explanation seems to be that judges conceive of international matters as being more complex. In international as in domestic commercial matters (namely, in the chamber for commercial matters) the single (professional) judge decided nearly all cases. This could be interpreted as a lack of factual complexity of international lawsuits because lay judges, who are necessarily businessmen, could help in understanding the economic aspects of cases. Both observations (preference for the bench in civil matters, preference for the single judge in commercial matters) seem to contradict each other, but the most plausible explanation is the business experience of the judges. Judges in commercial chambers are selected for this purpose whereas judges in civil chambers are not— and therefore need and seek support from other colleagues.

## 5. Hearings
German civil procedure is oral insofar as judgements, and (with exceptions) other decisions are based on oral pleadings in a hearing where attorneys and possibly the litigants themselves are

35    The corresponding values within domestic cases (in Bremen and Hamburg, 1988) are 30,000 and 46,000 DM. This smaller difference has led Rottleuthner and his team not to attribute decisive importance to the amount of claim in the selection of the single judge or bench. Cf. Rottleuthner, Böhm, and Gasterstädt *Rechtstatsächliche Untersuchungen*, 98.

present. The oral elements have been increased by a recent reform of procedural law, but in practice written pleadings still dominate. The intention of law reform was to concentrate everything (including the taking of evidence) in one hearing only, in order to accelerate the decision-making and to create a better ambience for compromise and settlement. This has been successful to a certain degree but, as we shall see in Table D–13, quite a number of proceedings need two or more hearings. Because the number of hearings seems to be an indicator for legal and/or factual difficulties, the table compares national and international proceedings.

### Table D–13: Number of Hearings in National and International Cases in the District Courts of Bremen and Hamburg (1988)

| Hearings | National % | National (N) | International % | International (N) | Total % | Total (N) |
|---|---|---|---|---|---|---|
| One | 75 | (5554) | 68 | (133) | 74 | (5687) |
| Two | 20 | (1455) | 20 | ( 39) | 20 | (1494) |
| Three or more | 6 | ( 449) | 13 | ( 25) | 6 | ( 474) |
| Total      % | 97 | | 3 | | 100 | |
|            (N) | | (7458) | | (197) | | (7655) |

In domestic cases three-quarters of the proceedings only have one hearing, whereas three or more hearings are needed in only 6% of the cases. In international cases a clear tendency toward more hearings can be observed—the difference being not spectacular but visible. We conclude from these data that international cases cause more problems, which means additional effort for both judges and attorneys. The problems have to do with the communications between domestic and foreign attorneys and, to a certain degree, also with the taking of evidence, which is more frequent in international than in national cases (25% compared to 21%). On the other hand, the taking of evidence—besides being more frequent—does not cause particular trouble: only in two of the 320 international cases of our sample did the evidence have to be taken in a foreign country (one in the Netherlands, one in Cameroon).[36]

36    The taking of evidence abroad has been facilitated by the Hague Evidence Convention 1970, which according to David McClean ("International Judicial Assistance", 86), has proved to be one of the most successful of the Hague Conventions—but this success relates more to the number of ratifications than to the actual use. Similarly legal literature overestimates the problems as well as the frequency of taking evidence abroad, cf. Coester-Waltjen, "Internationales Beweisrecht".

## 6. Duration of Proceedings

The greater number of hearings indicates a longer duration of international proceedings. In order to test the duration, we excluded from the data temporary injunctions, attachments, documentary proceedings, and proceedings about recognition as well as enforcement of foreign money judgements, because these do not represent the ordinary lawsuit.

Table D–14: Duration of National and International Ordinary Lawsuits in the District Courts of Bremen and Hamburg (1988)

| Duration | National % | National (N) | International % | International (N) | Total % | Total (N) |
|---|---|---|---|---|---|---|
| Less than 3 months | 31 | ( 3126) | 26 | ( 61) | 31 | ( 3187) |
| 3 - less than 6 months | 29 | ( 2943) | 23 | ( 56) | 29 | ( 2999) |
| 6 - less than 9 months | 17 | ( 1734) | 16 | ( 39) | 17 | ( 1773) |
| 9 - less than 12months | 8 | ( 777) | 12 | ( 28) | 8 | ( 805) |
| 1 - less than 2 years | 12 | ( 1154) | 18 | ( 42) | 12 | ( 1196) |
| 2 - less than 3 years | 2 | ( 228) | 5 | ( 12) | 2 | ( 240) |
| More than 3 years | 1 | ( 55) | 0 | ( 1) | 1 | ( 56) |
| Total    % | 98 | | 2 | | 100 | |
|          (N) | | (10,017) | | (239) | | (10,256) |

Table D–14 shows the significantly longer duration of international ordinary proceedings. Seventy-eight per cent of the national cases, compared to only 65% of the international cases, are concluded within nine months; 14% of the national cases, but 23% of the international ones, take more than a year. The mean duration of a national proceeding amounts to 201 days, whereas the mean duration of international proceedings is 253 days. This difference is in part a consequence of those problems that cause more hearings, but it may also be influenced by problems in the service of process. These problems occur if the defendant resides in a foreign country and has to be served either through diplomatic channels or with the judicial assistance of central authorities. We have described above how long that may take. Table D–15 clearly demonstrates the slowing down of proceedings by the delays of service of process abroad.

Table D–15: Duration of International Proceedings
in Relation to Domestic or Foreign Service of Process
in the District Courts of Bremen and Hamburg (1988)

| Duration | Domestic service | | Foreign service | | Total | |
|---|---|---|---|---|---|---|
| | % | (N) | % | (N) | % | (N) |
| Less than 3 months | 43 | (104) | 20 | (16) | 38 | (120) |
| 3 - less than 6 months | 24 | ( 58) | 19 | (15) | 23 | ( 73) |
| 6 - less than 9 months | 13 | ( 32) | 10 | ( 8) | 13 | ( 40) |
| 9 - less than 12 months | 6 | ( 15) | 18 | (14) | 9 | ( 29) |
| More than 1 year | 13 | ( 32) | 33 | (26) | 18 | ( 58) |
| Total    % | 75 | | 25 | | 100 | |
|          (N) | | (241) | | (79) | | (320) |

Whereas 67% of international proceedings with domestic service
of process (the defendant is a resident of Germany or has nominated an authorized representative) take less than six months, such
is the case in only 39% of the proceedings with foreign service of
process. At the other end of the columns we find the reverse picture: the first group of cases takes longer than one year only in
13% of the proceedings, but the second group in 33%. The decisive problem that causes enormous delays is clearly the service of
process abroad.

## 7. Role of Foreign Law or Unified Law
## in International Proceedings

Whereas courts all over the world apply their own procedural law,
they may not apply their own substantive law in the same way.
This last point either is subject to autonomous rules of private
international law, which refer entire legal cases or parts thereof to
domestic law or to foreign law, or the question is decided by the
parties if a contract contains a choice of law clause. Recent international conventions[37] stipulate a clear preference for the designa-
tion of the applicable law by the parties in order to avoid problems arising out of divergences between the conflict of law rules of

37    E.g., the Hague Convention on the Law Applicable to Interna-
      tional Sale of Goods (1955) and the more recent Hague Conven-
      tion on the Law Applicable to Contracts for the International
      Sale of Goods (1985); similarly Art. 3 of the EC-Convention on
      the Law Applicable to Contractual Obligations (1980).

national legal systems and in order to free attorneys and judges from the burden of studying and understanding specialized literature in the highly sophisticated disciplines of private international law. Germany, having signed the EC-Convention, also gives preference to choice of law in contractual obligations (Art. 27 EGBGB).

Private international law is further replaced in certain legal areas by unified law, for example, by the UN Convention on the International Sale of Goods (1980), and by quite a number of conventions on the unification of transport law, patent and copyright law, maritime law, and family law. As regards the European Community there are additional efforts of legal unification by way of directives.

In order to collect data on the law applied in international cases, we distinguished first between pleadings and judgements, then looked within this material for the legal basis of argumentation (distinguishing between German law, foreign law, and unified law), and, finally, tried to find out whether this legal basis was called for by choice of law (in a contract) or by private international law rules.

Table D–16: Law Applied in International Cases in the District Courts of Bremen and Hamburg (1988)

| Type of Law | Pleadings | | Judgements | |
|---|---|---|---|---|
| | % | (N) | % | (N) |
| German law | 79 | (248) | 86 | ( 98) |
| Foreign law | 14 | ( 44) | 7 | ( 8) |
| Unified law | 7 | ( 21) | 7 | ( 8) |
| Total % | 100 | | 100 | |
| (N) | | (313) | | (114) |

Nearly 80% of the pleadings in international cases did not mention foreign or unified law and/or argued in favour of the application of German law. More interesting for our purposes were those 44 pleadings where the application of foreign law was requested. But even in these cases foreign law was in general mentioned vaguely without indications of statutes and/or case law— only four pleadings pointed to specific foreign rules and six pleadings to foreign judgements (two of them were decisions of the European Court of Justice).

Those pleadings that made the existence of a conflict of law explicit (86 files contained such an argument) were mostly based on a choice of law clause (70), whereas only sixteen deduced the application of (German or foreign) law from German private international law. In relative figures the application of law in our sample of 320 international cases was, according to the pleadings, based on a choice of law clause in 22% of the cases and solely on the statutory rules of private international law in 5%. The large majority of the pleadings either pointed to the application of unified law (7%) or simply did not mention a possible conflict of law (66%). In theory the court, in view of foreign elements in the pleadings, must *ex officio* raise the question that foreign law might govern the controversy, but in practice the judges stay silent in regard to this question as a tacit or conclusive choice of law and apply German law without further discussion. In some files this understanding was made explicit by a short statement in the summary of the oral hearing.

As regards judgements, German law played an even greater role because 86% of the decisions were based on it, whereas the remaining 14% were equally distributed among foreign law and unified law. Again we observed an amazing lack of specification: only two judgements mentioned the wording of foreign statutory rules and two other judgements referred to foreign case law (one case being decided by the European Court of Justice). There were no attempts to interpret or discuss these foreign rules or cases. Foreign legal literature does not seem to be read at all in German district courts.

Table D-17: Foreign Law Applied in International Cases in the District Courts of Bremen and Hamburg (1988)

| Pleadings | | Judgements | |
|---|---|---|---|
| Great Britain, Italy | 6 | Austria | 3 |
| Switzerland | 5 | Italy | 2 |
| The Netherlands | 4 | Spain, Singapore, South Africa | 1 |
| France, U.S., Cyprus | 3 | | |
| Sri Lanka, Austria, South Africa | 2 | | |
| Argentina, Denmark, Spain, Japan, Finland, Sweden, Singapore | 1 | | |

Table D-17 gives more details about foreign law in German proceedings. The first observation is that judges are much more cautious or hesitant in applying foreign law than attorneys are in their pleadings. A second remark is very speculative: it seems that judges educated in a civil-law tradition are more ready to apply codified law than common law with its much more difficult access to legal knowledge and different methods of reasoning. If this last observation holds true (our data basis is unfortunately very small) legal-cultural elements appear as decisive variables in the handling of international cases.

As regards unified law, the main source used in international cases is the Convention on the International Carriage of Goods by Road (CMR) followed by EC rules. At a time (1988) when the UNCITRAL Sales of Goods Convention was not yet in force in Germany, its predecessor, the Uniform Law on International Sales, played a modest role in pleadings but no role at all in the judgements of our sample.[38]

Similar to universal practice, a German court may reject the application of foreign law for reasons of public policy (*ordre public*). German legal literature recommends a restrictive practice in order to tolerate foreign legal cultures and foreign values as much as possible—the limits of acceptance being only the fundamental rights of the German constitution. Our cases show clearly this liberal attitude: the two pleadings requesting rejection of foreign law (of the Netherlands and of Sweden) remained unsuccessful in the final decisions.

### 8. Hamburg Special Court Section for International Cases

German experts in private international law and comparative law used to complain about the incompetence of judges in dealing with international cases.[39] One of the proposals for improving the situation was to create special court sections for the decision of international cases, defined as matters where the application of private international law, unified law or international procedural law have

---

38    Only a few countries had ratified this convention in 1988.

39    Karl Arndt et al.,"Memorandum on the improvement of the German civil practice in international matters", *RabelsZ* 35 (1971): 323–31; Murad Ferid, "Auslandsrechtsfälle in der deutschen Rechtspraxis", in *Festschrift für Oskar Möhring*, ed. Rolf Beisswingert, et al. (Munich: Artemis, 1973), 1–11; and in Tugrul Ansay and Volkmar Gessner (eds.), *Gastarbeiter in Gesellschaft und Recht* (Munich: Beck, 1974), 144–58.

to be considered.[40] Although there are no legal obstacles at least for large courts to organize their workload accordingly (through court regulations in which for every case the competent judge or chamber has to be fixed upon beforehand) there has been created in Germany (in 1971) only one special "international" section, namely the fifth chamber in the Hamburg district court (which has been extended to three chambers recently).[41] Our data may help to evaluate its actual practice.[42]

The Hamburg international chamber is competent for cases, first, where one party is not German or is a company not domiciled in Germany, and, second, where foreign or international unified law may apply. This second element leads to a broader definition of "international cases" than the one we used for our file analysis. Nevertheless we used our access to the data of the official statistics to run a few cross-tabs and means on all cases (538) that were initiated in 1988 in the fifth chamber of the Hamburg district court. The results can be summarized as follows: the amount of claims is higher in the international chamber than in all other chambers of the court (57,000 DM vs. 42,000 DM), whereas the number of judgements and settlements is lower (more interim injunctions, attachments, and so on). The assumption of the former presiding judge of the chamber that, in comparison to domestic

40   Deutscher Rat für Internationales Privatrecht, "Denkschrift zur Verbesserung der deutschen Zivilrechtssprechung in internationalen Sachen vom 27.4.1982", *RabelsZ* 46 (1982): 743–5.

41   So as not to neglect recent developments that might have occurred, we inquired in all Ministries of Justice in other German *Länder* about their dealing with international matters and their steps to concentrate international cases in special sections. All answers were negative: international matters are part of the normal tasks of judges in all branches of the administration of justice. As regards Hamburg the family courts have also assigned international matters to specific judges.

42   Evaluations have already been published by the (then) presiding judge of the international chamber: Gerhard Luther, "Kollisions- und Fremdrechtsanwendung in der Gerichtspraxis", *RabelsZ* 37 (1973): 660–81, and Kurt Siehr, "Special Courts for Conflicts Cases". Both reports are outdated due to the change of jurisdiction in 1977: divorce cases, which were then 90% of the caseload of the international chamber, now have to be brought to the family courts.

cases, international proceedings take three times more time and energy[43] is not confirmed: the mean duration of cases of this chamber is 221 days (in all other chambers it is 202 days), the mean number of hearings without taking of evidence is 1.4 (all other proceedings 1.3), the mean number of hearings with taking of evidence is 1.3 (all other proceedings 1.2). These mean values may of course seem unfair to judges who suffer from the burden of some very time- and energy-consuming cases where foreign law has to be studied and language problems with parties and witnesses have to be resolved. But across all cases the additional burden is only 10%.

The remaining tests are carried out with international cases according to our own definition. Our main interest lies in comparing the handling of international cases in the special chamber and in ordinary chambers in order to learn about the effectiveness of specialization in international judicial decision-making.

First we calculated the mean duration of an international case in the special chamber and in other (ordinary) chambers: the special chamber needs 220 days, the ordinary chambers need 208 days. This result runs against our expectations, because one might reasonably expect specialized judges to gather experience and routine and, therefore, handle international matters more quickly than ordinary judges. The only way of explanation seems to assume a more thorough proceeding by way of extensive legal research in foreign law, taking of evidence abroad, writing of judgements, or preparing settlements.

The data do not clearly support this assumption. The special chamber does not carry out more oral hearings (less, rather) and does not take more evidence, although both cases that took evidence abroad proceeded from the special chamber; the special chamber does not show significant differences in the frequency of judgements and settlements. But these may not be the best indicators for a thorough disposition of complicated international matters. More meaningful are data about the consideration, discussion, and eventually the application of foreign or unified law. We find, on the one hand, twice as many pleadings requesting the

43  Luther, "Kollisions- und Fremdrechtsanwendung in der Gerichtspraxis", 672. See also Siehr, "Special Courts for Conflicts Cases", 677: "Conflicts cases anyhow require more time and effort than normal domestic ones (1.5 times more in divorce suits and 3 times more in all other cases)".

application of foreign law: 18 out of 79 valid cases ( 23%) in the special chamber and 26 out of 213 cases (12%) in other chambers; on the other hand, we find the reverse picture in pleadings based on unified law: one out of 79 valid cases ( 1%) in the special chamber and 20 out of 213 cases (nearly 10%) in the other chambers. The logic behind the weaker role of unified law in the special chamber seems to be that there is much more unified law in commercial matters than in others, the most frequently mentioned unified law being the CMR. These commercial disputes go to the commercial chambers rather than to the special chamber for international matters.

Table D-18: Role of Foreign and Unified Law in Pleadings Before the Hamburg International Chamber and Before Ordinary Chambers in the District Courts of Bremen and Hamburg (1988)

| Pleadings based on | | Special chamber | | Ordinary chamber | |
|---|---|---|---|---|---|
| | | % | (N) | % | (N) |
| Foreign law | Yes | 23 | (18) | 12 | ( 26) |
| | No | 77 | (61) | 88 | (187) |
| Total | % | 100 | | 100 | |
| | (N) | | (79) | | (213) |
| Unified law | Yes | 1 | ( 1) | 9 | ( 20) |
| | No | 99 | (78) | 91 | (193) |
| Total | % | 100 | | 100 | |
| | (N) | | (79) | | (213) |

This hypothesis is—although on a very low quantitative level—clearly confirmed by an analysis of judgements: whereas five out of 31 judgements of the special chamber are based on foreign law (16%), this is only the case in four out of 70 judgements in ordinary chambers (6%). A similar tendency is found as regards unified law.

Table D-19: Role of Foreign Law and Unified Law in Judgements of the Hamburg International Chamber and of Ordinary Chambers of the District Courts of Bremen and Hamburg (1988)

| Judgements based on | | Special chamber | | Ordinary chamber | |
|---|---|---|---|---|---|
| | | % | (N) | % | (N) |
| Foreign law | Yes | 16 | ( 5) | 6 | ( 4) |
| | No | 84 | (26) | 94 | (66) |
| Total | % | 100 | | 100 | |
| | (N) | | (31) | | (70) |
| Unified law | Yes | 10 | ( 3) | 6 | ( 4) |
| | No | 90 | (28) | 94 | (66) |
| Total | % | 100 | | 100 | |
| | (N) | | (31) | | (70) |

This special data analysis on the role of the Hamburg international chamber thus leads us to the following conclusions. Nearly 80% of the time, international cases are handled as if they were domestic cases. The remaining 20% are dealt with more thoroughly than the ordinary chambers, taking foreign law more seriously, encouraging attorneys not to grasp the first opportunity of a choice of (German) law, and even—in very exceptional cases—taking evidence in a foreign country. Nonetheless the additional effort of judges is not too impressive: in international matters they only had to write eight judgements based on foreign or unified law in 1988.

## E. Outcome of Proceedings

Our data allow us to analyse the outcome of international proceedings according to the types of formal decision as well as by the characteristics of winners and losers. As regards the enforcement there are no peculiarities in comparison to domestic proceedings. Therefore we only deal in the last section of this chapter with enforcement of foreign decisions in Germany.

### 1. Types of Formal Decisions

The specific structures of international proceedings lead to final decisions that are different from domestic cases.

Table D–20: Types of Formal Decisions in International Compared to National Proceedings in the District Courts of Bremen and Hamburg (1988)

|  | National % | National (N) | International % | International (N) | Total % | Total (N) |
|---|---|---|---|---|---|---|
| Judgement | 26 | ( 3042) | 23 | ( 73) | 26 | ( 3115) |
| Settlement | 18 | ( 2060) | 13 | ( 43) | 18 | ( 2103) |
| Judgement in default | 20 | ( 2304) | 19 | ( 61) | 20 | ( 2365) |
| Injunction/ Attachment of assets | 5 | ( 528) | 8 | ( 26) | 5 | ( 554) |
| Withdrawal of claim | 13 | ( 1503) | 19 | ( 60) | 13 | ( 1563) |
| Other | 19 | ( 2272) | 18 | ( 57) | 19 | ( 2329) |
| Total       % | 97 |  | 3 |  | 100 |  |
|             (N) |  | (11,709) |  | (320) |  | (12,029) |

The main differences between national and international cases were found in the relative frequency of judgements, settlements, and injunctions. Due to complications that may arise in an international proceeding, it is no surprise that judgements are less frequent. But, unexpectedly, settlements are also quite visibly more rare. Perhaps all possible ways of conciliation between the parties have already been exhausted before an international lawsuit has been initiated. Instead of concluding an agreement one party seems to prefer withdrawing the claim: the high frequency of this occurring (nearly one-fifth of the claims) indicates misunderstandings, confusion, and certainly poor communication between parties—a sign of legal-cultural distance.

It is tempting to create hypotheses as to possible influences of the plaintiff (resident or nonresident) on these different outcomes of proceedings. In particular one expects more default judgements against foreign defendants and more withdrawals by foreign plaintiffs. Although Table D–21 shows significant differences between lawsuits initiated by foreign plaintiffs and suits initiated by German plaintiffs, these hypotheses are only partly confirmed.

Table D–21: Types of Formal Decisions in International Cases Initiated by Foreign and by German Plaintiffs in the District Courts of Bremen and Hamburg (1988)

| | | Plaintiff | | | | |
|---|---|---|---|---|---|---|
| | Foreign | | German | | Total | |
| | % | (N) | % | (N) | % | (N) |
| Judgement | 23 | ( 49) | 22 | ( 24) | 23 | ( 73) |
| Settlement | 14 | ( 29) | 13 | ( 14) | 13 | ( 43) |
| Default judgement | 20 | ( 42) | 17 | ( 19) | 19 | ( 61) |
| Injunction/ Attachment of assets | 4 | ( 8) | 16 | ( 18) | 8 | ( 26) |
| Withdrawal | 20 | ( 41) | 17 | ( 19) | 19 | ( 60) |
| Others | 19 | ( 40) | 15 | ( 17) | 18 | ( 57) |
| Total   % | 65 | | 35 | | 100 | |
| (N) | | (209) | | (111) | | (320) |

The most visible differences shown in Table D–21 are those between the low number of injunctions/attachments of foreign plaintiffs and the corresponding high number of German residents who get this court decision. This decision is relatively easy to obtain—even without safeguarding the defendant's right to be heard—and can be enforced immediately within the jurisdiction of the court. In cities with a seaport, such as Bremen and Hamburg, this procedure is used frequently against foreign shipowners. Consequently the predominance of German residents in this type of procedure is no surprise.[44] Unexpected and difficult to explain is that foreigners obtain more default judgements in their favour than German residents—the picture of the foreigner who for lack of time and money or, because of difficulties in finding a local attorney, does not appear in court is not confirmed by the data. More in conformity with our expectations is the result that foreign plaintiffs—probably due to insufficient knowledge of German law and legal procedure—withdraw their claims more often than German residents, the only surprise being that this does not occur more frequently.

### 2. Winners and Losers

Winners and losers of a German civil proceeding are defined clearly according to who has to bear the judicial and extrajudicial costs. Because official court statistics contain reliable data about the judicial cost decision concluding the proceeding it is unproblematic to attribute to each party his/her relative success.

The normal picture is that plaintiffs win their cases more often than defendants: they normally check their risks carefully before commencing a lawsuit. Because international lawsuits create additional problems and risks, it is to be expected that plaintiffs bring only promising claims to court. They should therefore win even more often than plaintiffs of domestic cases. This hypothesis is clearly confirmed in Table D–22.

### Table D–22: Cost Decisions in National and International Cases in the District Courts of Bremen and Hamburg (1988)

| Costs imposed on | National % | National (N) | International % | International (N) | Total % | Total (N) |
|---|---|---|---|---|---|---|
| Plaintiff totally | 22 | (1797) | 20 | ( 45) | 22 | (1842) |
| Plaintiff predominantly | 6 | ( 535) | 3 | ( 7) | 6 | (542) |
| Plaintiff/Defendant equally | 12 | ( 979) | 10 | ( 23) | 12 | (1002) |
| Defendant predominantly | 12 | ( 971) | 9 | ( 21) | 12 | (992) |
| Defendant totally | 48 | (4023) | 58 | (134) | 49 | (4157) |
| Total % | 97 | | 3 | | 100 | |
| (N) | | (8305) | | (230) | | (8535) |

44  At the time when the attachment petitions of our sample were pending (1988), German residents had a privilege in § 917 para.2 ZPO: the danger of unenforceability did not have to be proved if a judgement would have to be enforced in a foreign country. This privilege might explain in part the predominance of German residents in the attachment procedures. The European Court of Justice has recently declared this provision void (European Court of Justice 10 February 1994—Case C–398/92, *Mund v. Hatrex*, NJW 1994, 1271).

The message of Table D–22 is that plaintiffs of international cases win three times more often than defendants of international cases. In addition it would be interesting to know whether this success in international lawsuits must be attributed predominantly to German plaintiffs suing defendants residing in a foreign country, or rather to foreign plaintiffs suing German residents. The first alternative is supported by the fact that German residents have everything in their favour: acquaintance with the legal system, contacts with local attorneys, application of German procedural and (mostly) substantive law, and so on. The second alternative again relies on the filter effect of foreseeable difficulties: foreigners only bring claims to a German court if they are certain to have a sufficient legal basis and all necessary evidence. The data discussed in Table D–21 did not necessarily support this alternative because more foreigners than German residents had to withdraw their claims during the proceedings.

### Table D–23: Cost Decisions in Relation to the Place of Residence of the Plaintiff in all Cases in the District Courts of Bremen and Hamburg (1988)

| | Place of Residence of Plaintiff | | | | | |
| | Germany | | All other | | Total | |
| Costs imposed on | % | (N) | % | (N) | % | (N) |
|---|---|---|---|---|---|---|
| Plaintiff totally | 22 | (1813) | 19 | ( 29) | 22 | (1842) |
| Plaintiff predominantly | 6 | ( 537) | 3 | ( 5) | 6 | ( 542) |
| Plaintiff/Defendant equally | 12 | ( 989) | 8 | ( 13) | 12 | (1002) |
| Defendant predominantly | 12 | ( 979) | 8 | ( 13) | 12 | ( 992) |
| Defendant totally | 49 | (4063) | 61 | ( 94) | 49 | (4157) |
| Total          % | 98 | | 2 | | 100 | |
|                (N) | | (8381) | | (154) | | (8535) |

Table D–23 tells us that plaintiffs who are not resident in Germany are significantly more successful in German courts than German residents normally in international or domestic lawsuits. They win completely or at least predominantly in 70% of the cases! If the mentioned filter effect must be discarded as a possible interpretation, an explanation must be sought in the subject matters of the foreign actions. As we have mentioned already in another context—and as will be shortly treated in the next section with more details—there are eighteen requests for enforcement of foreign judgements among the suits initiated by foreigners. These requests are obviously atypical lawsuits that normally lead to a quick positive decision. In our sample all such requests were successful and hence led to the imposition of costs to the defendant (the German debtor). If we eliminate these requests for enforcement of foreign judgements from our sample the apparent advantage of foreign plaintiffs disappears. In a normal international lawsuit they have about the same chance of winning as German residents—but this is already more than one might reasonably have expected.

### 3. Enforcement of Foreign Judgements

Our sample of 320 international cases of the district courts of Bremen and Hamburg contains eighteen requests for enforcement of foreign judgements. They were mostly based on the Brussels Convention. In addition five requests were based on a bilateral agreement with Austria and one on a similar agreement with Norway.[45] Not a single request came from a non-European country, particularly none from the U.S. Twice as many requests for enforcement of foreign judgements are brought to the municipal courts (Amtsgerichte),[46] in particular judgements on support claims in favour of children born out of wedlock.

The low number of requests for enforcement of foreign judgements at the district courts[47] is certainly surprising because these courts, according to Art. 32 of the Brussels Convention, must be addressed in order to obtain the exequatur.[48] We take these data as another indicator for our assumption that German residents (without foreign subsidiaries) are rarely taken to court, not only in foreign countries in general but also in other countries of the European Union.

## III. International Family Cases

### A. Frequency of International Family Cases

Because we were only interested in international cases in the sense of cross-border cases, the number of German residents

45  As regards the legal situation, cf. Martiny, "Recognition and Enforcement of Foreign Money Judgements", 721–59.

46  Cf. Martiny, Handbuch des Internationalen Zivilverfahrensrechts, 36. The data given in this book only cover the period until 1981 because, unfortunately, official statistics later abandoned special references to this item.

47  Our data are confirmed by the numbers given by Martiny.

48  Formal recognition for foreign judgements.

with foreign nationality (6.9% in Germany in 1988 and 7.2% in Bremerhaven) would not be a good indicator for the number of international family cases. Naturally this part of the German population appears in German family courts with its divorce, child support, and custody problems—cases that normally are decided not on the basis of foreign law but on German family law. For well-known reasons, such as different family structures and access-to-law problems, its share in the caseload of family courts—and generally in the use of the legal system with exception of the labour courts—is generally expected to be smaller than its share in the population. Although we found numerous cases of this type in the Bremerhaven archive, we did not count them and did not develop any assumptions regarding their possible share in the Bremerhaven caseload.

The phenomena of massive labour migration, of asylum seekers, of tourism, and in general of mobility across borders may lead to an assumption that international family relations—in our understanding of cross-border relations—are indeed frequent[49] and that this is also mirrored in the caseload of family courts.

The file analysis of the Bremerhaven family court does not confirm such an assumption: yearly only around 30 international cases are brought to the family section of the *Amtsgericht* Bremerhaven. Taking 1988 and 1989 together there were 59 international cases in a total caseload of 2534 family cases (2.3%). If one takes further into account that at least 19 of these 59 international cases have to do with the presence of a U.S. Army base in Bremerhaven, one must conclude that the average share of international family cases in a German family court is considerably even lower (approximately 1.5%).

---

49   E.g., 18.6% of married migrant workers living in Germany have their spouses and eventually their children in their home countries. Cf. Peter König, Günther Schultze, and Rita Wessel, *Situation der ausländischen Arbeitnehmer und ihrer Familienangehörigen in der Bundesrepublik Deutschland—Repräsentativuntersuchung '85* (Bonn: Der Bundesminister für Arbeit und Sozialordnung, 1986), 227. This fact alone could lead to massive cross-border legal family disputes (e.g., divorce, child support, parental care).

Table D–24: Country of Residence of Plaintiffs and
Defendants in International Family Cases in the Family Court
of Bremerhaven (1988 and 1989)

| Country of Residence | | | |
|---|---|---|---|
| Plaintiffs | | Defendants | |
| Germany | 56 | U.S.A. | 30 |
| Austria, Poland, Thailand | 1 | Poland | 8 |
| | | Germany | 3 |
| | | Spain, France, Sweden, Turkey, | 2 |
| | | Canada, Switzerland, Algeria, Italy, | |
| | | Norway, the Netherlands, Portugal, | |
| | | Taiwan, Rumania, Austria | 1 |

Table D–24 shows where plaintiffs and defendants of international family cases come from. Quite opposite from the picture in
our civil cases sample, the plaintiffs are nearly all German residents. It is a principle of international civil procedure recognized
in most countries to privilege plaintiffs in family matters as regards jurisdiction of their respective home countries. German law
as well as the Brussels Convention (as regards matters of maintenance) follow this principle by freeing the plaintiffs of the burden
of suing abroad. Our data, with their extreme predominance of
German residents as plaintiffs, quite clearly reflect this legal situation.

But the data are surprising from another point of view. They
show that international mobility only in part affects the caseloads
of family courts. The presence of U.S. soldiers, for example, is
much more visible than the quantitatively more important presence of migrant workers who either seem to prefer to sue in their
home countries or to abstain from legal steps in their family relations. The very important Turkish population in Bremerhaven took
only two cross-border lawsuits to the Bremerhaven family court—
in spite of the fact that nearly one out of five male married Turkish
workers left his wife and children in Turkey.[50] Mainly for cultural
reasons neither the wife nor children who live in Turkey pursue
their eventual money claims (maintenance and child support)
against the father who works in Germany. In the opposite case

50    Ursula Pasero, *Familienkonflikte in der Migration* (Wiesbaden:
      Deutscher Universitätsverlag, 1990), 40, 43.

where the mother (with children) lives in Germany[51] there is a structural explanation: they receive social security benefits without being obliged to sue the husband and father in court. Most divorces are taken to Turkish courts, which was a necessary choice of forum until 1982 when the exclusive Turkish jurisdiction in divorce matters of Turkish citizens was abandoned.[52] Since then, due to legal-aid schemes in Germany, it is rather preferable to take divorce cases to a German family court—but this is rarely done.

The intervening variable explaining legal behaviour is probably the plaintiff's German or foreign origin: most U.S. soldiers in the sample were married to German women, whereas migrant workers typically live with spouses from their home countries.[53] The social (and legal) situation if one of the spouses leaves Germany is different in both cases: if the U.S. soldier leaves Germany, his German wife eventually takes legal action in Germany, but if the migrant worker or his wife returns home and one of them takes legal action, he/she does it there in his/her own legal culture (if they do take legal action at all). The low visibility of asylum seekers from developing countries in the family court files is explained by their living conditions in Germany, which make the initiation of family relationships very difficult. If their potential family problems in their home countries are imported to Germany this becomes a problem for the social services, not for the family court.

In attempting to classify the cases into groups of countries, we found that 51 cases (86%) deal with non-EC, developed countries, four cases (7%) with developing countries, and only in another four cases (7%) did one of the parties reside in a member-state of the European Community.

51    According to the same source 6.3% of Turkish women living in Germany have their husband in Turkey (in 1985).

52    Tugrul Ansay, "Zur Scheidung von Türken in der Bundesrepublik Deutschland nach Inkrafttreten des neuen IPR-Gesetzes", *Das Standesamt* (1983): 29.

53    7% of married migrant workers from Greece, Italy, and Turkey have a German spouse. Cf. Claudia Koch-Arzberger, *Die schwierige Integration* (Opladen: Westdeutscher Verlag, 1985), 177. According to König, Schultze, and Wessel ("Situation der ausländischen Arbeitnehmer", 239), who studied a sample of migrant workers from Turkey, Yugoslavia, Italy, Greece, Spain, and Portugal, the share of foreign/German couples is only 4.8%.

## B. Characteristics of Parties

In addition to the social definitions of parties in view of their belonging to a certain group of migrants (which we deduced from their respective home countries), we learned from some scarce information in the Bremerhaven files that 64% of the (adult) parties had to be classified in lower occupational groups and 8% in occupational groups of the lower middle classes, 25% were (active or retired) soldiers and 5% were unemployed. Because many family problems are caused by economic difficulties, the predominance of lower strata seems to be typical for the family courts in general and not related to the international character of our cases. International lawsuits in family matters are in no way a privilege of the upper strata—rather the reverse.

**Table D–25: Family Status of Parties in International Cases of the Family Court in Bremerhaven (1988 and 1989)**

|  | Procedural Role | | | |
|  | Plaintiff | | Defendant | |
|  | % | (N) | % | (N) |
|---|---|---|---|---|
| Male | 17 | (10) | 83 | (49) |
| Female | 75 | (44) | 17 | (10) |
| Minor | 9 | ( 5) | | |
| Total | 100 | (59) | 100 | (59) |

The data shown in Table D–25 also give a picture typical of family lawsuits in general: women or minors sue the husband or father. The male party appeared in 83% of our international cases as the defendant and only in 17% as the plaintiff. The most frequent international case in a family court can therefore be described on the side of the plaintiff as female or minor and Germany-resident and on the side of the defendant as male with residence in a foreign, industrialized country.

## C. Characteristics of Family Cases

### 1. Subject Matters

The German family court, according to § 23 b *Gerichtsverfassungsgesetz,* has jurisdiction over proceedings for divorce and other matters of marriage; over matters of parental care, visitation rights, and support for legitimate children; maintenance for the spouse; compensation of pension rights; and the distribution of the household after the spouses separate. The family court is not competent for all claims raised by illegitimate children (filiation, support, and so on) and for claims between unmarried couples. These suits have to be taken to the civil section of the same municipal court, the *Amtsgericht*.

This limited jurisdiction has to be kept in mind in reading the following data. In particular one may miss cross-border claims of support for children born out of wedlock. They are to be found in the archives of general jurisdiction of the municipal court, which were not analysed for our purposes.

Table D–26: Subject Matters of International and National Family Cases in the Family Court of Bremerhaven (1988 and 1989)

|  | International cases | | National cases | |
| --- | --- | --- | --- | --- |
|  | % | (N) | % | (N) |
| Divorce | 40 | (32) | 30 | ( 868) |
| Parental care | 42 | (34) | 25 | ( 765) |
| Visitation rights | 1 | ( 1) | 5 | ( 169) |
| Child support | 3 | ( 6) | 12 | ( 373) |
| Support for spouse | 6 | ( 5) | 23 | ( 715) |
| Compensation of pension rights | 2 | ( 2) | 2 | ( 64) |
| Marital home and furniture | 1 | ( 1) | 5 | ( 154) |
| Total | 100 | (81) | 100 | (3108) |

The subject matters enumerated in Table D–26 exceed the number of cases because some cases had more than one subject matter (but in a divorce proceeding most other matters are jointly decided *ex officio*: according to § 623 ZPO, no petition is required for the determination of the parental care and the compensation of pension rights. An arrangement for personal contact with the child shall only be ordered if proposed by one of the spouses).

In comparing international cases with national cases, we mainly observe striking differences in the frequencies of cases concerning parental care and child support. The numbers of cases where support is claimed for a spouse are also far below the domestic level.

Petitions concerning parental care had a very simple bureaucratic background: in nearly all cases a wife living separated from her (foreign) husband claimed parental care for a common child in order to obtain an identity card or a passport for the child. The requirement of the father's signature may not cause major problems in a domestic case but raises enormous problems if the father lives abroad (mostly with unknown domicile). These petitions were particularly frequent if U.S. soldiers were involved.

By contrast international suits concerning child support were infrequent in comparison to the national sample. It is very improbable that the (male) debtors living in a foreign country comply more thoroughly with their support obligations than domestic debtors. Therefore the only explanation we can offer is that in spite of existing international conventions[54] and national legislation[55] in favour of support creditors, it is still very difficult to make use of the judicial system in order to get child support in a foreign country. Nonjudicial institutions seem to have completely replaced courts in the recovery of money claims in family matters: on the international level there is the International Social Service (Geneva), which helps to locate the debtor and attempts to reach an amicable settlement. On the national level the dominant institution is the *Deutsches Institut für Vormundschaftswesen* (Heidelberg), a private association that does not only confine itself to giving advice but even litigates in the debtor's home jurisdiction.[56]

Similar difficulties are to be made responsible for the low number of cases concerning support for a spouse. Here the risk of a lawsuit not being enforceable in a foreign country is even greater than in the case of child support, because legal cultures differ considerably as regards the obligation to pay support for separated or divorced spouses. One may recall that many cultures expect the abandoned wife to return to the family that has brought her up, while instead of paying a monthly support, the husband has a legal obligation to return the dowry. This kind of claim could potentially be brought to a German family court—but unfortunately this was not the case in 1988-89 in Bremerhaven.

## 2. Controversial Nature of the Cases
Before entering into procedural details one particular aspect of international family cases must be emphasized that seems to ex-

---

54    New York Convention on the recovery abroad of maintenance (20.6.1956); the Hague Convention concerning the recognition and enforcement of decisions concerning maintenance obligations (2.10.1973); Brussels Convention on Jurisdiction and the Enforcement of Judgements in Civil and Commercial Matters (27.9.1968).

55    Gesetz zur Geltendmachung von Unterhaltsansprüchen im Verkehr mit ausländischen Staaten (AUG)(19.12.1986).

56    Aungar Marx, "Wege zur Realisierung von Kindesunterhalt in Europa", *Nachrichten des Deutschen Vereins für Vormundschaftswesen* (1993): 374.

plain more than many other items: the extremely low degree of controversy. One aspect is the response rate on the side of the defendant. Table D–27 gives an impressive picture of the situation.

**Table D–27: Response of Defendants in International Family Cases in the Family Court of Bremerhaven (1988 and 1989)**

| The defendant was | % | (N) |
|---|---|---|
| Not found | 28 | (15) |
| Found but inactive | 40 | (21) |
| Active | 30 | (16) |
| Dead | 2 | ( 1) |
| Total* | 100 | (53) |

\* 6 cases not applicable or missing information.

In no less than 68% of our international cases did the defendant not react to the claims made through the lawsuit—either because the service of process remained unsuccessful, because the foreign defendant did not care about the German court procedure, or because the court decided without the defendant being heard (in the cases of parental care in particular[57]).

The picture of the international family case as an uncontroversial affair is confirmed by the fact that only in every fifth case were both parties represented by lawyers. In four out of five cases the defendant (who is generally, as we have seen, the foreign party) remained without legal counsel. Even the plaintiff was represented by a lawyer in only 60% of the matters.[58] As a consequence legal issues were raised in only three files (5%).

But even factual issues rarely became a problem (13% of our cases). This uncontroversial nature meant that most files were short

57    What should be the absolute exception (cf. Thomas Kersten, *Praxis der Familiengerichtsbarkeit* (Cologne: Carl Heymanns, 1986), 99) seems to be the rule in international cases: due to the expected long delays the foreign party is not heard from before decisions on parental care.

58    In divorce proceedings both parties must be represented by a lawyer (§ 78 ZPO), but if the defendant does not object to the divorce petition he is exempt from this obligation. All other matters within the jurisdiction of the family court do not require using a lawyer.

and without legal or social substance. Fifty out of 59 international family cases seemed to be more a matter of bureaucratic routine than a legal dispute.

## D. Procedural Aspects of International Family Cases

### 1. *International Jurisdiction*

In only one of our 59 international cases did the international jurisdiction of the Bremerhaven family court become an issue. A Canadian defendant questioned jurisdiction in a case about maintenance for his wife, but his arguments were dismissed and the defendant finally lost the case.

The singularity of this jurisdictional issue in the sample is first of all explained by the already described inactivity of the defendant party. In addition one should point to the generosity of German law in granting jurisdiction and to a clear and unambiguous legal regulation in the code of civil procedure (ZPO), the Hague Convention of 5 October, 1961, Concerning the Powers of Authorities and the Law Applicable in Respect of the Protection of Minors, and the Brussels Convention on Jurisdiction and the Enforcement of Judgements in Civil and Commercial Matters. Plaintiffs of family disputes may always bring their cases to domestic courts. Hence there are few situations inviting enough for a legal dispute on the choice of the forum if the case is already pending in the family court.

Foreign parties who try to avoid a German decision initiate court proceedings in a foreign jurisdiction before the case is made pending in Germany—a strategy chosen if possible by husbands in divorce cases in order to avoid the compensation of pension rights obligatory in a German divorce procedure. In two divorce cases of the sample a previous divorce procedure in a foreign jurisdiction was mentioned. One divorce was carried out in Mexico but the plaintiff's attorney did not expect it to be recognized in Germany (the judge recommended at least attempting recognition by the competent Ministry of Justice in Bremen[59]). The second, a U.S. divorce, was recognized in the Bremerhaven procedure. In a third case a previous foreign (Polish) judgement concerned support for

---

59    The attorney was obviously not familiar with the legal situation in the case of recognition of foreign divorces—just one of many examples of incompetence in international matters that we came across during our file analyses.

a child. Because the father had meanwhile moved to Germany, another forum (with higher monthly duties as regards child support) was created. Following a supreme court decision[60] the question of *res judicata*[61] raised by the defendant was decided in favour of the plaintiff.

## 2. Service of Process

The legal and factual situation of service of process abroad described for civil cases applies also to family cases. In view of these enormous difficulties, the family judges seem to avoid costs and delays for the plaintiff in matters of minor importance, particularly in cases of parental care where the foreign father does not bother about his child anyway and presumably will not object to a decision in favour of the mother. These cases are frequently very urgent because the mother realizes a few weeks or days before her vacation that the child needs an identity card or a passport to leave the country. The foreign defendant is—*contra legem*[62] but for very practical reasons—in those cases not served at all.

As regards the service of process, our cases can be arranged in the following order. In those 35 cases where a service of process abroad has been attempted, the Bremerhaven family court usually (68%) used diplomatic channels, and in only 12% did it use the facilities (via central authorities) of the Hague Service Convention. In the other 20% the foreign defendant was served by other channels. In comparison to our civil cases sample in Bremen and Hamburg where the average delay amounted to three months, the delays caused by the service procedures in family cases are slightly more dramatic: notwithstanding that in 43% of the cases it took only a month to serve the defendant, in the majority of the cases it took three or more months (with one extreme example of 24 months). The mean delay amounts to 3.5 months. The delays seem to be independent of the service of process mechanisms chosen.

60    Cf. Oberlandesgericht Düsseldorf, *Familienrechtszeitung* (1989): 97.
61    *Res judicata* being the legal concept that a judgement by one court serves as a bar against the same matter being brought again before the same court or another. The extent to which this bar goes as to the matter and parties involved differs between different states' laws.
62    Contrary to the law.

Both consulates and central authorities show extreme variance as to their efficiency in serving court documents.

## 3. Hearings

As in the civil cases sample, we compare national and international cases in view of the numbers of hearings because they indicate the legal and factual difficulties that occur during the proceedings.

Table D–28: Hearings in National and International Family Cases in the Family Court of Bremerhaven (1988 and 1989)

| Hearings | National % | National (N) | International % | International (N) |
|---|---|---|---|---|
| None | 31 | ( 771) | 34 | (20) |
| One | 38 | ( 942) | 29 | (17) |
| Two | 18 | ( 447) | 27 | (16) |
| Three or more | 13 | ( 315) | 10 | ( 6) |
| Total | 100 | (2475) | 100 | (59) |

Table D–28 does show a difference between the numbers of hearings in national and international cases. More international than national family cases need more than one hearing. But this tendency is not very accentuated and therefore no significant indicator for a more complex procedure in cross-border cases. A potential cause for more than one hearing and hence a source of complexity is certainly the taking of evidence abroad. But this cause must totally be excluded since in none of the 59 international cases was evidence taken abroad. Neither did we observe any other complications linked to the international character of the lawsuit such as, for example, inquiries about foreign law or correspondence with foreign authorities.

A picture similar to the number of hearings is offered if one measures the duration of national and international proceedings. The latter take longer but not more than can be explained by the time needed for the service of process abroad and the translations of various documents, which were required in 43 of our 59 international cases.

## 4. Role of Foreign Law or Unified Law

Because parties to family conflicts may not choose the applicable law, the role of private international law in resolving conflict of law situations is supposed to be greater than in other civil law areas. If one also takes into account that, in spite of a strong preference for the domicile or habitual residence principles, German as well as most other private international law systems frequently refer the resolution of international cases to the family law of the foreign party, one would expect foreign family law to be an important base for pleadings and decisions in those cases.

Table D–29: Law Applied in International Family Cases in the Family Court of Bremerhaven (1988 and 1989)

|             | Pleadings | | Decisions | |
|-------------|------|-------|------|-------|
|             | %    | (N)   | %    | (N)   |
| German law  | 80   | (40)  | 84   | (42)  |
| Foreign law | 20   | (10)  | 16   | ( 8)  |
| Total       | 100  | (50)  | 100  | (50)  |

The data shown in Table D–29 do not confirm the assumption of foreign family law being frequently applied in German family courts. In only 20% of the pleadings was foreign law mentioned, and even fewer court decisions were based on foreign law. Surprisingly the situation is quite similar to the one shown in Table D–16, referring to civil cases in general. Even in family cases judges and lawyers manage to avoid to a considerable degree the burden of studying a given situation under a foreign legal point of view.[63]

63    This statement is based only on a sample of "international" family cases in the sense that one of the parties must have his/her residence outside Germany. Whether foreign law is more "professionally" applied in cases (mostly divorce matters) *between two foreigners residing in Germany* is unknown to us. Family judges may have sufficient legal information and experience as regards certain legal orders where important groups of immigrants have lived before, but these cases were not included in our sample.

Not a single case was found where an argument was based on foreign legal texts (a statute, a supreme court decision, a law book). The only sources used were collections of foreign legal materials written in German, mostly divorce law materials, which gave only basic and not updated information.

**Table D–30: Foreign Family Law Applied in International Family Cases in the Family Court of Bremerhaven (1988 and 1989)**

|          | Pleadings | Decisions |
|----------|-----------|-----------|
| Poland   | 5         | 6         |
| Italy    | 1         | 1         |
| U.S.A.   | 1         | 1         |
| Portugal | 1         |           |
| Rumania  | 1         |           |
| Sweden   | 1         |           |

If one remembers that among our 59 international cases 30 were related to parties residing in the U.S., it is at first sight striking that U.S. law plays such a marginal role in Table D–30. But these cases mostly represent marriages of soldiers of the U.S. Army base in Bremerhaven. Divorce and parental care for the children residing in Germany are in these cases governed by German law.

There was no case where a problem of *ordre public* led to the nonapplication of foreign law. This issue, dealt with extensively in legal literature, was mentioned neither in the reasons for court decisions nor in the pleadings.

### E. Outcome of Family proceedings

As in our analysis of civil cases, we were able to compare the outcome of family proceedings according to the types of formal decisions.

Table D–31: Types of Formal Decisions in International Family
Cases Compared to National Proceedings in the Family Court
of Bremerhaven (1988 and 1989)

| | National | | International | | Total | |
|---|---|---|---|---|---|---|
| | % | (N) | % | (N) | % | (N) |
| No information | 2 | ( 39) | | | 2 | ( 39) |
| Judgement | 36 | ( 886) | 53 | (31) | 36 | ( 917) |
| Settlement | 13 | ( 311) | 3 | ( 2) | 12 | ( 313) |
| Judgement in default | 6 | ( 141) | 2 | ( 1) | 6 | ( 142) |
| Order | 15 | ( 375) | 19 | (11) | 15 | ( 386) |
| Order on costs | 1 | ( 12) | | | 1 | ( 12) |
| Withdrawal of claim | 12 | ( 300) | 10 | ( 6) | 12 | ( 306) |
| Suspension claim not renewed | 0 | ( 2) | | | 0 | ( 2) |
| Other suspension | 0 | ( 9) | | | 0 | ( 9) |
| Plaintiff inactive | 8 | ( 209) | 14 | ( 8) | 9 | ( 217) |
| No advance payment of costs | 0 | ( 4) | | | 0 | ( 4) |
| Referral to other family court | 1 | ( 21) | | | 1 | ( 21) |
| Referral to other court | 3 | ( 80) | | | 3 | ( 80) |
| Coupling with other case | 2 | ( 55) | | | 2 | ( 55) |
| Other type of disposition | 1 | ( 31) | | | 1 | ( 31) |
| Total     % | 98 | | 2 | | 100 | |
|            (N) | | (2475) | | (59) | | (2534) |

Table D–31 must be interpreted with caution because the
samples of national and international cases are quantitatively
so different. A test of significance was therefore not possible.
In spite of these caveats one message from the data seems to be
very clear: national and international family procedures are
not disposed of in the same way or even in a similar way. There
are in particular far more judgements and far less settlements
in international cases, which is not a sign of the controversial
nature of the family relationships in question but—as we have
already seen—the logical consequence of the defendants' inactivity. If in parental care questions the foreign father is often
not heard there is no opportunity for a peaceful settlement.
The frequent inactivity of the plaintiff may be caused by specific problems of cross–border family relations, for example,
the loose or lost contact between the spouses. These eight cases
should rather be understood as withdrawals of the claim—a
sign of intercultural conflicts.

Twenty-eight out of 31 judgements of the international sample
were divorces, seventeen of which were based on mutual agreement, five on breakdown of the relationship, and six on separa-

tion for a period longer than three years. Most of these divorces concerned soldiers from the U.S. Army base who, after returning to the U.S., lost contact with their German wives. Eighteen divorce judgements also decided upon parental care, one upon child support, and 22 upon compensation of pension rights.

As regards the success rates of the parties, the judicial cost decision is less significant than in the civil procedure because in family matters, as a principle, the costs are equally distributed between the spouses (§ 93a ZPO). Those few cost decisions that imposed the costs on one of the parties, imposed them in six cases completely or predominantly on the plaintiff and in four cases on the defendant. But not a single divorce petition was dismissed.

## IV. Conclusion: German Courts as a Bridge Between Legal Cultures?

Our final remarks will not go back to the detailed description of German international procedure where we have attempted to give a realistic picture of the handling of international cases in German courts and to test some of the assumptions found in legal literature. This attempt may have a value of its own.

The point we would like to raise concerns the issue of whether German law—understood as positive law and legal doctrine—and legal institutions keep pace with globalization processes. As regards law Germany is certainly globally oriented, taking part and sometimes taking the lead in legal harmonization and unification, in comparing and often integrating foreign legal approaches, and in abolishing the remaining barriers to legal interaction across borders. But law—particularly in the fields of private international law and international civil procedure—is nothing but a discourse among a very restricted number of people. Reading these discourses is mostly an intellectual pleasure, but one would err in attributing to it some kind of sociological reality. A "spill-over" to the real world always requires additional circumstances, which are mostly (but not necessarily) embedded in some kind of institution. Institutions may be guided to a certain degree by law but they mainly develop their own rules and routines. The behaviour of legal institutions, then, is a valuable source of information about the order of a particular segment of the social world. Other sources are noninstitutional actors like enterprises, associations, pressure groups, networks (criminal or not), and private individuals.

Courts were the object of our study, as one example of legal institutions that potentially play a role in cross-border legal interaction. We chose three out of approximately 650 first instance courts of Western Germany in 1988. Around 12,000 judges may be confronted yearly with one or several international cases in civil matters—only a few dozen judges handle such cases more often due to specialization. The legal education of German judges is confined to German law codes, German legal doctrine, and German case law. Private international law, international law, comparative law, and laws of the European Union play a marginal role and are unpopular among students (because these subjects are not part of their examinations). Very few law students are fluent enough in English to read English legal literature, not to mention other languages. German judges therefore have had at most a superficial education in foreign law and no information at all of foreign legal cultures. If they need such knowledge in a particular case, their court libraries are of little help. In view of this it would be somewhat utopian to expect courts to deal with international cases as legal doctrine wants them to behave, namely "to feel into the way of thinking of a foreign jurist".[64] German judges lack knowledge and experience for this kind of global empathy in international matters.

This critique has often been articulated.[65] In addition our data show that:

• foreign elements of the cases have virtually no chance of influencing the proceedings or the decisions. Foreign counsels appear neither in the files (pleadings) nor in the hearings—to say nothing of the foreign parties themselves. The taking of evidence in foreign countries is extremely rare (two cases in our sample). The German counsel is not familiar with the legal or legal-cultural situation of his/her foreign client and is therefore unable to explain this situation to the judges. In none of the international cases in Bremen, Hamburg, or Bremerhaven was there the slightest attempt of doing research in this direction—neither by the lawyers nor by the judges.

64    Ferid, "Internationales Privatrecht", 161.
65    Murad Ferid, "Überlegungen, wie der Misere bei der Behandlung von Auslandsrechtsfällen in der deutschen Rechtspraxis abgeholfen werden kann", *Festschrift für Möhring*, ed. Rolf Beisswingert (Munich: Artemis, 1973), 1–25; Deutscher Rat für Internationales Privatrecht, "Denkschrift zur Verbesserung der deutschen Zivilrechtssprechung in internationalen Sachen", 743–5.

• if foreign law was mentioned in the pleadings, it was never done in a way to fulfil the requirements of §293 ZPO, in other words, to assist the judge in his task of finding the foreign law applicable in the particular case.[66] No wonder then that application of foreign law in court decisions was extremely rare and that if foreign law was considered this was done without the use of literature, commentaries, or precedents,[67] in short, in a way one can only call unprofessional. None of the judges made use of the European Convention on Information on Foreign Law (1968) in order to get the necessary legal information from foreign ministries of justice,[68] nor were expert opinions requested from one of the university departments for comparative law or the *Max-Planck-Institut für ausländisches und internationales Privatrecht* in Hamburg.[69]

66    Kegel, "Internationales Privatrecht", 316; Siehr, "Special Courts for Conflicts Cases", 663, 667.

67    The German Supreme Court clearly states this requirement, cf. BGH FamRZ 82, 265.

68    Our sample correctly mirrors the actual situation: cf. Günter Ott, "Die gerichtliche Praxis und ihre Erfahrungen mit dem Europäischen Übereinkommen vom 7.6.1968 betr. Auskünfte über ausländisches Recht", *Firsching-Festschrift* (Munich: Beck, 1985): 209–32.

69    The leading commentary considers these expert opinions of university institutes as too time-consuming and recommends other experts: cf. Adolf Baumbach, Wolfgang Lauterbach, and Peter Hartmann, *ZPO-Commentary*, 51st ed. (Munich: C.H. Beck, 1993), § 293, 2. On the other hand these institutes complain about being used as expert witnesses too frequently: cf. Ferid, "Überlegungen", 4, who mainly refers to cases of families of migrant workers resident in Germany and not to international cases in our definition. As regards the legal and legal-cultural quality of these expert opinions, it is rather doubtful whether they are able to reproduce the way of thinking and arguing of the respective foreign system. The (German) jurists in charge of this unloved task generally have at most some limited foreign legal education and only scarce and outdated legal material at their disposal. As a consequence even cases where experts on foreign law are heard do not seem to fulfil doctrinal expectations of private international justice.

• the most frequent methods for the "nationalization" of international cases were either a proposal from the bench to agree that German law should apply (which is very much in the interest of the German lawyers representing the parties and was therefore always accepted) or a proposal for an amicable settlement, supported by the friendly advice that research in foreign law would be time-consuming and the hearing of experts in foreign law expensive.

It must therefore be stated that, in terms of internationalization of legal thinking, globalization simply has not reached German civil procedure. But international cases **are** taken to German courts and these courts **are** managing them quite effectively in terms of time and in terms of outcome. German courts therefore play a role in global legal interaction, handling and deciding cases according to German rules and routines. If we take the astonishing number of foreign plaintiffs into account who voluntarily use the German jurisdiction, this may be exactly what **both** parties in conflict want. Assuming the rationality of the parties and their legal counsels in choosing their forum, one must conclude that the German forum is considered adequate for certain kinds of cases, namely those of low economic and legal complexity and for cases where cultural and legal-cultural differences between parties are considered unimportant. All other cases—and this may be the great majority—are resolved otherwise, either in a foreign forum where a more adequate law than the German one is applied, in a forum with a more global reputation, or by arbitration and nonjudicial procedures developed for specific branches, conflict areas, and groups of persons.

## Abstract

This file analysis of international cases in civil matters in the district courts of Bremen and Hamburg and in family matters at the municipal court of Bremerhaven was only possible after searching some 15,000 files in the respective court archives. The information from the international files (320 in Bremen and Hamburg, 59 in Bremerhaven) was coupled with statistical data the German Statistical Office collects as a matter of routine from every single court case. The two data sets—international cases and national cases—were compared throughout the evaluation and interpretation. The comparison showed in civil matters the relative frequency of international cases (2.6%), the different composition of parties (considerably more firms as litigants), the distribution of subject matters (quite similar to domestic cases), and aspects of the procedure such as duration (which is longer in international cases mostly due to the time-consuming service of process abroad) and outcome (less judgements and more withdrawals). It was surprising to find more foreign than domestic plaintiffs in civil matters. Also surprising was the result of an equal distribution of winners and losers between domestic and foreign parties, which was interpreted as an indicator that foreign parties only bring promising cases to court. The hypothesis of a "homeward trend" of private international law literature was clearly supported: German judges rarely apply foreign law. In German courts international cases are disposed of relatively efficiently but only by sacrificing all foreign elements of the cases. This is true for civil as well as for family matters, which nevertheless show some peculiarities as to relative share of international matters (1.5%), plaintiffs (very few foreign residents), subject matters, and outcome.

## The Author

Volkmar Gessner. Degrees in Law and Sociology. Prior practice as lawyer and as judge. Currently Professor of Comparative Law and Sociology of Law at the University of Bremen, Germany. Research areas (mainly empirical) lie in the fields of litigation in national and international contexts, alternating forms of dispute resolution, legal culture and globalization of law. Heavy involvement also in policy research for the German government and the European Commission.
*Address*: ZERP, Universitätsallee GW 1, 28359 Bremen, Germany.
*e-mail*: VGESSNER@ZERP.uni-bremen.de

# 4  Cross-Border Litigotiation in Italy

VITTORIO OLGIATI

## I. Foreword

The study is based on the results of the first empirical survey carried out on cross-border litigotiation in Italy. It deals with a court file's analysis of the "universe" of cross-border disputes—each case involving at least a foreign (non-Italian) party—registered throughout 1988 and archived by May/June 1993 at the Central Chancellery of the Civil Court of Milano.

The main report is divided in two parts. The first part enlightens the theoretical and methodological framework of the research project. The second part analyses the data and discusses the results of the survey as a whole. Needless to say historically determined space-time features of the context under examination are at the core of the study.

## II. Theoretical and Methodological Framework

### A. The Research Design

As has been illustrated in the introductory chapter to this volume, the general design of the cross-border international research project that frames this study is based on a multilayered but selective theoretical approach. The notions of legal culture and conflict of cultures have been assumed as basic explanatory tools. In turn these notions sustain a cluster of other concepts that seem to offer a refined entry point to the topic: in particular, the concept of *anomie*, implying a situation of low-norm orientation, contradictory normative expectations, and operational helplessness vis-à-vis legal complexity, and so on; the concept of a third culture, to be referred to as a set of values, behaviours, and attitudes developing between different levels or types of legal culture; and the concept of cognition, inherent to those learning processes that are required to deal with an unstable, unpredictable, and largely unknown situation. What happens when social actors from different cultures—and with conflicting interests and values—meet within a given context such as a state court?

Taking the above question seriously, at least three basic theoretical assumptions provide this study with its particular heuristic rationale.

The first theoretical assumption is based on the perception of the importance of state courts for a comparative understanding of cross-borders sociolegal relations in contemporary Western society.

As is well known the evasion of state court conflict settlements involving transnational issues has been an ongoing theme of discussion in the last decades. According to a number of analysts, national states, especially in Europe, have somehow directly and indirectly favoured such a phenomenon, by means of legislative and/or administrative inertia. In turn powerful semiautonomous sociolegal orders have also extended their branches in the field of law, creating not only special legal systems, but also in-house legal expertise and exclusive dispute treatment devices. According to these discussions conflicts at the transnational level seem to be increasingly channelled towards and/or performed within such new legal realms. Thus it also seems that the state legal system is no longer a primary structure for handling these litigation matters.

On the other hand, nation-states have also enacted a number of international agreements, among which the Brussels, Lugano, and the Hague Conventions on international jurisdictional matters and the Vienna and Rome Conventions on international goods' trade and international contractual law, respectively, are probably the best known. These agreements and conventions have been explicitly depicted as ways of resolving the problems of justiciability precisely at cross-borders level, which leads one to assume that there are in fact (1) issues that could be treated by state court litigation, and (2) a governmental interest in fostering or at least reassessing cross-border state court litigation.

So far the intertwining of these opposing trends has not been put to the fore as a topical object of an empirical enquiry, nor has it been seriously considered as a source for interpretive and empirical research projects. To venture into this unexplored fieldwork from the point of view of social actors leads one to hypothesize that a plausible and socially adequate study of cross-border court disputes in contemporary Western society requires a broader analytical framework and an up-to-date interdisciplinary approach.

This hypothesis joins, in turn, with a second theoretical assumption: the necessity to revise the traditional idea of state court jurisdiction as a single-loop system.

Although the amount of law and social change literature now at one's disposal gives full evidence of a growing space-time contingency in the overall province of law and a diffuse ambiguity in sociolegal interactions, it is really surprising to note that, all the above notwithstanding, the analysis about (Western) state law in general, and state court disputes in particular, are still based on, or recall to a large extent, traditional (formal) modelling of rational goal-oriented procedures, actions, and decisions. A rational actor in a state court aims at a formal decision, for a formal decision is the rationale for a court proceeding (otherwise, a dysfunction or an irrational choice occurs); this, in short, is the theoretical model that still leads to explanations of variations in dispute rates in current longitudinal and/or comparative sociolegal dispute treatment analysis.

Quite paradoxically no serious attention is paid to the possibility that a (self-defined) formal-rational organized subsystem such as a state court proceeding can also be considered a veritably complex organization.[1] Consequently empirical conditions for bounded rationalities,[2] step-by-step goal orientations,[3] opportunism,[4] transpositions of ends, and so on, are not seriously considered as coessential, constitutive devices. The possibility that such *de facto* conditions could structurally and logically lead to quasi-solutions,[5] rather than authoritative formal decisions, is thus almost ignored— for it is assumed that a quasi-solution is not rationally coherent to normative structures, expectations, and so on.

If the above is realized, a leading hypothesis comes to the fore: the hypothesis that, due to their very nature, cross-borders interactions might imply and/or embody—more than any other type of

1   Michel Crozier and Jean-Claude Thoenig, "The Regulation of Complex Organized Systems", in *Administrative Science Quarterly* 21, 2 (1976): 547–70.

2   Herbert A. Simon, "From Substantive to Procedural Rationality", in *Philosophy and Economic Theory*, ed. F. Hanhn and M. Hollis (Oxford: Oxford University Press, 1979).

3   Georgiou, 1973.

4   Oliver Williamson, *The Economic Institutions of Capitalism. Firms, Markets, Relational Contracting* (New York: The Free Press, 1986).

5   James G. March and Johan P. Olsen, *Ambiguity and Choice in Organization* (Gergen: Universitetforlaget, 1976).

interaction—a high mixture of adversarial, inquisitorial, and co-operative patterns.

In other words one might hypothesize that a sort of multilayered reinstitutionalization process,[6] or, as Goffman would put it, a veritable secondary adjustment might occur as a prerequisite condition for a reasonable court dispute. Consequently one might also argue that the notion of sociolegal reaction—as a way of relocalizing behavioural and cultural patterns—is among the conceptual key terms and methodological grid of comparison required to assess the sociolegal dispute treatment nexus in cross-border legal relations in contemporary Western society.

Given such a hypothesis it follows that the intertwining of litigation and negotiation dynamics, both performed in the course of the same proceeding—often at the same time and for the same purpose, by the same actor—should not be sociologically viewed as a dysfunction or a corruption of the classic state court model of dispute treatment, but as a potential (individual and collective) accomplishment of all the variables which are anyhow constitutive of its organizational design. The neologism "litigotiation"[7] that—as we will see—summarizes the content of this empirical study stresses precisely the heuristic concern for such a too-often ignored and so far underestimated, but increasingly apparent, sociological dimension of procedural state law.

The question, therefore, is twofold: why do certain social actors still apply for a state court proceeding to treat their cross-border disputes? Who are they?

The hypothesis of this study is that, in order to account for the above questions, the judicial process should be conceptualized, as ancient Roman jurists would suggest, both as a method and structure of cybernetic—in other words, as the Greek etymology of the word indicates not only as a selective technical tool, but also and above all as a socioinstitutional place for navigating—controlling and driving relevant social issues—throughout problematic fluctuations. More precisely it could be conceived of as a techno-struc-

6    Paul Bohannan, "Law and Legal Institutions", in *International Encyclopedia of the Social Sciences* IX (New York: MacMillan Free Press, 1968).

7    Marc Galanter, "Worlds of Deals: Using Negotiation to Teach About Legal Process", *Journal of Legal Education* 34 (1984): 268.

ture, to the extent that—as a rhapsodic event—it can foster a har-
monic, or modular, combination of contrasting voices. But it must
be firmly assessed as a spatially localized social construction in
order to enlighten the broader functions of control/management
of the social complexity that it embodies anyhow.

Given such premises this study will present a contextualized
account of the cross-border disputes under scrutiny. Consequently
one would expect to find regional differences in comparison to
any court file analysis carried out elsewhere—those carried out
within this international research project included. On the other
hand, however, one will also perceive the high degree of generali-
zation that the experience of the Milano court is able to offer, for
the quantitative sample of cross-border cases that have been studied is, in fact, a qualitative sample of the contemporary Western
sociolegal universe.

### B. The Research Project

Given the structure and aims of the general project, it was
agreed to carry out the Italian survey in the Milano area, hypoth-
esizing that the metropolitan jurisdiction of Milano could represent an appropriate fieldwork for comparative research due to its
national as well as international socioinstitutional and economic
character. As in other countries a city court was selected, the
Tribunale Civile di Milano—hereinafter named the Civil Court of
Milano, or the court—was sorted out as exclusive fieldwork. Additionally, to match the other studies, it was agreed that only court
files registered in that court in 1988 could be taken into consideration. Needless to say both decisions were particularly selective,
and the latter (as will be shown) became a serious difficulty.

The year 1988 was chosen by the project team in Bremen under the assumption that it was, on one hand, recent enough to
allow conclusions on current practices and, on the other hand,
that the research period from 1988 to 1992/93 would be long
enough for the overall majority (if not all) of the cases to be closed.
Thus conclusions on the outcomes of the cases would be possible.[8]

As we will see, in Italy the period was too short to gather all the
potential data. A number of other constraints also had to be overcome. To begin with, court disputes dealing with cross-border cases

8    For mere practical reasons of accessibility, in New York eventu-
     ally the year 1986 was selected.

are not recorded as such by official sources, as Italian court registers are based on more traditional criteria so that what the research project defined as cross-border cases had to be sorted out, so to say, in spite of the rationale of the formal-legal asset of the national legal systems. Additionally, as in most administrations, computerized systems for recording court files are a very recent development, appearing in the selected court as of 1991. Therefore, as 1988 was the period of time chosen to fit with Bremen, Hamburg, and New York court file analyses, there was no alternative solution: the Milano cross-border cases required a manual selection, classification, and listing.

All the above, in turn, had to be related to the constraints of the real functioning of the court. For example, record lists of the Central Chancellery, once completed, are all transferred to, and placed in, the General Archive of the Chancellery. The same happens for all court files that have been defined. Consequently the empirical part of the research had to be performed to a great extent in the archive, along its labyrinthic corridors and multiple-level dusty shelves.

In brief, at this first stage, the Milano unit was aware of the fact that, to cope with the general project's comparative aims, it had to scrutinize eighteen General Roll Registers filled up in 1988; sort out from the total amount of 20,036 files registered that year, those apparently involving at least a foreign (non-Italian) party; register these cases in a separate list; analyse all the selected files in order to ascertain whether they were, in fact, cross-border disputes; and finally, report the data pertaining to each file in the questionnaire. All this, manually.

## 1. Approach to the Fieldwork

Apart from the manual recording, the very first part of the enquiry—the scrutiny of the General Roll Registers and the listing of cases separately—did not raise any particular obstacle, for registers are public devices and the General Archive hall of the Central Chancellery is generally open to the public for consultation. On the contrary the actual access to, and study of, the listed files—both those still open and kept in one or the other Chancellery of the twelve Court sections of the Civil Court of Milano, and those already closed and kept in the General Archive—appeared quite problematic.

First, to gain access to the inner system of the court section Chancelleries or the court archive, it is necessary to obtain not only a formal authorization from the president of the court, but also substantial collaboration on the part of the court sections' and archive's clerks. Secondly, there is a dispersion of the files. Open files normally are located in the court sections' Chancelleries and assigned to court sections' judges according to selective criteria of division of court labour. Moreover, the same files are continuously transferred from the Chancelleries to the judges' rooms for the hearings. In turn already closed files are put in broader file folders, which are then placed on the shelves running along internal corridors of the archive, and these (as there is no proper place for consultation) are not by rule accessible to the public. In short, before making the basic, final decision about which type of file—still open, already closed, or both—had to be selected for data analysis, it seemed necessary to verify whether such analysis could be reasonably carried out in actual practice.

As both a formally authorized personal access to court files and a positive attitude and/or collaboration on the part of court officers during the manual research and study of the files were absolutely necessary, various exploratory meetings were arranged. Quite surprisingly, the President of the Civil Court of Milano, once informed about the general aims of the research, showed great interest in the matter and, without hesitation, signed, on 8 January 1993, a formal authorization allowing us access both to the court sections' Chancelleries and to the General Archive.

Provided with such a bypass, equally surprising was the positive attitude and open collaboration of the clerks, particularly of the clerks at the archive. Not only did they not seem annoyed in any way by our presence in the archive corridors, but they were also very helpful and allowed us to access and review the registers and the archived court files even on days when the office was closed to the public.

## 2. The Research District

Before describing the actual progression of the survey, it seems opportune now to move the attention to the broader context of the research area and to give some information about the sociolegal dimension of the jurisdictional district of the Civil Court of Milano.

From a formal-legal perspective a jurisdictional district such as that of the Civil Court of Milano is basically defined by the formal-legal level of competence established nationally by state law. Such competence concerns the objective criteria of the value and nature of the dispute, as well as that of the territoriality of the jurisdiction and the subjective criteria of capacity (namely, active/ passive legitimation) to act in that court on the part of a legal subject. While the former criteria refer to the objective limits of the assets of the given court as regards other courts or jurisdictions, the latter refers to the subjective potential action of a given legal actor in the same court. From a socioinstitutional perspective, on the contrary, the jurisdictional district of the Civil Court of Milano is basically defined by regional variables, such as socioeconomic structure, demographic composition, and so on.

Given such a sharp distinction let us consider the socioinstitutional variables. From these vantage points one might gain a better understanding of both national and international relevance of the data that the study is concerned with.

### 3. Socioinstitutional Variables
No matter how relevant a general overview of the formal-legal framework of the Civil Court of Milano jurisdiction[9] cannot exhaust the real dimension of the research district. A sociolegal approach to our study, in fact, cannot ignore the other side of the coin, that is, the social, economic, and other assets of the area.

As far as the population of the area is concerned, the inhabitants registered as official residents amount to about 2,800,000, of whom about 1,500,000 live in the city of Milano. However a total of nearly 4,000,000 people currently live de facto within the province (that is nearly half of the whole population of the Lombardy region, which is about 9,000,000). On the part of foreign citizens, in the last decade the number of residents coming from Africa, Asia, and South America has notably increased, while the traditional communities of residents coming from the European Union or North America remained relatively steady. The number of tourists that in each season visit or pass through the city is also very important.

With regard to the number of productive and commercial agents, within the territorial jurisdiction of the Court of Milano, figures show about 300,000 companies and about 120,000 small firms— firms that in Italy are usually owned and run by members of a family. These numbers include about 5000 banks and credit institutions, about 200 insurance companies, and more than 7000 trans-

9     See Enzo Vial, herein.

port firms. However, to have a better idea of the economic setting of the area, one must also look at the total amount of commercial interchange (value and quantity of import/export) and keep in mind that the vocational calling of the whole region—more particularly of the province of Milano—has always been and still is concerned with goods/services intermediation and transformation. With reference to foreign trade only, a recent report published by the Milano Chamber of Commerce shows that from 1985 to 1990 the province of Milano dealt with about 70% of all imports and 54% of all exports of the Lombardy region, as well as more than 25% of all imports and about 17% of all exports of Italy. Finally the international dimension of Milano's economic system can be appreciated by looking at the commercial fairs' systems and at the type of foreign settlements in the area. In 1990, out of a total of 1000 foreign industrial corporations settled in Italy, 376 were located in Milano, of which 30% were American, 17% German, and 12.5% French. In the same year 76% of service firms with foreign shareholders operating in Italy were also located in Milano.[10]

As one can see, the Milano area can rightly be defined as a real coupling-pin of the Italian economy, as well as an open space as regards cross-border interactions in the broader international networking economy.

## C. The Research Fieldwork

Let us now turn our attention back to methodological problems of our research project. As a part of the research fieldwork, the actual organization of a court can positively and negatively condition a research programme at two levels: at the level of its structural/functional dimension and at the level of its performative conditions. The first level mainly concerns the division of labour within the organizational set of the court as a whole. In turn the second level mainly concerns the selective strategy that had to be adopted to surmount the obstacles that such a dimension might put to the fore.

### 1. Organizational Set of the Court
In Italy one can find some data about court files not only in the General Roll Register of the year under consideration, but also in other sources: in the Court Decisions Register and Court Files

10   Benito Boschetto, "Le reti di collaborazione fra Milano e le altre metropoli europee", in *Impresa e Stato*, 14 (1991).

Archive Register, both kept by the General Court Archive, once the cases are closed; in the Court Section Files Registers, kept by each court section Chancellery throughout the period in which the cases are still in process; and in the Plaintiffs' and Defendants' Name Registers, kept by the Central Chancellery. From an organizational as well as from a qualitative point of view, the General Roll Register seemed to be the best choice.

At the moment of the registration of a file, a lawyer has to fill in a sheet indicating, besides his name and the parties' names, a description of the matter or nature of the case, *causa petendi* and *petitum*. To facilitate the description of the claim on the part of the lawyers and, indirectly, the prospective assignment of a file to a court section on the part of the court presidency (and consequently the routine work of clerks) the Civil Court of Milano created a special guideline: a general list containing, so far, 104 different work-area or key-word items.

As far as the variety of court cases is concerned, it is significant to note that according to the list, a claim can be defined according to a two-level grid. It can be classified with reference to different standards: type of contract; type of proceeding; type of legal effect of the prospective decision; type of legal subject concerned; type of socioeconomic context of the dispute; type of act or fact on which the claim is based; type of right; type of rules or legal system involved; and so on. Once a standard has been chosen, the same claim can be further specified accordingly. For example, the typology of contracts includes 35 specifications, which is about one-third of the entire list items.

Interestingly such a classification to some extent disregards various formal-legal distinctions of Italian law although legal formalism is clearly at its core. The typology of legal subjects involved in the case includes items such as associations and foundations, legal persons, region disputes, public administration disputes, and RAI-tv and telecommunication disputes. The typology of contexts includes items such as agriculture, labour, navigation, and town-planning. The items related to the typology of acts or facts on which the claim is based concern motor vehicle accidents, professional responsibility, bequests, unilateral promises, action for falsehood, and action for defamation by the media. Concerning the typology of rights, one finds these items: copyright, trademark, patents, family, estate, and personality.

Finally, the typology of rules or legal systems includes one item only: EC law. However, in another part of the general list, two other items are mentioned: ritual and nonritual arbitrations and opposition to arbitration decisions.

Significantly a key term such as cross-borders relations is not included in the list. Yet the above classification and specification scheme is an interesting reference point for our research project, as it outlines how the main topics of court disputes in the Milano area are perceived and handled by the court administration.

Given the minute description of types of claims, however, one might suppose that the above list also constitutes a standard model for the division of labour among either the twelve court sections or the number of judges of each court section. This supposition is supported by the fact that the list was meant to help the president of the court when assigning the cases according to each section or judge specialization. Yet if one compares the description of the claims in the General Roll Register and the actual assignment of the file to a certain specialized court section or judge, one soon realizes that quite often the two sets of data do not coincide at all.

In fact the functional jurisdiction of each court section is also defined by its specific list of claims, which is much more refined and detailed than the general list discussed above. This accounts for the fact that, by rule, each court section has an exclusive jurisdiction about certain claims as defined by its own special list, as well as a mixed—that is, concurrent—jurisdiction about other claims also included in other court section lists. As a consequence of such highly refined arrangements, therefore, only a few cases are assigned according to the principle of exclusive specialization, while the majority of cases, especially if they are of some importance, are distributed among the sections.

In addition the distribution of the files on the part of the president of the court is also based on the actual amount of each section's work, that is, not on the above qualitative criteria, but according to the number of cases currently in progress, the number of judges available, and so on. Thus the intertwining of the very incoherent variables makes the overall system extremely inconsistent, even from a bureaucratic point of view.

Given all of the above one can easily realize why a court file screening and analysis of cross-border cases throughout the registers of the twelve court section Chancelleries of the Civil Court of Milano could not be carried out and had therefore been excluded from the research agenda. The research could only be done by starting from a review of the Central Chancellery General Roll Register, as the following paragraph indicates.

## 2. *Approach to the Files*

As has been said, in 1988 the Central Chancellery of the Civil Court of Milano filled up eighteen volumes of the General Roll Register, for a total of 20,036 enrolled cases.

For each case the register shows, in progressive order:
- chronological registration number,
- date of registration,
- file number,
- primary plaintiff's name, plus the number of coplaintiffs,
- primary defendant's name, plus the number of codefendants,
- lawyers' names,
- *causa petendi,*
- type of the introductory act,
- court section to which the file had been assigned, and
- judge to which the court assigned the case.

The cluster of data that one can gather from these items is significant indeed, although, for the reasons already discussed, they do not give a clear indication about the main concern of the research.

It was decided to select the cross-border files by the names of the registered primary plaintiffs and defendants. With regard to corporate entities, which we assumed to be the major actors on the international fore, this seemed to be an apparently reasonable option. Italian corporate names differ from those of other countries. It was thus quite easy to sort out foreign companies, banks, and so on, due to the explicit indication of their formal-legal nature (Ltd; Inc.; GmbH; S.A., and so on) as opposed to Italian companies (Spa; Srl; Snc; S.acc.; S.acc.p.a.; S.a.). In cases of doubt the file was selected. It was also possible to identify, and therefore exclude, Italian branches of foreign companies. Briefly, to the extent that the attention was concentrated upon corporations that, according to Italian law, could not be defined as Italian companies, it was possible to reach a good approximation of our issue. In retrospect this kind of selection proved, altogether, to be basically correct, even if at this preliminary stage of the research it was still impossible to ascertain, for example, whether foreign companies acted in court through Italian or foreign citizens provided with special powers of attorney.

Unfortunately the same formal legal criteria was not useful at all in the case of individuals. Among the names of individuals that were undoubtedly foreign by spelling and meaning, one could indeed find foreign people, but also foreigners living in Italy or Italians with foreign ancestors (and therefore foreign names). Thus, as far as this cluster of cases was concerned, one could only hope to gather the proper information by intuition and verify its correctness afterwards during the file documents' analysis. In reality, as we will see in detail in the second part of this study, this hope has been largely frustrated. In fact, notwithstanding an explicit rule of the Italian civil procedure code, the duty to mention explicitly the domicile of the parties on each party's first act was usually ignored by the lawyers who drafted these.

After leafing through each page of the eighteen register volumes, of 20,036 enrolled files, a total of 546 prospective cross-border cases were selected and recorded on a separate list, from mid-January to mid-April 1993. We then proceeded to look at the actual file content in the files stored in the general archive.

At this point a first important finding was made. Out of 546 selected cases, just over half (286) were still open after about five years and had not been closed and filed in the archives. Apart from the fact that this suggests that Italian legal proceedings have a duration that might appear unusual in some other parts of the world and that the Civil Court of Milano is no exception to this phenomenon of delay in court, there are other implications, as will be described.

In the meantime, looking through each closed file kept in the archive and by analysing the enclosed acts and documents from April 1993 to June 1993, the group of 260 closed cases was further reduced:

• two files could not be found, as they were not in the right folders;

• one file concerned a case registered by mistake and immediately withdrawn by the same lawyer;

• one file had absolutely no act or document;

• three files, upon closer inspection, concerned Italian branches of foreign companies (two plaintiffs, one defendant);

• three files, upon closer inspection, concerned Italian firms representing foreign companies (one plaintiff, two defendants);

• 37 files, upon closer inspection, concerned foreign citizens (mainly extra European Union immigrants) provided with formal Italian residence (22 plaintiffs, 15 defendants);

• six files, upon closer inspection, did not concern any foreign party (merely foreign names of Italian citizens); and

• nine files concerned the same Italian fashion firm and its Japanese counterpart, sued for alleged unfair competition. For a number of questions it seemed reasonable to involve only one of them.

In conclusion the final group fitting with the basic research project guidelines was thus of 197 cases, 189 cases if only one of the nine Italian-Japanese files was included.

Unfortunately in a number of these cases file documents were partially incomplete; some data were also missing. However, any available information was recorded and put in the questionnaires, which had been prepared for computerized analysis in the meantime.

## D. The Data

### 1. Validity of the Data

The two steps mentioned above, namely the selection according to names and the limitation of time, caused the data to be highly selective and probably biased.

As a result of the name selection, the data miss all individual foreign residents with an Italian name. Therefore, there is most likely an underrepresentation of countries with an Italian emigrant history as well as the Ticino area in Switzerland. If one assumes that these emigrant communities (be it recent or historical emigration) have somewhat closer commercial and private ties to Italy than the remainder of the world population, a not insignificant number of cases may be missing from the data. It might even be a significant difference regarding the behaviour of these parties in comparison to other foreign parties. In addition a number of residents of other Latin countries may also have been excluded. On the other hand, the data set was cleared to exclude all noncross-border files. Thus, the number of cross-border cases found must be regarded as a minimum. The actual number is probably somewhat higher, yet, fortunately, this issue only concerns individuals and the fault might therefore be tolerated.

The second issue is far more serious indeed. The time limitation of five years, which served well for other jurisdictions proved to be completely inadequate for Italy. On the other hand, there were few alternatives. As mentioned, a filing year of 1988 was chosen to obtain up-to-date results. Going back up to ten years or more, as would have been necessary in Italy, would have provided outdated results from a legal as well as from a socioeconomic point of view. Using the judgement roll rather than the registry would have been unsatisfactory as well, as it would have excluded all files closed without a judgement.

Unfortunately this exclusion of more than half of the cases from the research has more implications than a simple reduction of the number as it is not a random selection. Rather, from all that can be assumed, a strong bias is introduced with the effective likelihood of changing the levels of most of the data. It may particularly exclude certain—yet unknown—types of parties and disputes and definitely serves to systematically exclude the more complex disputes, the more uncooperative and combative parties, and the more problematic procedures, particularly those where service of process used much of the initial periods of time.

In effect this means that all data have to be read and evaluated *cum granu salis*, in other words, that all conclusions need to be made subject to scrutiny and great caution. Additionally it is worth noting that court proceedings concern merely the phase of cognition, not execution or enforcement. Finally, eventual or prospective enhancements of the cases under scrutiny (namely, appeals) before other jurisdictional levels have not been considered.

Yet we nevertheless believe that the data provide some initial insight into cross-border litigation in Milano. Even on this limited basis some conclusions can be made with relative certainty and others seem reasonably secure. And in connection with the other research conducted in Bremen, Hamburg, and New York, the study provides empirical information on cross-border conflict resolution on a larger scale that was not available before.

## 2. Representativeness of the Data

The overall frequency of cross-border cases registered in the Civil Court of Milano in 1988 could be used here as a rough indicator. As has been said, out of a total of 20,036 cases, those intuitively sorted out as cross-border cases were 546, that is, 2.7%. If we maintain the rate of error that resulted from the cleansing of the closed files (260–197 = 63), one could reasonably correct the above proportion to about 2.0%. On the other hand, considering the number of foreign individual residents with Italian names, the actual number might be slightly higher again. Significantly such a frequency is not too far from that found in the Bremen and Hamburg courts as well as in the New York data.

The rationale for such an analogy is supported by the fact that both the Milano and Hamburg areas have about the same population and are characterized by a comparable level of industrialization and international relations. The difference, however, lies in that both areas benefit from their specific geographical position. Hamburg develops its international affairs throughout the natural environment of the harbour. Milano, on the contrary, performs its international business relations throughout a functionally equivalent, but artificial device: a number of specialized and/or general trade fairs. In 1989 the Milano fair system concerned 89 exhibitions, involving a total of 42,899 exhibiting firms—of which about 20% were foreigners—and a total of 4,296,746 visitors, for a total expenditure on their part (equipment, purchases, food, travel and hotel charges, and so on) of a total of 3270 billion liras.[11]

To what extent similarities and differences actually influence the typology of actors and the nature of cross-border disputes in these two territories is thus a question that our research project as a whole could not comparatively ignore. In any case the potential for generalizing these data at national and international comparative levels can be referred to the emblematic role of the Milano area—for the Italian, as well as for the European system—as regards financial, industrial, commercial, and cultural worldwide linkages.

### 3. Questionnaire Fields of Enquiry

In its structure the Italian questionnaire corresponds to a very large extent to the model format used in the New York, Bremen, and Hamburg studies. This was done to allow the highest possible comparative outcomes. However, it has also been framed by taking into account the specific features of the local research context, by adding to and/or deleting from the reference model a few topics related to differences in the procedural legal system.

The questionnaire's fields of enquiry have been constructed with specific regards to four main thematic issues: typology of the parties, typology of the disputes, typology of the proceedings, and outcomes of the cases, for a total of 32 fields. Data about each field were analysed by frequency counts and percentage, as well as by cross-tabulation. The input and analysis of the data contained in the above-mentioned 197 court file questionnaires was carried out in Madras (India) by an independent Indian software firm. What follows is a descriptive presentation and analytical commentary of said computerized calculations.

11    Enzo Vicari, "La Fiera di Milano nella Business Community Milanese", in *Impresa e Stato*, 14 (1991): 36–44.

### III. Data Analysis

The importance of disaggregating and intertwining the three main items of the questionnaire (the type of parties involved in cross-borders relations, the subject matter of the disputes, and the nature of the proceeding) throughout a computerized data analysis is found not in relation to abstract theorizing on international disputes' treatment in state courts, but with direct reference to the local context of our study. Type of actor, nature of the case, and enactment of the proceeding are local variables strictly embedded in a formal and substantial cultural network.

### A. The Typology of the Parties

The set of questions (questionnaire's fields) about the typology of the parties concerns three items: the legal status in the case, the country of residence, and the area of origin of both plaintiffs (and plaintiff intervenors) and defendants (and defendant intervenors).

These indicators constitute the references for deciphering not only the respective normative attitudinal imprintings, but also the amount and fluctuation rates (direction, content, and so on) of the issues involved.

*1. Sociolegal Status*

As far as the legal status of the frequency of parties is concerned, let us focus on the following figures.

#### Table I–1: Legal Status of Plaintiffs and Defendants

|  | Plaintiffs | | Defendants | | Total | |
|---|---|---|---|---|---|---|
|  | % | (N) | % | (N) | % | (N) |
| Private individuals | 36 | ( 67) | 26 | ( 48) | 31 | (115) |
| Small firms | 4 | ( 7) | 4 | ( 8) | 4 | ( 15) |
| Companies | 51 | ( 95) | 61 | (112) | 56 | (207) |
| Insurance companies | 3 | ( 6) | 3 | ( 6) | 3 | ( 12) |
| Banks | 4 | ( 8) | 3 | ( 5) | 4 | ( 13) |
| Other | 2 | ( 4) | 2 | ( 4) | 2 | ( 8) |
| Total    % | 100 | | 100 | | 100 | |
|    (N) | | (187) | | (183) | | (370) |

As Table I–1 shows, at the Civil Court of Milano cross-border disputes to a large extent involve companies (55.9%) and private individuals (31.1%) while small firms (3.7%), banks (3.5%) and insurance companies (3.2%) are rather rare in court. Even if one considers the limitations of this study, these numbers are probably somewhat indicative of the relationship among the different types of parties. Significantly, the results obtained in Bremen/Hamburg and in New York are approximately similar. The figures about companies do not raise any particular question, for it is a widespread assumption that international court cases mainly concern business issues. The figures about private individuals, on the contrary, are astonishing indeed, either per se or in comparison with any other item. Even if the missing half of the files were to contain far fewer private individuals, the numbers would still be impressive (also taking into consideration that there may be a number of individuals missing at the initial selection level). They deserve therefore a detailed comment.

If one reviews scientific literature about court disputes, one finds a number of arguments trying to demonstrate that individuals are no longer the core players. In Anglo-American studies a common explanation is that individuals are quantitatively and qualitatively marginal in mobilization of court lawyering precisely because, by rule, they are mere one-shot players.[12] This is even more so in the international context. Cultural patterns, fee costs, language difficulties, lack of stable communication networks, space-time constraints, and so on are all variables invoked to support the thesis that individuals are in trouble—up to the point of giving up the matter in advance—if and when they have to deal with a foreign court or a foreign party.

Yet here we have data that—although neither putting into question the one-shot player definition nor the plausibility of the above constraints—clearly require a more convincing explanation. Why, according to our empirical findings, are individuals among the most active players in state court cases involving cross-border matters?

For the cases in point, a plausible explanation could be that suggested by Blankenburg.[13] In Blankenburg's view what really

12      Marc Galanter, "Why the Haves Come Out Ahead: Speculation on the Limits of Legal Change", *Law and Society Review* 9 (1974); Marc Galanter, "Reading the Landscape of Disputes: What We Know and Don't Know (and Think We Know) About Our Allegedly Contentious and Litigious Society", *UCLA Law Review* 31 (1983).

13      Erhard Blankenburg, *Legal Cultures Compared* (paper delivered at the International Conference on Comparing Legal Cultures, Macerata, 1994).

matters about the access to, as well as the escape from, a contemporary (state) justice system is not so much the demand side, but rather the supply side of a legal action, that is, the functioning of an intermediary infrastructure that facilitates certain legal behaviour. To support his statement Blankenburg outlines in his studies, among others, the experience of road accident tort cases in Germany and the Netherlands: an experience that shows that insurance agencies routinely handle these cases out of their respective national courts.[14]

Paradoxically enough—as we will see when illustrating the *causa petendi* (the file object)—the highest rate of private persons in our cross-border court cases is due to the number of road accident disputes, a type of dispute that is clearly sponsored by generalized infrastructures such as insurance agencies.

### Table I–2: Plurality of Parties, i.e., Number of Plaintiff and Defendant Intervenors for All Cases and for Motor Vehicle Disputes

| Number of Intervenors | All Plaintiffs | | All Defendants | | Motor Vehicle Plaintiffs | | Motor Vehicle Defendants | |
|---|---|---|---|---|---|---|---|---|
| | % | (N) | % | (N) | % | (N) | % | (N) |
| 0 | 95 | (179) | 68 | (128) | 89 | (41) | 15 | ( 7) |
| 1 | 4 | ( 7) | 25 | ( 47) | 7 | ( 3) | 67 | (31) |
| 2 | 2 | ( 3) | 6 | ( 12) | 4 | ( 2) | 17 | ( 8) |
| 4 | | | 1 | ( 2) | | | | |
| Total % | 100 | | 100 | | 100 | | 100 | |
| (N) | | (189) | | (189) | | (46) | | (46) |

Table I–2 shows that in motor vehicle tort cases, in which private individuals are most represented, almost 85% of the defendants have intervening parties, whereas overall this is true only in 32% of the cases. Apparently, in cross-border cases, Blankenburg's findings hold true and are confirmed for the first part, namely, the intermediary function of insurance agencies.

---

14   Blankenburg, "Legal Cultures Compared"; Erhard Blankenburg, *The Infrastructure of Avoiding Civil Litigation: Comparing Cultures of Legal Behaviour in the Netherlands and West-Germany* (paper delivered at the International Conference on Comparing Legal Cultures, Macerata, 1994).

On the other hand, in the Italian cross-border disputes, the insurance companies generally seem to be not as opposed to litigation as they are on a domestic level—at least in Germany and the Netherlands, according to Blankenburg's findings.[15] The cases are, in fact, not routinely handled out of court. This result is interesting, particularly if one considers the efforts that have been made to create insurance resolution schemes within Europe (from which most of the foreign parties come). These results should hold valid also in light of the incompleteness of the file sample, because the longer and more complex motor vehicle tort litigation involving private individuals is even more likely to involve insurance company intervenors than not.

Turning back to the original issue regarding the parties' sociolegal status, (Table I–1), the results are confirmed by looking at the data concerning small firms. Here one could argue that the low figures reflect more or less directly the insufficient or even lacking support (counselling, intermediation, and so on) on the part of ad hoc intermediaries or agencies. The argument is supported by the prestigious review *Impresa e Stato* edited by the Chamber of Commerce of Milano. In fact it is not by chance that the policy of this chamber in the last decade has been devoted precisely to providing infrastructural networks at any territorial and functional level.[16]

Finally, one might wonder if current opinions about overrepresentation of the wealthier parties, particularly as plaintiffs, in international disputes are correct,[17] as has also been found in the New York study. The Milano study rather suggests that although one might reasonably hypothesize that wealthy parties numerically dominate, nevertheless state courts maintain a somewhat democratic, or open, access to justice: a hypothesis that is also supported by the empirical findings in the Bremen and Hamburg research.

About 35% of the cases were set in motion by private individual plaintiffs. As the rate of corporate business defendants is higher than that of business plaintiffs, there is no doubt that a

---

15    One should also note that, of course, the data are comprised of more than Dutch and German insurance companies.

16    Piero Bassetti, "Il cameralismo tra regionalismo e europeismo", *Impresa e Stato* 25 (1994): 9-13.

17    Galanter, "Why the Haves Come Out Ahead".

number of private plaintiffs have been first movers not only against other private persons, but also against corporations.

**Table I–3: Cross-tabulation About the Summarized Parties' Legal Status (Private/Business): Plaintiffs by Defendants**

| Defendants | Plaintiffs | | | | | |
| | Private | | Business | | Total | |
| | % | (N) | % | (N) | % | (N) |
| Private | 53 | (35) | 11 | (13) | 26 | (48) |
| Business | 47 | (31) | 89 | (107) | 74 | (138) |
| Total    % | 36 | | 65 | | 100 | |
| (N) | | (66) | | (120) | | (186) |

As Table I–3 shows, almost half of the cases (47%) set in motion by private plaintiffs are against business defendants. This result seems quite surprising indeed, as it somehow recalls the disproportionate dispute between David and Goliath. Yet it also suggests that one should not underestimate the variety of manifest and latent opportunities that, in spite—and/or by virtue—of its constitutive formal-legal design, state law still offers to any social actor.

## 2. Country of Residence and Area of Origin
A deeper cognition of the typology of legal actors can be also achieved by looking at their origin. Let us look first at the breakdown of Italian and foreign plaintiffs and defendants. Here, again, conflicting trends would appear to lead to different results. On the one hand, both dispute-immanent rational factors, such as ease of service of process and enforcement and the rules set by the Brussels Convention for Europe, would lead to an overrepresentation of foreign plaintiffs over Italian plaintiffs. On the other hand, the thought that it might be preferable for any party to attempt to find a jurisdiction at home and the above-mentioned advantage to the defendants (and disadvantage to plaintiffs) that is inherent in Italian court proceedings would lead many foreign plaintiffs to abandon their claim if faced with the necessity to commence an action in Italy.

**Table I–4: Groups of Foreign/Italian Plaintiffs and Defendants**

| Plaintiff-Defendant | % | (N) |
| --- | --- | --- |
| Foreign-Italian | 48 | (90) |
| Italian-Foreign | 49 | (92) |
| Foreign-Foreign | 4 | (7) |
| Total | 100 | (189) |

In the analysed files nearly the same number of cases have foreign as Italian plaintiffs. Table I–4 offers also a further detail: seven cases (3.7%) concern exclusively foreign parties who seem to have chosen Italian jurisdiction voluntarily. Overall the data seem to support the second rather than the first option; however, here the limitations of the data come to full force and effect as the origins of the ongoing litigants cannot even be guessed. Thus any further conclusions would be illegitimate.

Table I–5 offers a general overview of the data about plaintiffs' and defendants' country of residence frequencies.

## Table I–5: Country of Residence of Plaintiffs and of Defendants*

|  | Plaintiffs | | Defendants | | All | |
|---|---|---|---|---|---|---|
|  | % | (N) | % | (N) | % | (N) |
| Austria | 1 | ( 2) | 2 | ( 3) | 2 | ( 5) |
| Belgium | 2 | ( 4) | 1 | ( 2) | 2 | ( 6) |
| Bangladesh | 1 | (1) |  |  |  | ( 1) |
| Bahamas | 1 | ( 1) |  |  |  | ( 1) |
| Switzerland | 2 | ( 4) | 6 | ( 9) | 4 | ( 13) |
| Costa Rica | 1 | ( 1) |  |  |  | ( 1) |
| Germany | 14 | ( 23) | 12 | ( 19) | 13 | ( 42) |
| Algeria |  |  | 1 | ( 1) |  | ( 1) |
| Spain | 1 | ( 1) |  |  |  | ( 1) |
| Egypt | 1 | ( 1) |  |  |  | ( 1) |
| France | 8 | ( 14) | 12 | ( 19) | 10 | ( 33) |
| Liechtenstein | 1 | ( 2) | 1 | ( 2) | 1 | ( 4) |
| Great Britain | 3 | ( 5) | 2 | ( 3) | 2 | ( 8) |
| Greece | 1 | ( 1) | 2 | ( 3) | 1 | ( 4) |
| Italy | 53 | ( 90) | 52 | ( 85) | 52 | (175) |
| Israel |  |  | 1 | ( 1) |  | ( 1) |
| Japan | 1 | ( 1) | 1 | ( 2) | 1 | ( 3) |
| Libya | 1 | ( 1) |  |  |  | ( 1) |
| Norway |  |  | 1 | ( 2) | 1 | ( 2) |
| The Netherlands | 2 | ( 4) | 1 | ( 1) | 2 | ( 5) |
| Portugal |  |  | 1 | ( 1) |  | ( 1) |
| Rumania | 1 | ( 1) |  |  |  | ( 1) |
| Philippines |  |  | 1 | ( 1) |  | ( 1) |
| Thailand |  |  | 1 | ( 1) | 1 | ( 2) |
| Finland | 1 | ( 2) |  |  |  | ( 1) |
| China | 1 | ( 1) |  |  |  | ( 1) |
| Tunisia | 1 | ( 2) |  |  | 1 | ( 2) |
| Turkey |  |  | 1 | ( 1) |  | ( 1) |
| U.S.A. | 4 | ( 7) | 4 | ( 7) | 4 | ( 14) |
| Nigeria | 1 | ( 1) |  |  |  | ( 1) |
| St.Vincent |  |  | 1 | ( 1) |  | ( 1) |
| Yugoslavia |  |  | 1 | ( 1) |  | ( 1) |
| Total    % | 100 |  | 100 |  | 100 |  |
| (N) |  | (170) |  | (165) |  | (335) |

* Figures in this table that are not subsequently discussed have been provided for informational purposes only. For such discussion the figures are too low in light of the incompleteness of the file sample.

With regard to the proportion among foreign parties, one notices that the numbers of German (12.5%) and French (9.9%) parties are higher than those concerning any other European and non-European party. This would tend to confirm the socioeconomic relationship between North Italy, Germany, and France. Indeed it is possible to argue that the data give evidence of the fact that the Milano area takes a significant part in the European Union core system.

The rate of geographical distribution of parties from other countries is quite dispersed indeed, yet if one aggregates the countries of origin one finds foreign parties from a total of 32 countries. This finding raises the problem of the missing or potential foreign parties in absolute and relative rates, as the number of countries in the world, actually existing in political terms, is more than 150. One might thus wonder what type of—and how many— cross-border interactions are performed altogether among these countries. As far as the Milano area is concerned, it is possible to say only that Milano is strongly attached to continental Europe in the first place and to other OECD member states in the second, which conforms with the data in Bremen and Hamburg and New York, respectively, and is hardly surprising. Again, at this point any further conclusion would be illegitimate in light of the limitation of the data.

### B. Typology of the Cases

The enquiry into the nature of the cases is the second general item characterizing our empirical study. Its importance lies in the fact that it gives evidence of the substantial areas of conflict as well as of the special areas of substantive law mobilized by international relations, as defined by the official legal system. Not by chance, the list of file objects has been made according to the same (formal) description found in the General Roll Register of the court Chancellery.

### 1. File Objects

Let us look now at the table directly concerned with the details of the file object's field frequencies.

## Table I–6: File Object in Milano District Court Files (1988)

| File Object | % | (N) |
|---|---|---|
| Motor vehicle tort | 25 | ( 46) |
| Bankruptcy | 14 | ( 26) |
| Family law / Testament / Personal rights | 5 | ( 9) |
| Tenancy contract / Condominium | 4 | ( 8) |
| Advertising contract / Work contract | 3 | ( 5) |
| Bank / Stock exchange contract | 4 | ( 8) |
| Patent / Trademark / Copyright / Unfair competition | 9 | ( 16) |
| Exclusive right of sale | 3 | ( 6) |
| International transport contract | 5 | ( 10) |
| Agency / Brokerage | 3 | ( 5) |
| Insurance | 2 | ( 3) |
| Other contracts | 21 | ( 39) |
| Extracontractual liabilities | 2 | ( 3) |
| Objection to fiscal injunction | 1 | ( 1) |
| Labour contract | 1 | ( 1) |
| Total | 100 | (186) |

\* Figures in this table that are not subsequently discussed have been provided for informational purposes only. For such discussion the figures are too low in light of the incompleteness of the file sample.

As already mentioned cross-border motor vehicle tort cases are one of the most important types of cases and are represented in the data by almost 25%. In Milano—and, more generally, in Italy—this fact is hardly surprising, as the number of motor vehicle tort disputes is considered to be a problem for the Italian justice system as a whole. In the last decade about 40% of all court disputes in Italy concerned car accidents, so that a recent law reform (L.374/1991, enforced in 1994) lowers the jurisdiction about traffic accidents from the Tribunale to the Pretore, in an effort to speed courts' activity.

From an international comparative perspective, even if one considers the limitations of the data, the numbers are absolutely shocking at an analytical as well as at a practical level: tort cases are a basic issue in cross-border disputes. To underline this evidence does not imply that the overall cases about contractual matters are quantitatively or qualitatively less relevant (these cases, in fact, are simply dispersed throughout other questionnaire items) and may be much higher overall if one considers the missing half of the cases.

In summary, out of a total of 186 valid cases, 65.6% concern business matters and 34.4% nonbusiness matters. Altogether these data offer an univocal picture of the sample (based on an extralegal reference item such as business). Table I–7 gives a more detailed picture.

### Table I–7: Summarized File Object (Nonbusiness/Business), Compared for Foreign and Italian Plaintiffs in Milano District Court Files

|  | Plaintiff | | | | | |
|  | Foreign | | Italian | | Total | |
|  | % | (N) | % | (N) | % | (N) |
| Nonbusiness | 27 | (24) | 43 | (39) | 35 | (63) |
| Business | 73 | (64) | 57 | (52) | 65 | (116) |
| Total    % | 49 | | 51 | | 100 | |
|           (N) | | (88) | | (91) | | (179) |

As one can see foreign plaintiffs set in motion a higher number of court disputes about business matters than Italian plaintiffs. In turn Italian plaintiffs are concerned rather with nonbusiness cases. These results are intertwined and could indicate that foreign plaintiffs with nonbusiness matters face higher barriers to the Italian court than Italians, or, in other words, that only business actors possess the necessary resources and incentives to pursue such a dispute. Unfortunately this issue cannot be further elaborated as the limitations of the data could have a significant influence on this aspect. It should be noted, however, that a majority of the individual parties (59.6%)—with little difference between Italian and foreign individual parties—are concerned with motor vehicle torts, which seems to be the one major dispute the origin of which can hardly be avoided by the parties involved.

### 2. Relationships Between the Parties

The questionnaire items about the typology of the cases also deal with the substantial structuration of the relationships between the parties. Unfortunately, it has not been possible to gather empirical evidence of either the amount of money or the actual legal content of each case claim as precise information was largely missing in the General Roll Register as well as the files, a number of disputes were nonmonetary in nature, and, even in cases that explicitly mention a claim for money, the amount is often left undetermined. In many of the remaining files, there is conflicting information. Having said that, one might suppose what is otherwise intuitive,

namely, that cross-border disputes could deal with high values and/
or be more expensive than domestic disputes (in terms of travel
costs, double-lawyers' fees, act translations, and so on) and therefore also more important in terms of the money involved. However, the limitations of the data would also rather prohibit conclusions on this aspect.

## C. Typology of Proceedings

Our survey not only offers information on some relevant
procedural issues comparable to those of any other judicial system
(services, hearings, decisions, and so on), but gives evidence of the
actual functioning of a state court as regards the treatment of the
cases in point (time, expertise, awards, and so on).

### 1. Procedural Devices and Hearings

If one looks at the introductory acts of the cross-border cases under scrutiny, one notices that petitions (83.4%) largely dominate
over summonses (15.5%).

Table I–8: Introductory Acts in Milano District Court Files

| Introductory Act | % | (N) |
|---|---|---|
| Petition | 83 | (156) |
| Summon | 16 | (29) |
| Other | 1 | (2) |
| Total | 100 | (187) |

At first inspection, the dominance of petitions—a sort of functional equivalent of the order to show cause in the common-law
system—could hardly be considered significant, given the relative
autonomy to mobilize the law that the Italian legal system grants,
in principle, to any legal actors. On closer inspection, however,
one realizes that it puts indirectly to the fore once again what is
too often underestimated, that is, that within the province of a
state court there is an area of competence related to a cluster of
subject matters that by no means can be opportunistically selected
by any party, as they are strictly related to the symbolic power of
state law.

To what extent such a symbolic power affects the decision-
making process of a foreign party to promote a cross-border dispute or influences the technicalities of cross-border legal expertise
at a cultural and material level is difficult to say here, particularly

in light of the limitations of the study, as it may well be that it is the proceedings commenced by petitions, rather than those commenced by summonses that tend to have a shorter duration.

## 2. Legal Frame of the Procedure

Initially, one can note that only 17% of the files contained any reference to the basis of jurisdiction and that none of these references were insightful to any degree. Interestingly the Milano jurisdiction, once selected by the plaintiff, is rarely questioned.

### Table I–9: Battle over Jurisdiction in Milano District Court Files (1988)

| Battle over jurisdiction | % | (N) |
|---|---|---|
| Yes | 3 | ( 6) |
| No | 97 | (170) |
| Total | 100 | (176) |

Only a very small number of files (3.4%) dealt with the issue of the incorrect determination of the jurisdiction or mentioned a jurisdiction clause. Of course, such a low rate could also be ascribed to the missing cases, whose long procedure may have been predicated by such a dispute over jurisdiction. On the other hand, where successful a defendant may be able to obtain an early dismissal by raising this issue. Thus, the total share may only be slightly higher, if at all. This would suggest that, when state law is mobilized, a defendant is almost bound by the limited discretionality that the same law leaves either to the other party or to the court about the acceptance or rejection of its jurisdiction. Finally, one should consider that both plaintiffs' and defendants' correspondents do not have a professional interest in raising this issue, which might lead to the case being brought in another jurisdiction.

Interestingly, similar results on the same item have been found also in the Hamburg and Bremen and the New York data, which finally points to a normalizing rhythm of the proceeding, the routine work of the court, and the communicative role-playing of lawyers, which tends to domesticate any dispute.

The allotment of the files among the twelve court sections in which the Court of Milano is functionally articulated offers further support for this thought. The cross-border cases were not treated any differently by the assignment system than any other case. Particularly the short period of time incurred from the files' registration to the files' allotment is an indirect indicator of the lack of jurisdictional conflicts within the inner organizational setting of the court, in other words, over the court sections' division of labour according to judges' professional expertise.

On the contrary various problems arise just after the introductory act has been prepared, as far as foreign defendants are concerned. Plaintiffs are due to serve the introductory act. According to Italian law the service of any act on the part of any party is a complex procedural action that includes the formal request to a public office (Ufficio Notificazioni) to serve the act as well as the formal service performed by the office by means of a public officer (acting as Ufficiale Giudiziario). The formal request simply indicates who is in charge of the service and how the act has to be served (personally in the hands of the prospective defendant, by mail, by mail through an official authority, such as consulates, and so on).[18]

Given all of the above, the service performance is thus actually taken not only out of the control of the parties, but also of the lawyers, as it is conceived of as a pure state action in accordance to the operations of the office. In theory such a system seems to favour the party—particularly the first mover, the plaintiff—for he/she is not materially involved in the research of his/her counterpart. In practice, however, the opposite is true: not only because the same system has been constructed with reference to general public order issues, but also because it is based on a mere presumption about its own efficient functioning. The implications of both items, in turn, are particularly serious in the case of cross-border relations: bureaucratic controls of state administration do not seem to favour a prompt and effective result.

Given the above legal arrangements field frequencies of the item thus reveal that only 6% of introductory acts had been served by means of diplomatic carriers or consular agencies, while 17.9% were served by mail and 76.2% were served into the counterpart's hands by personal delivery.

18    Sandro Merz, *Le notofiche in Italia e all'estero* (Milano: Giuffre, 1994).

Table I–10: Service of the Introductory Act in
Milano District Court Files (1988)

| Type of Service | % | (N) |
|---|---|---|
| In the party's hand | 76 | (64) |
| By mail | 18 | (15) |
| By diplomatic means | 6 | (5) |
| Total | 100 | (84) |

As one can see, contrary to what one could have expected and putting aside the files devoid of any information, our cross-border cases suggest that international conventions aimed at easing (inter)national service procedures are almost ignored, that mail service is not considered reliable enough, and that, rather, most Italian plaintiffs have been in pretrial negotiations with the foreign defendants wherein it was somehow agreed to utilize the local lawyer as recipient of the service.

In fact this prior availability of local service would seem to be a prerequisite for litigation against a foreign defendant or, considering the limitations of the data, at least for disputes with a comparatively short duration.

A further procedural burden, particularly relevant in cross-border cases, is the service of acts other than the introductory one, such as those concerning formal requests, exhibitions, and assumption of proofs; witness testimony; party depositions; and so on to be taken in a foreign country or reported from abroad. Here the Italian legal system requires either serious factual reasons or a *fumus boni juris* to enhance these procedural devices. Moreover, to save the costs of acts' translations and/or asseverations, parties often limit their respective power to action. Although our study does not offer enough information to make serious generalizations about this topic, it seems reasonable to affirm that these variables play a relevant role. Altogether, we found only one request of proofs and one testimonial hearing taken abroad; nine acts translated in a language other than Italian; one assumption of proofs; and one expert witness consulted from abroad. We also found one act served by facsimile, and one might suppose again that it did not concern a basic procedural issue nor was challenged by the party concerned, for Italian law—and dominant Italian legal doctrine—does not give official recognition to such a type of service due to the reasons of public order given above. Overall, this would confirm the above theory. These findings would further point to our initial assumption: that the court proceeding is just another step in the ongoing negotiation process.

Another aspect needs to be considered. According to Italian law civil proceedings are based mainly on written acts and proofs and on the lawyers' performance in court. Here again it seems that Italian law is favourable to the parties, because it neither requires necessarily their permanent physical presence during the hearings nor compels them to plead orally. The other side of the coin, however, is that in actual practice both parties stay at the margin of the proceeding and rarely make any appearance in court. The dispute formally and substantially flows according to a time-table and a *ratio juris* largely determined by legal professionals. Lawyers discuss and record the issues of the dispute. Judges certify, by rule, such communicative interactions.

Table I–11: Number of Hearings in Milano
District Court Files (1988)

|                        | %   | Cum. % | (N)   |
| ---------------------- | --- | ------ | ----- |
| Less than 3 hearings   | 27  | 27     | ( 53) |
| 3 - 5 hearings         | 33  | 61     | ( 65) |
| 6 - 10 hearings        | 35  | 96     | ( 69) |
| More than 10 hearings  | 4   | 100    | ( 8)  |
| Total                  | 100 |        | (195) |

As one can see, the number of hearings performed by the lawyers is quite substantial (73% of the cases have three or more hearings) and this despite the fact that we have only considered cases with a comparatively short duration. The distribution does not vary substantially if we analyse the same item with reference to whether the disputes have been initiated by local or foreign plaintiffs, but they are, as one could expect, directly related to the duration of the proceeding.

Because of the above, the number of hearings has to be considered mainly as an indicator of the heteronomous guidance of the cases on the part of lawyers, rather than as a sign of slowness of the judges, although judges' workloads might be decisive as far as the overall duration of the dispute is concerned. This suggests that the number of hearings is also related to the lawyers' performance outside the court. In fact, if it is true that hearings mark the time of the formal-legal enhancement of procedure, they also mark the time of the informal and semiofficial steps that lawyers are able to set up before and after their interaction in court. Consequently the number of hearings, in itself, is not a mere sign of the technical (formal-legal) difficulty of a case, but rather a synthetic indicator of the space-time interactional cleavages and reference points— complexity in cybernetic terms—that formal/informal and strategic/communicative ways of treating legal disputes can imply.

Thus, these data provide further support for the hypothesis of domestication, as the need to hire a local (correspondent) lawyer on the part of foreign parties presupposes a professional attitude by the same lawyer, which seems to be decisive in the overall dispute treatment.

### 3. Case Claims

The relationship between the type of claim and the type of law inherent to our cross-border cases was approached at a different level of enquiry. First, we looked at whether each dispute started with a conflict over jurisdiction, that is, with a procedural claim about law. As has been mentioned only 3.4% of files dealt with a claim of incorrect determination of Milano jurisdiction or put a jurisdictional clause to the fore.

A brief description of two of the six cases could further underline the point. In the first case the jurisdictional conflict concerned the passive legitimation to act on the part of a foreign company characterized by a complex nationality (seated in a country but ruled by foreign law). The legal issue concerned the notion of contract stipulation in Italy. The dispute was abandoned by both parties after five hearings. In the second case the jurisdictional conflict concerned the enforcement of a contractual clause. The dispute went on for about two years, and six hearings were held before the Civil Court of Milano formally recognized its own incompetence.

Significantly both files did not give evidence of any doctrinal quotation or legal argumentation requiring a particular study. In fact quotations of law, overall, were quite infrequent.

Table I–12: Frequencies of Questions of Fact and Questions
of Law Involved in the Proceedings
in Milano District Court Files (1988)

| Involved | % | (N) |
|---|---|---|
| Questions of fact | 60 | (102) |
| Questions of law | 6 | ( 10) |
| Both | 35 | ( 59) |
| Total | 100 | (171) |

What is striking here is not so much the low percentage (5.8%) of cross-border disputes about legal, doctrinal, or jurisprudential controversies, but that a total of 39.5% involved questions of law. This result contrasts with the findings in Hamburg and Bremen and New York, and this despite the large number of cases without formal resolution and the limitations of the data. It hints at a legal-cultural peculiarity, a ritually formalistic attitude of Italian lawyers to relate facts to norms more than in other legal cultures.

On the part of foreign and uniform law, the Italian picture is back to normal and conforms with the other studies. Only twelve cases mention foreign or international laws, conventions, treaties, doctrines, jurisprudence, and so on. As for the rest national (state) law dominates the whole scenario. Of these, treaties and conventions take the majority (8), while foreign law is even less important. Again the limitations of study are problematic, yet the evidence strongly suggests that these findings provide further support for the domestication hypothesis.

## D. Outcomes of the Cases

The last item of our study concerns the outcomes of the cases.

It has been previously noted that the duration of the case was correlated to the number of hearings. From a sociolegal perspective, in fact, hearings mark the time of the formal-legal enhancement of the acts of procedure, as well as the steps necessary to the socioinstitutional construction of a motivated dialogic understanding between the parties. With regard to the duration it is interesting to note that about 39% of the analysed files—only about one-fifth of all cases initiated in 1988—were completed within one year. In comparison to the findings in Hamburg and Bremen and in New York, this would once again emphasize the comparative length of Italian procedures.

Let us now turn our attention to the conclusion of the proceedings, namely, to the types of formal solution of the disputes.

### Table I–13: Concluding Acts in Milano District Court Files (1988)

| Concluding Acts | % | (N) |
|---|---|---|
| Sentence / Order | 35 | ( 67) |
| Failure / Voluntary withdrawal | 54 | (104) |
| Failure to appear | 11 | ( 21) |
| Total | 100 | (192) |

Before analysing these data a brief comment on two specific formal-legal features of Italian civil procedural law seems opportune. Italian civil procedural code states that court proceedings are carried out by a single judge up to the final decision, which is then made by a chamber of three judges. The *ratio juris* of setting up a chamber is not related to the technical difficulty of the prospective decision, but rather to the political opportunity of depersonalizing the legal responsibility of the decision-making process. Additionally, due to the jurisdictional competence of the court, decisions can vary in form and content. For this reason one finds various items concerning this matter in the questionnaire.

According to Italian law, court proceedings can also be concluded by the judge of the proceeding alone by means of a special decree (file archivation). By rule this happens in two cases. The first instance is when the judge formally ascertains that both parties failed to appear at the last two hearings (Art. 309 c.p.c.). In such circumstances, the parties' failure to appear is a mere formal device. In actual practice it implies that both parties have informally agreed for an undeclared voluntary withdrawal from the proceeding and the accomplishment of an undeclared out-of-court dispute settlement. Another case of archivation can be related to a formally declared out-of-court settlement, which prevents proper court decisions. Due to a normal recurrence of these last hypotheses in Italy, the questionnaire item was thus prepared accordingly, mentioning each possible outcome as a distinct topic.

Looking at Table I-13, one notices a neat prevalence (54.2%) of proceedings interrupted *ex* Art. 309 c.p.c., because of the parties' failure to appear (in actual practice, because of informal out-of-court settlements) and a high rate (10.9%) of abandoned disputes or court withdrawals. Whether this is generally true in cross-border disputes or a result of the limitations of the data cannot be determined. However, the figures are relatively comparable to official Italian statistics.

Table I-14: Total First Instance Proceedings — Civil Courts Within the Court of Appeal of Milano District

| Year | Registered during year | Closed by court decision | Closed without a Court Decision | | Pending suits at year end |
| | | | Out of court | Judge's mediation | |
|---|---|---|---|---|---|
| 1988 | 39,818 | 17,545 | 17,535 | 468 | 96,534 |
| 1989 | 44,414 | 19,435 | 19,435 | 336 | 102,534 |
| 1990 | 43,079 | 9,388 | 17,638 | 272 | 111,483 |
| 1991 | 47,178 | 11,038 | 20,045 | 280 | 121,313 |

Source: ISTAT

Table I–14 deals with first-level cases only (as in our research) and includes all the Tribunali within the jurisdiction of the Milano Court of Appeal. As one can see 39,818 files were registered in 1988: as 20,036 were registered in the Milano court only, about half (19,782) concern other courts located in the same region. At least those cases, which were part of the limited data set, confirm these figures. It seems that the authority of state law was invoked for its mere potential power of intimidation, in other words, as a mere pressure device in 64.1% of cases. Thus one can assume that the court proceeding was basically used as a contingent socio-technostructure.

We do not know how the other disputes were resolved, and there may be significant differences. A comparison between the results obtained by foreign and by Italian plaintiffs show substantial differences.

Table I–15: Concluding Acts Compared for Foreign and Italian Plaintiffs in Milano District Court Files (1988)

| | Plaintiff | | | | | |
|---|---|---|---|---|---|---|
| | Foreign | | Italian | | Total | |
| Concluding Act | % | (N) | % | (N) | % | (N) |
| Sentence/Order | 51 | (45) | 20 | (19) | 35 | ( 64) |
| Failure/Voluntary withdrawal | 41 | (36) | 68 | (66) | 55 | (102) |
| Failure to appear | 8 | ( 7) | 12 | (12) | 10 | ( 19) |
| Total        % | 48 | | 52 | | 100 | |
| (N) | | (88) | | (97) | | (185) |

Cases with foreign plaintiffs tend to be closed by a court sentence or a court order (51%) more than cases with Italian plaintiffs (20%). Thus a dependence of the formal result on procedural factors is likely. This prohibits further deliberations on the formal result as well as, unfortunately, on the question of winners and losers of the cases that were closed by formal sentence or order. The remaining numbers would be too small to be significant.

## IV. Concluding Remarks

One of the leading hypotheses of our research project is that in order to ascertain the actual nature of sociolegal relations in the international arena, it is essential to empirically focus on state legal systems. The data that have been presented and discussed in this study offer—we hope—a range of interesting unprecedented insights. As these insights provide a general meaning to the whole research project, we shall attempt to provide a few tentative interpretive-reflexive answers to the questions presented in the first part of this study: why do certain actors apply to state courts, and who are they?

A real jurisdictional choice about state court disputing reasonably arises in certain circumstances. Only to the extent that state law jurisdiction is not exclusive and compulsory can one really evaluate the pros and cons of a given legal setting. In these cases—given the number of obstacles at structural, functional, and cultural levels—the above questions, therefore, can also be put as follows: why are state courts (still) appealing to deal with in cross-border cases? What resources do they offer to parties involved in cross-border conflicts?

Our analysis suggests that the state court is mobilized according to attitudes, expectations, and strategies that imply a sort of contingency approach. The court setting is conceived not only as a sociotechnical frame of reference, but also as a somewhat democratic space, relatively closed by certain formal rules but relatively open to any prospective solution. Procedural norms are used as technical tools as well as temporal structures of communication. Substantive law is enhanced to ritualize the conflict, in order to assess a mutual convergence based on the most convenient award, not necessarily to obtain a formal-legal ought-to-be.

Such results are not really surprising. Advanced studies on dispute treatment have already outlined that court proceedings are to a large extent losing their formal-legal function: they are now increasingly set up as mere pressure devices. In particular scientific literature stresses that civil court judges are losing their traditional role as masters of the proceeding, as they are increasingly mobilized to perform, in the last instance, a mere notarial role, certifying solutions that have been made outside the court.[19] Needless to say, this might also be due to lawyers' opportunism about the transaction costs of the proceeding.[20] In fact it is well known that the

---

19 Herbert M. Kritzer, *Let's Make a Deal: Understanding the Negotiation Process in Ordinary Litigation* (Madison: University of Wisconsin Press, 1991); Valerio Pocar and Paola Ronfani, *Coniugi senza matrimonio. La convivenza nella società contemporanea* (Milano: Cortina, 1992).

20 Olson, 1992.

cultural gap between clients and legal professionals on the one hand and judges on the other, as far as out-of-court dynamics are concerned, further reduces the judges' role even in the cases in which he/she tries to act as a mere mediator. Last, but not least, legal experience indicates that state court decisions lacking efficient enforcement apparatuses—as in the case of the Italian legal system—dramatically erode symbolic and material appeals about formal court decisions.

These variables, however, just describe the surface of the matter. We argue that a civil court dispute is basically set up to create the premises and/or implement the chances to treat an otherwise problematic interaction. The problem, once again, does not concern so much the technicalities required by the given legal setting, rather it derives from the fact that social actors are distant and increasingly separated parties—even within the same place of origin. Functional, structural, and/or performative barriers, obstacles, and cleavages permeate, in fact, any social context at present, and only expert systems—as places for meaningful social encounters—can provide a substantial connection.

The data that have been gathered seem to give evidence that the above analytical framework holds true for cross-border court disputes in Milano. We also have found that it seems that both local and foreign parties were not directly oriented, by necessity, towards the maximization of a Paretian optimal individual solution—the formal rationale of a court decision—but rather to a Simonian bounded outcome, based on a satisfactory substantial result.[21] A result, it must be added that also seems rationally congruent with the limits and resources of the local sociolegal context, namely, the actual conditions of the Milano court organizational setting. Data about the frequency of voluntary withdrawals from the court by means of the failure to appear, therefore, should not be interpreted as indicators of misunderstandings, confusion, poor information, or lack of determination in pursuing the technical (formal-legal) aim of the dispute. Surely all these variables occurred due to the cultural distance between the parties. Yet their occurrence might indicate something different.

Once a positivistic approach to state law is abandoned, one might assume that truly strategic (programmed) courses of actions are constructed by rule throughout a continuum of (partial) decisions. In turn these decisions transform, from time to time and at

21    Simon, "From Substantive to Procedural Rationality".

each stage, the aims into means, to the point that negotiated, co-operative, often informal quasi-solutions are perceived as prefer-able to a strict formal, deterministic outcome.[22] In a contingent but relatively structured framework such a cross-border court dis-pute, the basic ability—and the major problem—of a party could be thus oriented, not towards the conditional devices of the pro-ceeding but rather towards the capacity to compel a distant and cognitively unstable counterpart to sit at the same table for a cer-tain length of time, notwithstanding the contingency of all the vari-ables involved.

In synthesis our findings suggest that cross-border court dis-putes appear plausible and socially adequate to certain social ac-tors not so much because of the potential coercive power of state law (which is too often a mere virtual reality), but because of its paradoxical transcendental-contextual—localized and localizing—implications. Here lies the hard core of state court disputes' technostructural and socioinstitutional complexity: the possibility to enhance a veritable litigotiation.[23]

Reflecting on the data that have been presented here, it is also possible to reach a reasonable approximation to this last question. In fact, if we consider the group of cases as an average qualitative sample, it is possible to hypothesize that the parties involved in our cross-border court disputes were/are effectively distant social agents: to a large extent, they had/have neither deep-rooted sociolegal interactions nor stable sociolegal contacts. In short they did/do not belong, as a rule, to a closed relational system or small community.

Because of this condition both the constitutive ambiguity of state law[24] and the maturity of court lawyering[25] could thus have

22    March and Olsen, "Ambiguity and Choice in Organization".

23    Galanter, "Worlds of Deals".

24    Eligio Resta, L'ambiguo diritto (Milano: Angeli, 1984).

25    Vittorio Olgiati, "Positive Law and Sociolegal Orders: An Op-erational Coupling for a European Sociology of Law", in On Complexity and Sociolegal Studies: Some European Examples, Oñati Proceedings, 14, ed. André-Jean Arnaud and Vittorio Olgiati (1993): 33–55; Vittorio Olgiati, "Assetto locale e posizionamento strategico: le questioni di fondo del professionalismo giuridico europeo", in Sociologia del diritto, 1st ed. (Milano: Angeli, 1993), 129–60; Vittorio Olgiati, "Il pluralismo giuridico come lotta per il diritto", in I diritti nascosti, ed. Alberto Giasanti and Guido Maggioni (a cura di) (Milano: Cortina, 1995), 71–104.

played, paradoxically, a positive role: throughout the structural and communicative potentials of state court they were somewhat able to normalize a relational distance[26]—or, if one prefers, a state of anomie[27]—otherwise problematic and immeasurable. These conclusive remarks seem to be supported, in particular, by the data concerning the frequency of file object and party status, which enlightened the role of state compulsory jurisdiction as a filter institution in mobilizing certain disputes. It could also be inferred by the data concerning the voluntary withdrawals from the proceedings, which enlighten the client-lawyer relationship with regards to the complexity of the dispute and the contingency of the court setting.

The counter-evidence of the above, in turn, is given by the current experience of nonstate court dispute systems: international cases are, by rule, treated according to a strict elective affinity. For each type of matter, type of actor, type of relation, and so on, there is a proper type of law, a special chamber, a particular procedure, to the point where relational norms[28] prevail, in the last instance, over any other normative device. The same counter-evidence also explains why the specialized legal press constantly warns certain social strata (for example, business people) already provided with local (extraterritorial) legal arrangements (such as *lex mercatoria*), about the (alleged) difficulty and uncertainty of cross-border state court disputes.

In short it seems that a specific trait of state courts, in contemporary Western society, is that they permit the construction of closed/open sociolegal interactions for parties otherwise lacking self-regulatory communicative standards and infrastructures.

Thus if the primary issue in crossing boundaries is the need to reassess the space-time nexus, the particular mix of functional and

26    John Griffiths, "The Division of Labour in Social Control", in *Towards a General Theory of Social Control*, ed. Donald Black (Academic Press, 1984).

27    Volkmar Gessner and Angelika Schade, "Conflicts of Culture in Cross-border Legal Relations: The Conception of a Research Topic in the Sociology of Law", in *Theory, Culture & Society* 7, (1990), 253–77.

28    Ian MacNeil, "The Many Features of Contracts", in *Southern California Law Review* 47 (1974): 691–816.

territorial nature of state law is far from becoming marginal in overall prospective international relations.

## Abstract

The escape from state court disputes involving transnational issues has been an ongoing theme of discussion in the last decade. In the meantime, however, a number of international conventions and agreements have been enacted at official levels precisely to regulate and foster cross-border conflicts' settlement at the state court level.

The intertwining of these opposite trends therefore raises a number of questions about the type of parties, the type of case, and the type of proceeding concerning the topic.

The study tries to answer these questions by focusing on the results of an empirical survey carried out on cross-border disputes in Italy. More precisely it deals with the universe of cases—each one involving at least one foreign (non-Italian) party—registered throughout 1988 and archived by May-June 1993 at the central Chancellery of the Civil Court of Milano. The neologism litigotiation that summarizes the results of the files' analysis also gives evidence of the main theoretical premises and conclusive remarks of the research as a whole. Given the high number of informal out-of-court settlements and voluntary withdrawals from official decision-making, the study suggests, in fact, that—at least in the Milano court—cross-border cases are treated according to a veritable contingency approach. Court setting and proceedings are conceived as a sociotechnical frame of reference, but also and above all as a space-time communicative context that realizes a mutual convergence among parties otherwise lacking stable relationships and self-regulatory infrastructures.

## The Author

Vittorio Olgiati. Lawyer. Researcher at the Faculty of Law, University of Milan. Currently Reader on Sociology of Organization, Faculty of Sociology, University of Urbino, and Sociology of Law, Faculty of Law, University of Macerata, Italy. Extensive writings on sociolegal issues and legal professionalism.

Address: Istituto di Filosofia e Sociologia del Diritto, Via Festa del Perdono 7, 20122 Milano, Italy.

# 5 Italian Civil Procedure from a Foreign Party's Perspective

ENZO L. VIAL

## I. Introduction

The difficulties of the cross-border legal procedures studied by Vittorio Olgiati must be considered against the background of national procedural law and the legal and judicial culture. Accordingly the objective of this chapter is to present the legal and practical peculiarities of Italian civil procedure as addition to the analysis of files of the District Court of Milano. Because the largest group of foreign plaintiffs and defendants in the analysed procedures at the District Court of Milano represents German parties, it seems reasonable to examine the peculiarities of Italian civil procedure from the point of view of a German legal practitioner.

For the purpose of this study and in order to become acquainted with the Italian legal and judicial culture, participant observations were conducted for one month in 1995 in Padua, Italy. In addition to studies in civil and procedural law, this participant observation consisted mainly of a stay at a civil-law-oriented law firm in Padua, where the author attended hearings in court, held discussions with clients, and processed files. This work was accompanied by numerous interviews and discussions with lawyers, judges, and social scientists in Padua, Venice, and Milano.

## II. The Civil Procedure in Italy

### A. Initial Problems

By pointing to the unpredictability of judicature and the lengthy duration of procedures, juridical literature for practitioners warns all foreigners against litigating in Italy.[1] In a particular

---

1    Alberto Cristanelli and Hans-Jürgen Zahorka, *Beitreibung und Zwangsvollstreckung von Forderungen in Italien* (Sindelfingen: Libertas, 1991), 6.

case, which had been pending in Italy, the German Federal High Court held a second action to be admissible in Germany.[2] This decision stands in contradiction to a general rule of German procedural law, which provides that a procedure already pending elsewhere serves as a bar to the institution of a second proceeding by any of the parties involved (§ 261 Section 3 Number 1 of the German Code of Civil Procedure). The court reasoned that the duration of Italian civil procedure effectively denied the plaintiff his constitutional right of access to court and legal remedies.

This serves to demonstrate that, from the German participants' point of view, the Italian civil procedure obviously has a reputation of being rather ineffective and offers, particularly for foreign plaintiffs, little promise of success.

Under the concept of "litigotiation" Olgiati describes his hypothesis that the Italian civil suit possibly does not serve the solution of legal controversies as a technical instrument but as a framework, offering the parties various options of settling their differences. Is it possible that such criticism by German practitioners emerges from the fact that this way of solving problems remains closed to them? Does the Italian civil procedure, due to its practical formation, constitute a social rather than a technical means of solving conflicts, and do foreign parties possibly fail for this reason?

## B. The Procedure at the *Tribunale*

### 1. *Legal Framework*

Recently the Italian legislation subjected the civil procedural law to a comprehensive reform. The aim of this reform was to shorten the duration of procedures and to reduce the backlog of pending civil procedures.[3] As the files examined by the Milano analysis were registered in the year 1988, which is to say, before the reform occurred, the procedure will be presented here first in the version

---

2    BGH NJW 1983, 1269.
3    Law No. 353 of 26 November 1990 and No. 374 of 29 November 1991; for further details, see Virgilio Andrioli, "Sulla Riforma del Processo Civile", *Rivista di Diritto Civile* 37, 2 (1991): 217ff.; Peter Winkler, "Die Reform des italienischen Zivilprozeßrechts", *Jahrbuch für Italienisches Recht* 6 (1993): 137ff.

which was in force at the time. The most important changes subsequent to the reform will be presented later.

In 1988 the Italian Code of Civil Procedure (codice di procedura civile - c.p.c.) provided three courts for first instance claims:[4]
- the Justice of the Peace *(conciliatore)*;
- the Inferior Court *(pretura)*; and
- the Superior Court *(tribunale)*.

*a. Justice of the Peace (conciliatore)*     The *conciliatore* has jurisdiction over small claims and does not require the parties to be represented by a lawyer. According to Art. 7 c.p.c. (prior version) the *conciliatore* is competent for disputes about movable goods having a value of not more than one million lire, unless there is a special assignment to another court. In addition the *conciliatore* has exclusive jurisdiction over some special types of claims.

*b. Inferior Court (pretura)*     For claims with a value from one million up to five million lire, the *pretura* has jurisdiction, notwithstanding any exclusive jurisdiction of the *conciliatore*.[5] Regardless of the value in dispute, the *pretura* also has jurisdiction over different real estate matters. In addition the *pretura* is exclusively competent for labour disputes (Art. 409, 413 c.p.c).

*c. Superior Court (tribunale)*     The *tribunale* is competent for all disputes that do not fall under the jurisdiction of the *conciliatore* or *pretura,* in other words, all claims of a value exceeding five million lire or where the value cannot be determined.[6] The *tribunale* also has jurisdiction over family disputes and disputes about personal status, fiscal injury, civil rights, and forgery.

Finally, the *tribunale* serves as an appellate court for the *pretura* and *conciliatore* if the lower courts' decisions are not based on principles of equity, explaining why a number of disputes, which in first instance fall under the jurisdiction of the *conciliatore* or

---

4     See Cristanelli and Zahorka, *Beitreibung und Zwangsvollstreckung von Forderungen in Italien,* chapter 2.

5     Art. 8 c.p.c. (prior version); Elio Fazzalari, "La Giustizia Civile in Italia", in *La Giustizia Civile nei Paesi Comunitari,* ed. Elio Fazzalari (Padova: Cedam, 1994), 258.

6     Art. 9 c.p.c. (prior version).

*pretore,* have been found among the researched files of the *tribunale.*

*d. Venue*        Under Art. 18 c.p.c. a claim falls under the jurisdiction of the court in the district in which the defendant has his residence or domicile. Alternatively, if the defendant's residence is unknown or abroad, the court is competent in the district in which the plaintiff has his residence.

## 2. Judicial Proceedings in Practice

According to the observations made the procedure is carried out entirely in writing, being based on numerous individual dates for the hearing *(udienza).*[7] The lawyers of both parties appear in the office of the examining judge for the hearing. An obligatory appearance of the parties themselves only exists in exceptional cases, by special order of the court.[8] The lawyers of both parties confirm their due appearance by written entry into the official file on display there and, also by entry into the file, submit their respective motions. Thereafter the file is presented to the judge for a decision and generally he will immediately decide on the motions and assign the next date for the hearing. The first impression of these hearings is one of total chaos. The first thing one notices is that the hearing itself generally lasts only a few minutes, as only one individual motion is processed at a time. Within a few hours per day, one judge will perform up to 50 hearings of this nature. As many hearings are assigned simultaneously, the effect is that up to ten or twenty lawyers rummage in the judge's office, looking for the lawyer of the opposing party (often by calling aloud), rooting through the open pile of official files for their process, or shoving in front of the judge's writing desk in order to present their file with the enclosed motions for his decision. Not altogether wrongly, these hearings have been jokingly referred to as "mercato" (market) by the lawyers themselves.

---

7        For a summary of the proceeding at the *tribunale,* Elio Fazzalari, "La Giustizia Civile in Italia", 262ff.; Angela Krages and Nicoletta Contardi, "Der Zivilprozeß in Italien", in *Deutsche Unternehmen in Italien,* ed. Henning von Boehmer (Stuttgart: Schäffer-Poeschel, 1993), Chapter 2.3.

8        See Art. 117 c.p.c.

During the research period the author never observed a thorough discussion of the issue taking place; if there was anything unclear, some queries would possibly be made and the problem would be briefly discussed. Only when problems are more complicated will the judge reserve to adjourn his decision and not pass it until thorough examination. In such cases he also has the option to appeal to a panel of three judges for a judgement on the motion (also see Olgiati, chapter 4). Another possibility is to adjourn the hearing to another date when the issue would be discussed with the parties at greater length.

At the end of this hearing of evidence extending over many days of appearance, the pleadings will be specified at the hearing for putting final motions *(precisazione delle conclusioni)* and will be enclosed into the official file. With this hearing the judge terminates the hearing of evidence and assigns a date for the final hearing *(udienza di discussione,* Art. 275 c.p.c. et seq.—prior version). The waiting times for the final hearing that were observed extended from two to four years (the work overload being cited as the reason for this delay). During this time the judge presents the case for judgement to the panel of three before which the final hearing will take place. Art. 275 et seq. c.p.c. (prior version) provide that the case shall be discussed once more at this final hearing. However, contrary to this regulation, in practice arguments rarely take place: if one party does not specifically register the need for a discussion, the hearing will generally be limited to the pronouncement of the judgement. Subsequently, the judgement is deposited by the judges at the court registry and the judgement clause is served on the counsels. Not until the judgement has been registered, following an application submitted by the victorious party, may the complete text be served on the parties.

The unusualness of this procedural structure for German and many other European participants emerges by comparing it with the German civil procedure: the German Code of Civil Procedure provides that at the court hearing the parties will first be heard, directly followed by the taking of evidence and the discussion with the parties (§ 278 of the German Code of Civil Procedure). If at all possible the pronouncement of judgement, too, occurs at the same date as the hearing (§§ 310, 311 of the German Code of Civil Procedure). In Italy, on the other hand, no verbal discussions of the case take place during a hearing. The framework of the hearing alone would hamper any profound entering into the case or its verbal discussion. Consequently the procedure merely forms a framework leading to the option of filing numerous written motions and of rendering judgement.

A further peculiarity consists in the possibility that the evidence may in fact be dragged on to an unlimited length, as the parties are entitled to file any number of motions.

On being questioned about the average number of hearings for any given civil procedure at the *tribunale*, lawyers stated that twenty hearings would be a realistic value. Each hearing at the *pretore* leads to a time loss of about two months and at the *tribunale* of four to eight months with the consequence that a simple civil lawsuit takes up to several years to finish evidence proceedings.

Furthermore the procedure also enables the lawyers to purposely delay the action indefinitely, as the parties can apply for an adjournment of the procedure *(rinvio)* at any given time. As long as the opposing party agrees, or does not contradict, the judge will grant such a motion. On being questioned several Italian lawyers stated that they indeed would be quite prepared to use a motion for adjournment as a tactical means for an action, in order to delay procedures, for example, to pressure the opposing party to come to a settlement or to conceal a temporary insolvency of the debtor sued. It was pointed out that the readiness to come to a settlement would depend on the individual situation of the creditor: if the latter was interested in a prompt solution of the case, a compromise would generally be offered to the opposing party to avoid a lengthy procedure.

On the basis of the procedural circumstances described and the multitude of hearing dates involved, a further peculiarity to be noted, finally, is that the constant presence of lawyers at court is indispensable during the procedure.

## C. The Reform of Civil Procedure

### 1. Legal Framework

The reforms of the civil procedure of 1990 and 1991 introduced in order to shorten the duration of civil cases have changed the jurisdiction of the various courts.[9]

The competence of the *conciliatore*, now called the *giudice di pace*, has been considerably extended. The highest value in dis-

9   Winkler, "Die Reform des italienischen Zivilprozeßrechts", 137.

pute concerning proceedings about movable cases was increased from one million to five million lire. In motor vehicle torts the *giudice di pace* is competent up to a value of 30 million lire.

In addition, the *giudice di pace* has jurisdiction over various cases that were previously brought before the *pretura,* such as condominium disputes.

Disputes about goods and real estate up to twenty million lire are allocated to the *pretore,* unless they do not come under the jurisdiction of the *giudice di pace* or the law allocates the dispute to another court.

The jurisdiction of the *tribunale* has not been changed. Nevertheless the *tribunale* is greatly relieved through the increase of the maximum values in dispute for *giudice di pace* and *pretura.*

*2. The Course of Procedures after the Reform*
In addition to the redistribution of jurisdiction described above, the reform of civil procedure also aims to limit considerably the number of hearings and the duration of procedures.

An important aspect here is that of the initial hearing at which the defendant must in the future present his entire defence strategy. In contrast to previous procedures, the appearance of the parties—including participants from abroad—is obligatory. By an examination of the parties, the judge is thus able to clarify the issues from the beginning, and he can limit the matter to its decisive aspects. During this initial hearing the parties may still amend or supplement their motions. By these means the subsequent taking of evidence is supposed to be limited to a few hearings.

After completion of the evidence and lodgement of the final motion, the judge decides whether he will adjudge the case as sole judge, or whether he will appeal to the panel. In the future, a decision by a sole judge is supposed to become the rule.[10] Finally, a final hearing will take place only on application by the parties. If the latter do not explicitly register a need for discussion, the judgement will be rendered and deposited in the official file without any further discussion with the parties.

### D. The Role of Lawyers and the Protest Against the Reform

On 1 May 1995 the Italian bar stated their opinion on the planned enforcement of the reform of civil procedure and on the

10    Art. 43 legge sull ordinamento giudiziaro.

establishing of *guidice di pace* and called on the lawyers to raise a
national protest against the enforcement of these regulations.[11] In
detail, the lawyers criticized in their call that the structural and
personal conditions for establishing *guidici di pace* are not even
rudimentarily present; that the conditions for enforcing the reform of civil procedure are not given; and that the planned enforcement of the reform would bring the already impaired civil
jurisdiction process to a total collapse. According to the bar it
would be "foolhardy" to believe that the planned enforcement of
the reform would be suitable for overcoming the backlog of
2,600,000 pending civil procedures. The bar also pointed out the
consequences for the citizens affected, whose rights they have to
safeguard, and called on the Italian lawyers to boycott all current
procedures for two weeks. In practice this boycott—similar to a
strike—meant that the lawyers of both parties in dispute would
appear on the scheduled day of hearing, but, instead of filing motions to receive evidence, they would mutually apply for a postponement of the hearing.

This call, as well as the fact that the lawyers followed it almost
unanimously, illustrates the attitude of the bar vis-à-vis the judiciary: for reasons of their personal and professional deficiencies alone,
the judicial authorities are met with considerable distrust; the cause
of the inefficiency of Italian civil jurisdiction is not regarded primarily as a problem of its procedural law but as one of its structure. This criticism is not unjustified. The condition of the Italian
administration, of which the judiciary is a part, has recently been
investigated by the Italian Ministry of Public Service, showing that
the inefficiency of public administration costs the Italian taxpayer
several billion dollars annually. Even the processing of simple applications takes an average of six months.

These efforts by the bar to influence the civil procedure leads
to the assumption that the lawyers regard themselves as protago-
nists of the procedure not only on a political level but also for
individual lawsuits. As has been described, the course of the procedure is largely determined by the number and the content of the
motions, which are filed by both parties. Although the judge decides in accordance with the procedural law previously in force,

---

11    This declaration was made at the special meeting of the delegates
      of the Italian bar association on 22 April 1995.

he is bound to the motions filed by the parties. Consequently he has in practice very little influence on the course of the procedure. In practice the judge only rarely makes suggestions for a solution or compromise, and he is not able to speed up the procedure. This means that the number of hearings involved, and, therefore, the duration of the procedure, is determined exclusively by the lawyers. The possibility of delaying the procedure, or bringing it to a standstill by a motion for postponement, is lastly an expression of this influence. The thesis that lawyers play a dominant role in civil procedures is reinforced by a practical observation: lawyers regard their contact with each other as an important part of their work; much time is used at court for corridor talks and side discussions of the hearings. A lawyer who was questioned about this practice considered this communication more important than the close contact with his client or a discussion with the judge. Any suggestion for a compromise, any offer for a settlement, or questions on procedural tactics are, if possible, discussed directly with the opposing lawyer. Characteristic of this attitude is the following statement made by a lawyer: he would only speak to his client in order to obtain the basic information from him. After this, he would do "his own thing"; when planning his procedural strategy the client would only interfere with his amateur opinions. Through the multitude of hearings and the constant presence of lawyers at court in connection with it, the outer structure is established here, too, in order to ensure a constant flow of information among lawyers.

It becomes clear how the legal structure of the procedure and the legal and cultural identity of the participants are connected with one another: the organization of civil procedure constituted by procedural law and accompanied by many hearings and little room for discussion in the presence of the judge favours the largely independent working method of lawyers. Or, to return to Olgiati's picture of litigotiation: the legal organization of civil procedure produces the structure for informal ways of settling disputes.

If this assumption is correct, a further explanation for the vehement protest of the lawyers against the enforcement of the reform emerges: a successful realization of the reform, which would lead to an obligatory attendance of the parties at the judicial hearing and to reinforced conciliatory proposals by the judge, would reduce their power in this area and would at least limit their role as the central figure of the procedure. The well-greased system of litigotiation would be thrown out of balance by the new regulations of civil procedural reform.

Such a functionalization of the procedure would finally explain, too, the distrust of German participants towards the Italian procedure. A foreigner, by his different cultural understanding, his lack of presence at the place of action, and his missing insight into the negotiating structures, will inevitably be confronted with significant problems when he asserts a claim in Italy.

## III. Particularities in Cross-Border Procedures

### A. Choice of Venue

Olgiati describes that, as a result of the legal rules of procedure (by the Brussels Convention, in particular) in international procedures, a majority of foreign plaintiffs were to be expected, whereas the individual plaintiff himself, on the basis of practical considerations, would rather endeavour to sue at his native place of residence.

This poses a question as to the practical ramifications and the extent to which the latter stand in contradiction to the pertinent procedural regulations.

#### 1. *Legal Framework*
*a. Competences Regarding Italian Civil Procedural Law*        Notwithstanding the jurisdiction of the court, where no distinction is made between Italians and foreigners or between the plaintiff's residence or domicile regarding the legal capacity to act as a plaintiff before Italian courts,[12] Italian law distinguishes between foreign and Italian nationals as regards the ability of the same to be sued in Italy: foreign citizens may be sued in Italy only in certain cases specified under Art. 4 c.p.c.[13]

---

12    Giuseppe Campeis and Arrigo De Pauli, *La Procedura Civile Internazionale* (Padova: Cedam, 1991), 29.
13    These cases are:
       • if he has a place of residence or is domiciled in Italy;
       • if he has formally elected a representative in Italy, who is legally able to act in court; or
       • if he formally accepts the Italian jurisdiction; and
       • unless the claim concerns real estate located abroad.
       Foreign citizens can also be summoned before an Italian court, or

According to Art. 2 c.p.c., the parties can derogate Italian jurisdiction in favour of a foreign jurisdiction only by written agreement, if the claim is about an obligation, and if the parties are either both foreigners or a foreigner and an Italian, the latter having his place of residence abroad.

*b. Competences Pursuant to the Brussels Convention*    In lawsuits in which the foreign party has his place of residence in a member state of the Brussels Convention,[14] Italian procedural rules are accordingly replaced. The application of Art. 2 and 4 c.p.c. is expressly excluded by the convention. Rather the convention provides for the defendant's place of residence as the principal place of jurisdiction (Art. 2 of the convention). Furthermore, the convention provides various cases in which a jurisdiction can be established against the rules of national procedural law. Here it is of interest that, according to Art. 17 and contrary to Art.2 c.p.c., the parties may generally select the jurisdiction of any member state by written agreement.

*2. Practical Problems*
*a. Criteria for the Choice of Venue*    The comparison of legal principles with the practical considerations of lawyers has shown that a lack of practice of the actors involved and an increased

- if the claim concerns goods located in Italy, cautionary proceedings that have to be enforced in Italy, mortis causa of an Italian citizen, or testamentary succession in Italy;
- if the claim is connected with another lawsuit pending before an Italian court, or concerns cautionary proceedings that have to be enforced in Italy or legal relationships which come under the jurisdiction of an Italian judge.

Finally, Art. 4 c.p.c. contains a reciprocity clause providing that Italian courts entertain any claims against foreign citizens in circumstances where the courts of the foreigners' countries could deal with the same claims made against Italian citizens.

14    *Convention on Jurisdiction and the Enforcement of Judgements in Civil and Commercial Matters* of 27 September 1968 (law no. 804 of 21 June 1971; law no. 756 of 1 October 1984; law no.745 of 29 November 1990).

distrust of foreign procedural parties may be important factors in the choice of forum and in the outcome of the procedure.

The problems of Italian civil jurisdiction described above would lead one to assume, at first, that a plaintiff would avoid taking legal action in Italy if possible. When questioned about this, Italian as well as German lawyers stated that, above all, one reason not to sue in Italy was indeed the long duration of Italian procedures.

However, as far as Italian lawyers are concerned, these statements must be modified to the effect that they would only apply to those lawyers, who themselves possess a respective command of language and of practical experience in cross-border disputes. An inquiry held among several lawyers inexperienced in this area showed that on no account would they venture into a procedure abroad. It must be taken into consideration that the majority of Italian law firms, as always, are characterized by the personality of the individual lawyer, whereas law firms of the U.S. pattern and large law firms with international experience and constant connections abroad are the exception.[15]

One lawyer with international experience, on the other hand, pointed out a problem that he called the "home advantage of the plaintiff": according to which judges in most countries usually privilege the native party. Henceforth, if the issue was in dispute, an action abroad would always be more risky. Independent of whether such an attitude of "hostility to foreigners" by the courts can indeed be verified by empirical data, it is notable that practitioners take this attitude for granted, which would at least present a direct barrier to cross-border litigation.

*b. Additional Costs of Procedures Across National Boundaries*      A further criterion in the choice of venue may be the question of costs: the Italian regulation of fees enables the lawyer to assess his fees, according to the value of business, between minimum and maximum amounts, which are to be determined in accordance with the regulation.

---

15      See Gerardo Broggini, "Europäische Dienstleistungsfreiheit auf dem Gebiet der rechtsberatenden Berufe (Rechtsanwälte): Situation in Italien", in *Jahrbuch für Italienisches Recht* 4 (1991): 149ff.

In cases of particular complexity or importance, the Bar Council grants the lawyer fees in excess of those provided by the regulation. In addition the lawyer has the possibility of exhausting the scope of fees at his discretion, in any given case. As has been stated few specialized lawyers exist on the international level in Italy.

As a result of less competition, therefore, it is possible to charge higher fees right from the start. When asked, lawyers working in this field admitted that this was indeed current practice. Consequently it automatically becomes a question of costs to find a lawyer who is prepared and competent to conduct a procedure abroad.

On top of these fees there are further additional costs, such as for translations, services, and increased costs of communication.

*c. Correspondence Lawyers*      A further factor to be observed with international procedures, which also may contribute to an increase in costs, is the need for a second lawyer residing at the place of jurisdiction.

In Italy this problem first arises both for domestic procedures as well as for cross-border disputes. If an Italian lawyer wants to bring an action at a different domicile than home, he needs a local lawyer, for at the *tribunale* the parties must be represented by a lawyer who is enrolled in the register of the respective *tribunale*.[16]

The opinion is also held that in those cases in which this legal prerequisite does not exist (which is to say, when no procedural acts are to be performed) a lawyer who is not acquainted with the local rites and social structures will always call for a local cocounsel.[17] Lawyers who were asked confirmed that within the limits of Italy they would always consult a lawyer residing at the forum.

For cross-border disputes the foreign party needs a correspondence lawyer as well, as foreign lawyers are not generally admitted to practice in Italian courts.[18] A condition for admission to practice, among others, is Italian citizenship or a place of residence in

16   Art. 82 c.p.c. in connection with law no. 1578 of 27 November 1933.

17   Gerardo Broggini, "Europäische Dienstleistungsfreiheit auf dem Gebiet der rechtsberatenden Berufe (Rechtsanwälte)", 150.

18   For special rules regarding lawyers of the EU member states, see law no. 9 of 9 February 1982.

Italy.[19] This system of correspondence lawyers leads to additional costs on the international level.

On the domestic level the initiating lawyer draws his written pleadings and transmits it to the correspondence lawyer at the place of jurisdiction. The latter will then submit the completed written pleadings under his letterhead to the court, without any further treatment.

On the international level, on the other hand, the rule is that the matter is always processed, once again, by the lawyer at the place of jurisdiction, and that the written pleadings are drawn by the latter, himself. Even in cases in which the initiating lawyer has a sufficient command of the language and the law of the place of jurisdiction, it is not customary that the correspondence lawyer would adopt the written pleadings of his foreign colleague. Consequently the result is that for cross-border disputes one more fee arises for each written pleading. In comparison to domestic disputes cases, an increase in costs must be expected.

A further problem that may arise is that the initiating lawyer, as a rule, will revert to a correspondence lawyer whom he knows and trusts due to a long-term relationship. However, the latter will not inevitably reside at the place of jurisdiction. The consequence is that the foreign correspondence lawyer will have to consult cocounsel at the forum so that three lawyers may now be involved in the procedure. Given the case, finally, that the lawyer engaged by the client does himself not entertain any contact with any foreign lawyers, it is conceivable that he may first engage a colleague at home, who then passes on the case to the foreign colleague. In such an event, four lawyers may even be engaged in the case, as well as a respective increase of costs.

*d. Summary*     The results of the analysis of files by Olgiati and Gessner indicate that many plaintiffs are discouraged from suing abroad because of the practical difficulties involved. The interviews and observations made in practice support the assumption that in this area there are, quite obviously, problems that might play a decisive role in the choice of forum.

19     Law no. 1578 of 27 November 1933.

## B. Recognition and Enforcement of Foreign Judgements

The possibility of having a judgement recognized or enforced in Italy may be an important reason for the choice of the place of jurisdiction or for conducting a procedure. One lawyer stated that the question of how complicated a recognition procedure or the enforcement of a judgement is might well decide the choice of the place of jurisdiction in a particular case.

### 1. Legal Framework

*a. The Procedure of Enforcement*    The enforcement requires the existence of an executory title.[20] According to Art. 474 c.p.c. various legal and nonlegal documents can be recognized as executory titles, such as judgements and orders, which by law are expressly granted executory force.[21] In order for an Italian judgement to be enforceable, it must be endorsed with the executory formula by the court. Judgements are directly declared provisionally enforceable by the court upon application by the creditor. After the reform of the civil procedure the general rule is that a first instance judgement will generally be provisionally enforceable (Art. 282 c.p.c.).[22]

Under Art. 479 et seq. c.p.c., the creditor has to deliver a demand note *(precetto)* to the debtor before commencing an enforcement procedure. With the *precetto* he requires a set deadline. This note is a required step for the enforcement procedure. After delivery of the *precetto* and the enforceable title, the enforcement procedure can be commenced within 90 days after the expiration of the term set in the *precetto*.

---

20    See James Richardson, *Debt Recovery in Europe* (London: Blackstone Press, 1993), 84ff.; Cristanelli and Zahorka, *Beitreibung und Zwangsvollstreckung von Forderungen in Italien*, Chapter 3.

21    Richardson, *Debt Recovery in Europe*, 355.

22    See Andrioli, "Sulla Riforma del Processo Civile", 217; Richard Guy and Hugh Mercer, *Commercial Debt in Europe: Recovery and Remedies* (London: Longman, 1991), 109ff.

*b. The Recognition of Foreign Titles*        Under Italian law recognition and enforcement of a foreign title is achieved by a special
proceeding *(procedimento di delibazione).*[23] Art. 796 c.p.c. provides that the plaintiff has to obtain the recognition of a foreign
judgement by application and suit at the court of appeal *(corte
d'appello).*

The court of appeal reviews whether the foreign judgement
meets the requirements of Art. 797 c.p.c.[24] After this examination
the court recognizes the foreign judgement. In such cases the judgement is enforceable as an Italian judgement.

Applications under the Brussels Convention are also made to
the court of appeal (Art. 32 of the convention), but recognition is
provided without any further proceeding and without the process
of *delibazione,* described above.

## 2. Concerning the Practice of Recognition and Enforcement Procedures

As for the practical realization of these regulations, the practitioners questioned described the Italian appellate courts as working quickly and effectively. Concerning the competence, or the readiness to apply the Brussels Convention, none of the lawyers asked
had had bad experiences with the Italian courts. The recognition
of a foreign judgement would need about six to eight weeks. The
speedy dispatch of these procedures indicates that here the lawyers are obviously not offered any opportunity for litigotiation.

The system of correspondence lawyers—connected with the
additional costs for the second lawyer—has also established itself
for recognition and enforcement procedures. In accordance with
the regulations of the Brussels Convention, the recognition and
enforcement of a German judgement, for example, could be ap-

23    Campeis and De Pauli, *La Procedura Civile Internazionale,* 114.
      In particular, it examines whether
      • under Italian law, the foreign court had jurisdiction;
      • the defendant had adequate opportunity to be heard;
      • the judgement is final pursuant to the foreign law;
      • the judgement is not in conflict with an Italian decision or an
      anticipated decision in the same dispute; and
      • the judgement is not contrary to Italian public policy.
24    Edoardo Vitta and Franco Mosconi, *Corso di diritto internazionale
      privato e processuale* (Torino: UTET, 1994), Chapter 3.

plied for by a German lawyer without any problem. Astonishingly enough, however, this course of action is not customary. In Italy any motion on the recognition or enforcement of a foreign judgement is categorically filed by an Italian correspondence lawyer.

This leads one to assume that for the foreigner, who is less experienced in his dealings with the Italian administration anyway, the infrastructural problems of the Italian administration present a special burden and cause him additional difficulties in taking action in Italy. When looking at the reverse case, however, the same picture emerges. In legal practice an Italian lawyer, too, will always call in a German correspondence lawyer for enforcement in Germany. Practitioners call it "as good as impossible" for an Italian lawyer to directly engage the services of a German bailiff for an enforcement, as the distrust of the authorities towards a foreign applicant were too great.

One should note, therefore, that this distrust is not specifically a problem of the Italian administration of justice. At least as far as German-Italian legal relations are concerned and contrary to the wording and the spirit of the Brussels Convention, practice is a long way away from allowing a foreigner to take legal action in another state. Instead a system of correspondence lawyers has established itself. This system may be effective, but it increases the costs of procedures across national boundaries, and, with this, it relativizes the facilities that international conventions aim for.

Differences in the national legal system and in the application of law may also cause problems and misunderstandings when applying the Brussels Convention. The handling of sanctioning of noncompliance with time limits, for example, varies in different legal systems. In German procedural law, in the event of the defendant's failure to appear following an application filed by the plaintiff, the court may take this failure as admission of claim and render a judgement by default (§ 331 of the German Code of Civil Procedure). The Italian law, by comparison, does not know of any judgement by default; a failure to comply with the time limit may only be sanctioned by bar dates, so that the defaulting party can no longer plead. As a rule only a loss of time is caused by the default as a result of an adjournment of the hearing. For procedures across national boundaries the Italian lawyer is thus confronted with more severe sanctions by the German courts. In practice these differences can sometimes be decisive for a procedure.

## C. Summary Procedure

On evaluating the number of foreign plaintiffs in Italy, the possibility of recovering one's claim by means of a summary procedure must also be taken into consideration.

### 1. Legal Framework

A creditor who does not have an executable title can, instead of commencing a lawsuit, order payment (or delivery) within a summary procedure *(procedimento d'ingiunzione).*[25] The summary procedure can be utilized when the claim relies on written evidence or if the debt arises out of certain fees, rights, or reimbursements as specified by Art. 633 c.p.c. If the requirements are met, the court draws up a default (or delivery) order *(decreto ingiuntivo),* which will be delivered to the debtor without prior hearing.

Having received the order the debtor may file an opposition or objection, in which case, the procedure reverts into an ordinary civil lawsuit. If the debtor neither files an opposition nor pays the debt within twenty days, on application of the creditor the court can pronounce the order as enforceable. In this case the order becomes an executory title and may be enforced within the ordinary enforcement procedure.

While the summary procedure can be initiated by a foreign creditor, delivery of the *decreto ingiuntivo* abroad is explicitly excluded by Art. 633 c.p.c. Therefore the procedure is not available when a debtor has his place of residence outside Italy.

There is no special summary procedure in Italy for debts to be recovered from abroad; the respective foreign country's summary system alone can be applied.

### 2. Practical Significance

In the literature it is recommended to foreign creditors that, before commencing litigation, he should first attempt to enforce his claim by means of a summary procedure.[26] This is in accordance

---

25    See Cristanelli and Zahorka, *Beitreibung und Zwangsvollstreckung von Forderungen in Italien,* Chapter 4; Krages and Contardi, "Der Zivilprozeß in Italien", Chapter 3.1.

26    Cristanelli and Zahorka, *Beitreibung und Zwangsvollstreckung von Forderungen in Italien,* 6.

with the impression gained in Italy: as long as a claim can be supported, a judicial summary procedure will be preferred to an immediate action. Consequently many a claim will not even appear as a lawsuit in the court file registries. Nevertheless, clear evidence notwithstanding, the author observed a debtor filing an opposition against the default summons, thus provoking an action. As the lawyer of the suing party was able to disclose, the debtor happened to be insolvent. This particular case may serve as a confirmation of Olgiati's thesis of litigotiation: its purpose is to delay payment or lower it by means of an extrajudicial settlement. An Italian lawyers' proverb, which says that a lean settlement is better than a fat judgement is hereby also brought to mind.[27]

### IV. Summary

An inspection of the background of the procedural law in the analysis of files presented by Olgiati renders the following picture. The structure of civil procedure in Italy positively provides the conditions for the phenomenon of litigotiation described by Olgiati. The conduct of lawyers, as well as the observations of procedural practice, reinforce this finding.

However, a comparison of the regulations governing procedural law with those practical particularities that the author was able to observe, and which are a special consequence of cross-border procedures, leads to the assumption that considerations of tactics and of the costs of the proceedings must in practice play a large role. In addition to the empirical data examined, an inspection of the theoretical and practical problems involved would indicate that the particularities of law and culture exert a considerable influence on international procedural practice.

### Abstract

The problems of cross-border cases must be considered against the background of national procedural law and the relevant legal and judicial culture. Therefore, as an addition to the file analysis carried out by Vittorio Olgiati, the study presents the legal and practical peculiarities of Italian national and international civil procedure. The description of procedural law, influenced by the legal and cultural identity of the participants, confirms that the organization of civil procedure produces the structure for

27    Cristanelli and Zahorka, *Beitreibung und Zwangsvollstreckung von Forderungen in Italien*, 31.

informal ways of settling disputes as it is described by Olgiati, using the neologism litigotiation. This leads to the assumption that a foreigner who commences an action in Italy, by his different cultural understanding, by his lack of presence at Cristanelli and Zahorka, *Beitreibung und Zwangsvollstreckung von Forderungen in Italien*, 31, the place of action, and by his lack of insight into these negotiating structures, will inevitably be confronted with significant problems. The comparison of international procedural law with particularities of the Italian procedural practice explains the results of the Milano file analysis. Many plaintiffs may be discouraged from suing abroad because of the practical difficulties, for example, the duration of Italian civil procedure, the system of correspondent lawyers, additional costs in international disputes, and differences in the national legal system that cause problems and misunderstandings when applying international conventions. Therefore these characteristics of Italian law and culture have a considerable influence on cross-border disputes. Contrary to the wording and spirit of the international conventions, practice is far from allowing a foreigner to take legal action in Italy.

## The Author

Enzo L. Vial. Lawyer. Research Assistant at the Centre for European Law and Policy at the University of Bremen (ZERP). Prior work as an assistant in German and Italian law firms and in the German Consulate in Venice, Italy. Currently conducts research on German and Italian legal cultures as well as policy research for the European Commission.
*Address*: ZERP, Universitätsallee GW 1, 28359 Bremen, Germany.
*e-mail*: ENZOVIAL@ZERP.uni-bremen.de

# 6 The Role of Courts in Global Legal Interaction

HANNO VON FREYHOLD

VOLKMAR GESSNER

VITTORIO OLGIATI

Our concluding chapter will take up the assumption of structural and cultural differences between the domestic and international settings and will, in particular, attempt to answer the question of whether domestic courts are able to cope with the complexities and uncertainties of the global legal arena. The common goal of all three studies is not only to uncover legal problems and particularities of international litigation but also to take a position in the controversy about the role of law and of state courts in what may already be called a world society. They attempt a contribution to the understanding of institutions that may reduce the transaction costs of international exchanges.

## I. Quantitative Role of Courts in International Matters

Even taking into account the overrepresentation of international matters in our three German courts, it seems to be a cautious guess that every year approximately 10,000 cross-border complaints are litigated before German district courts *(Landgerichte)*. In addition, there are approximately 5,000 such disputes litigated before the family courts and an unknown number at the county courts *(Amtsgerichte)*, the labour courts, and in other branches of the judiciary. Because Italy shows a quite similar share of international matters in the Milano court *(tribunale)*, with an unknown number in other courts, and even the New York data lead to a similar picture, a projection regarding the number of international matters in the court caseload of industrialized societies may be permitted. Taking the fifteen member states of the European Union as an example, one would have more than 100,000 (and possibly even 200,000) international disputes entering the civil courts of first instance in Europe every year.

This number shows that courts are certainly not an insignificant institution in the international legal arena. On the other hand, our research so far does not allow us to describe or even to estimate the *relative* share of litigation in international dispute resolution. Despite the seemingly high number of court cases, it may well be that even more disputes are taken to arbitration, mediation, or other alternative dispute resolution mechanisms created by international or national trade institutions. It is also possible, and even probable, that more international than national actors give up early in pursuing a claim due to time and cost considerations. This is certainly true for consumers and for creditors of maintenance claims who get less support by autonomous structures for a cross-border dispute than trade actors.

Regarding the characteristics of the cases taken to court, our data indicate the rather marginal role of courts in complex and—in terms of money—important disputes. Their number was extremely low in the files of all three jurisdictions. The assumed uncertainty of cross-border litigation is—if not for all international matters—probably decisive for this kind of case, where actors are more deterred by the risk of unpredictable third party intervention than in minor cases. If it is true that complex and important disputes are frequent in international trade the *lex mercatoria* promoters so far are right in attributing little relevance to judicial decisions in global legal interaction.

On the other hand, smaller cross-border claims also need to be enforced, and domestic courts do not seem to create too many problems of access as regards jurisdiction, legal representation, and judicial costs.

## II. Judicial Reasoning in International Matters

As regards the way international disputes are decided in court, one obstacle may be found in the fact that the judges assigned to these matters are insufficiently accustomed to foreign legal cultures, and they can therefore not adequately consider the foreign or international aspects of the cases. Legal cultures consist of norms and behaviours. We have tested which of these legal-cultural elements of foreign legal cultures are acknowledged by German and U.S. judges when deciding international disputes.

### 1. Foreign Law

In Bremen and Hamburg as well as in New York, the application of foreign law to international disputes is comparatively rare: in 93% of the judgements the decision is based exclusively on domestic law.

Notably, as a matter of quality, it can be observed that, as far as foreign law is utilized for the reasoning of decisions in Germany, such reasoning is obviously made without any actual knowledge, without efforts of interpretation, without the interrogation of expert witnesses, and without the reception of applicable case law or literature. In New York, on the other hand, references to foreign statutes can be found as frequently as the discussion of foreign cases and legal literature. In seventeen of the 24 cases found, the foreign law was discussed extensively and, as far as can be determined in hindsight, was applied correctly. In any event this is true for a judgement in which German law had to be applied.

A closer view at the basis of these discussions provides insight into the reasons for the more skilful application of foreign law in New York judgements. At the beginning of the reasoning of a number of cases, one can find wordings such as the following:

> This action brought by an Italian corporation against a French corporation and involving parties from the United Kingdom and the United States, arises out of allegedly negligent acts occurring in Greece and causing an accident in international waters off the United States coast. The controversy is truly international in nature and hardly "localized" in any way.[1]

In fact, the phrase "truly international" is used quite frequently. Two conclusions can be drawn therefrom. First, it shows the importance of New York as a marketplace for international legal interactions, which also expresses itself by the presence of a large number of foreign corporations, by the activities of international law firms, and by the fact that there are certain areas of commerce in which New York law and jurisdiction are agreed to in contracts and *ad hoc*, even where the matter otherwise has no connection to New York.

Second, it shows the sensitivity of New York judges who realize that an international case is before them and treat the case accordingly in a special manner:

> [S]ensitivity to the interests of other jurisdictions is perhaps most compelling in the international arena.[2]

---

1    *Carbotrade SpA v. Bureau Veritas*, 1992 U.S. Dist. LEXIS 17689 (SDNY 1992).

2    *Golden Trade, S.r.L. et al. v. Lee Apparel Company et al.*, 143 F.R.D. 514 (SDNY 1992).

In addition the more competent application of foreign law may be caused by the fact that large firms, as well as some smaller boutique speciality firms, employ a not-insignificant number of foreign lawyers. For example, at least 37 New York law firms employ German lawyers. The importance of conflict of law is also enhanced by its potential application to interstate matters, as happened in three more cases of our 352 international judgements.

However, the most important reason for the more frequent and intensive discussion of foreign law probably lies in the fact that, in New York, foreign law—as is generally the case—is subject to presentation by the parties. Not the judge, *sua sponte* or *ex officio*, but the law firms, who have more time and resources, have to research, present, and prove foreign law:

> [T]his court is not mandated to take judicial notice of foreign law and may require testimony at a hearing. The extensive disagreement among the parties' experts as to the applicable French law, coupled with the experts' meagre citation of authority for their respective positions, necessitates a hearing to resolve the disputed issues of law.[3]

Before the court, in many cases, this is achieved by expert party witnesses, who may even argue before the court. In half of the cases in which foreign law was applied, the court based its decision on these experts. For example,

> [W]e are presented with affidavits from and testimony by two extraordinarily well qualified Bahamian attorneys: Sir Leonard Knowles for defendant and Michael R. Scott, Esq. for plaintiff.[4]

This effect of the presentation principle is increased by other factors. Particularly for law firms that have a foreign lawyer in-house, the research of foreign law creates a financial benefit. The fees, which are billed on an hourly basis in most commercial disputes, allows them to directly profit from any in-house research. The presence of lawyers who are able to summarily predetermine the content of foreign law causes a higher probability for the proposition of foreign law, where it is of advantage for the respective party even where the final expertise and presentation is made by

---

3    *In Re Will of Reine-Marie Duysburgh*, 154 Misc. 2d 82; 584 N.Y.S.2d 516, (N.Y. Co. Surr. Ct. 1992), references omitted.

4    *Sundance Cruises Corp. et al. v. American Bureau of Shipping*, 799 F. Supp. 363, 1992 AMC 2946 (SDNY 1992).

foreign cocounsel. As far as financial benefits from the proposition of foreign law are concerned, where foreign law is of advantage for the respective party the profit incentive also exists in the case of a contingency fee schedule. Finally, the possibility that one side might present foreign law forces the other side to do the research as well.

In contrast a German lawyer who bills pursuant to the statutory fee schedule has basically no financial benefits from dealing with foreign law. Even where an hourly fee schedule is agreed upon, lacking in-house competence a summary investigation cannot be done and outside expert analysis is not profitable for the law firm itself. Lacking the possibility of a contingency fee, there is no direct profit from the results of the case. Finally, if the matter is handled carefully, the possibility of being held liable for not presenting foreign law is remote.

Yet even in New York the application and discussion of foreign law is not substantiated and qualified in all cases. In particular a difference can be observed with regard to the application of common law and civil law. With the former the court's discussion often concentrates on foreign case law that has been presented to the court in its original (English) language. The case law is analysed and applied to the matter before the court, sometimes even independently from the expert witnesses.

In two of the cases reviewed, even the application of foreign law was quite unusual: in the opinion of both expert witnesses, the law of the Bahamas applicable to one of the cases had no solution for a question that arose. The court helped itself by looking to an older British judgement. This judgement, in turn, had referred to a leading case from New York. Thereupon, and with this reasoning, the court applied New York law.

In the application of civil law, the courts had serious difficulties in four cases, apparently because the lawyers had also failed to provide substantial information and had not presented expert witnesses. In one case the result reads as follows:

> [T]he law of Venezuela applies . . . . [Plaintiff] does not dispute that Venezuela has no law of unfair competition (statutory or otherwise) . . . . Therefore, [Plaintiff's] unfair competition claim must be dismissed . . . for failure to state a claim upon which relief can be granted.

In all nine cases in which the application of common law was considered, the foreign law was discussed intensively. In seven cases foreign experts participated, five times foreign case law was analysed, and four times foreign statutes. In only one case was the foreign law not applied after all.

In the judgements in which civil law was to be applied, this was only discussed intensively in six out of the thirteen cases. In only four was it applied in the end. In three cases the foreign law was not expressly applied; in four cases it was only mentioned in passing. The basis of discussion in four cases were expert testimony, foreign statutes, and general statements, as the one cited above on the law of Venezuela.

An equivalent reluctance to bridge the gap between common law and civil law can also be observed in German courts. If foreign law is ever applied in the reasoning, it is usually the more familiar civil law. In 1988 common law was applied only two times in the district courts (Landgerichte) of Bremen and Hamburg (namely, the law of the Republic of South Africa and of Singapore, respectively).

## 2. Behaviour Abroad

The legal program of the judge concerned with international matters also assigns the task of considering foreign behaviours to a certain degree. In German law such (in a narrow sense of the word) legal-cultural considerations are indicated in the context of recognition of foreign judgements. The behaviour of and before the foreign court is to be tested in light of the German constitution; in addition, where mutuality is to be observed, the judicial practice also needs to be kept in mind. Another gateway is the right to a trial doctrine, allowing litigation in Germany to proceed despite parallel prior proceedings abroad or lack of German jurisdiction if the plaintiff cannot expect justice in the foreign court (due to extreme duration of proceedings, or desolate conditions of the foreign judicial system). Finally, many other behavioural aspects may come into the consideration of ordre public or public policy. However, in the case analysis at the district courts (Landgerichte) of Bremen and Hamburg, not one case was found in which a judgement or a party's brief reflected any such argument.

Again the New York international matters appear more open. Likewise public policy considerations as such do not play any role. In the aforementioned discussions the justice of a foreign law was never doubted by the court. Nevertheless, and in contrast to German law, New York law has one more gateway in the context of which respective discussions could be found. The relatively broad jurisdictional powers of New York courts are eased by the judges' discretionary power under the *forum non conveniens* doctrine, which a court allows to dismiss a case despite the existence of jurisdiction where another court that would have jurisdiction appears to be the more adequate forum with regard to the matter before the court. In at least 8% of the surveyed judgements, the defendant had made a motion to dismiss for *forum non conveniens*, which was successful in about half of the cases. In this situation the plaintiffs several times opposed the motion with arguments disputing the foreign courts' fairness or the justice of the other countries' legal system.

In fact some of the plaintiff's arguments seem absolutely plausible. In one case it was feared the Polish courts would be prejudiced in a libel action between the Polish Cardinal Glemp and the American Rabbi Weiss arising in the context of a highly political dispute about a nunnery on the Ausschwitz grounds. The same was alleged for the Israeli courts in a case involving high officials of the Bank of Israel after a parliamentary investigation commission had ended without results. Regarding an arbitration case in which arbitration in Moscow had been agreed on, the plaintiff moving for a change of venue was concerned about his personal security in Moscow shortly after the 1992 attempted coup d'état (this case did not, in fact, concern *forum non conveniens*). In a final case the extremely long duration of Mexican proceedings was noted.

Yet none of these quite serious arguments were successful. It appears that even the New York judges, who are more generous in the application of foreign law than German courts, are not willing to even sometimes deal with other cultural elements of foreign legal systems.

## III. Contribution of Domestic Courts to the Globalization of Law

According to our data courts provide only a very limited contribution to global integration. There is a swift glance across borders within the common law and also, moderately, in civil law regions of a common language such as Germany, Austria, and Switzerland. However, between these legal families there is no discussion whatsoever about the "right" law, and in the individual matter there is no chance for the foreign party to be judged pursuant to his/her own legal standards. It must also be doubted whether the proposals by the German *Rat für Internationales Privatrecht,* referring to a better international legal education of judges and the institution of chambers of special jurisdiction, can possibly impede the "homeward boundedness" of the judges.

In any event the model of the European Court of Justice cannot be established on a domestic level, due to the relatively sporadic occurrence of cross-border matters. Nevertheless this model shows what a court with international jurisdiction could ideally resemble. At the European Court the justices come from different member states of the European Community. The parties are represented by lawyers from their own country. The briefs (and the courts' questions in preliminary ruling procedures) are written in the respective language of the country, and the language of the procedure is adapted to the changing parties. One aspect has to be emphasized above all others: the court applies uniform European Law and not, as may happen to domestic courts, the law of Burkina Faso. The justices of the European Court are usually appointed in their capacity as experts in European Law, which they may even have developed in their prior activities as professors or at the court. A large number of cross-border contacts during their professional career has made them acquainted with the different legal cultures in Europe as well as with the slowly developing "European legal culture". Particularly when they decide in senates or in plenary session, they have considerable apprehension on regulatory policies and mechanisms in Europe, on styles of administration and decision-making, and on economic policies, business cultures, legal awareness, conflict orientations, and attitudes towards the state. All this is knowledge that is required for any act of judicial lawmaking but that also becomes part of the analysis and interpretation of law. Thus European law has been interpreted and developed by these justices with both foresight and consideration. All this combined explains the undisputed legitimacy of the European Court of Justice and its bearing for legal policy.

None of these multicultural elements can be found in domestic courts and, accordingly, they have considerable difficulty in adequately adjudicating international disputes. Through education, professional practice, and common knowledge, domestic judges have even more of this highly complex understanding, albeit only on elements of their own legal culture. Their legal-culturally induced preunderstanding allows the "anticipation of meaning"[5] or,

5    Josef Esser, *Vorverständnis und Methodenwahl in der Rechtsfindung*, (Frankfurt / Main: Athenäum, 1970).

in the language of the theory of science: "Hermeneutic understanding is the interpretation of texts on the basis of an already existing understanding, it leads to processes of generation of new knowledge based on already accomplished processes; it is a new step of socialization based on a socialization that has already taken place—as it appropriates tradition it continues tradition".[6] This hermeneutic circle of understanding social norms ends at the horizon of life experience of the judge—which, as a rule, is identical to the social and geographical limits of his own legal culture. Thus the language of foreign legal texts remains out of context and, making the problem even more serious, is combined with the judge's own prior understanding, leading almost inevitably to misinterpretation.

Some business branches such as the banking, insurance, and maritime industries evade the courts by self-regulation. Many trade organizations extend this trend of developing global communities by drafting standard contracts and establishing arbitration tribunals. Research on the costs and duration of arbitration procedures shows that these are not the elements making them attractive. Rather, they are selected for their expertise, namely, their knowledge of the particularities of the trade area under scrutiny. This indicates that the future of global legal culture seems to lie in processes of social differentiation and in the independence (autonomy) of globally acting areas of life possessing their own norms and forms of conflict resolution. The multinational enterprise is obviously the most extreme example of the "internalization" of cultural and legal differences. But business branches may also reach a high degree of global autonomy, as was brilliantly demonstrated by Bernstein in her study on the diamond trade.[7]

## IV. Domestic Courts and the Uncertainty of Cross-Border Exchanges

The attempts of nations, international organizations, and legal scholars to uphold the claim of law for universal authority, which largely abstracts from particularisms and which lies trans-

---

6      Jürgen Habermas, "Zur Logik der Sozialwissenschaften", *Philosophische Rundschau*, Beiheft 5 (1967): 157.

7      Lisa Bernstein, "Opting out of the Legal System: Extralegal Contractual Relations in the Diamond Industry", *Journal of Legal Studies* XXI (1992): 115–57.

verse to said differentiations through the creation of unified law
or at least by the approximation of laws, are essentially obstructed
by the legal-cultural constraints of domestic courts. This statement
holds true in spite of indicators that international matters are disposed of in court quite effectively.

As we have seen in our data the conflict resolution tasks of
courts are fulfilled in international cases in almost the same way
as in domestic cases. Unexpectedly there are few signs that foreign
parties have less chances to win their cases. The application of
domestic law does not seem to systematically prevent foreign parties from being successful. Although both parties may suffer from
considerable delays, such delay is either explained by mere technical problems of service of process, translations, and legitimations
of foreign documents or by autochthonous elements peculiar to
the entire caseload of the court. There do not seem to be major
legal or cultural barriers against international matters in general
or against foreign parties in particular.

Nevertheless state courts are far from securing the rule of law
in cross-border exchanges. In order to understand this argument,
one has to remember that courts, in addition to resolving conflicts
case by case, make other important contributions to social stabil-
ity and development, in particular by reducing the uncertainties
involved in human interaction. By legitimating some values and
behavioural patterns and sanctioning others, courts continuously
produce relatively stable orientations and expectations. This long-
established legal sociological knowledge is now one of the core
concepts in Douglass C. North's Institution Economics,[8] where
the formalization of constraints—as opposed to informal constraints—is taken as a key variable to explain economic performance in complex societies.

> More complex economic exchanges need reliable institutions that al-
> low individuals to engage in complex contracting with a minimum of
> uncertainty about whether the terms of the contract can be realized
> . . . . A coercive third-party enforcement is essential . . . . (It) is never
> ideal, never perfect, and the parties to exchange still devote immense
> resources to attempting to clientize exchange relationships. But nei-

8    Douglass C. North, *Institutions, Institutional Change and Eco-
     nomic Performance* (Cambridge, England: Cambridge University
     Press, 1990).

ther self-enforcement by parties nor trust can be completely success-ful. It is not that ideology or norms do not matter; they do and im-mense resources are devoted to attempting to promulgate codes of conduct. Equally, however, the returns on opportunism, cheating, and shirking rise in complex societies.[9]

Although cautious in ascertaining the efficiency of legal insti-tutions, North attributes the courts essential tasks in reducing the risks of economic exchanges. What he has in mind are domestic courts and domestic economic exchanges, but he seems to assume that the international economy has achieved a similar degree of legal institutionalization. A general pattern of exchange based on kinship ties, bonding, exchanging hostages, or merchant codes is found in the early development of long-distance and cross-cul-tural trade and the fairs of medieval Europe. In that period "the state was often an increasing source of insecurity and higher trans-action costs as it was protector and enforcer of property rights".[10]

Our data clearly indicate that domestic courts still do not pro-vide this institutional security for long-distance and cross-cultural trade, or for any other global legal interaction. If in most coun-tries—Italy being just one example that could easily be general-ized—a judicial decision of a case simply cannot be reached in a reasonable period of time; if the choice of law applied eventually in these decisions rarely follows the rules of private international law; if foreign law is mostly unknown to judges and if these judges prove to be unable to take foreign elements of the case into con-sideration when they decide on the basis of domestic law; if com-peting jurisdictions invite parties to "forum shop"; and if there is a risk that the claim has to be abandoned early for reasons of service of process or taking of evidence—if only one of these situ-ations occurs, then the "property rights" in international exchanges remain unprotected due to rational risk calculations. The claim will be abandoned or at best renegotiated.

Uncertainty and unpredictability in legal sociological and eco-nomic theory are elements of generalized expectation structures. These generalized expectation structures are not easily changed by the strategic behaviour of individual actors, like those few liti-gants of international cases whom we have been able to observe.

9   North, *Institutions*, 34–35.
10  North, *Institutions*, 35.

Some more or less successfully resolved conflicts only hide the fact that other—and probably many more—actors remained outside the unpredictable legal system. In order to create a generalized expectation structure of trust and predictability, a complex legal-cultural environment around the judicial process would have to be established. Domestic courts in some societies can rely on such a cultural environment, but they completely lack such a support structure in the "global marketplace". An adequate legal-cultural environment for an international civil procedure would require widespread information among judges, legal professionals, business actors, and so on about international rules and practices, the approximation of attitudes and behaviours by way of scientific and intellectual exchanges, and the worldwide creation of efficient judicial organization and support structures. This is, according to most theories of the world society, not what is expected to happen. They doubt that the history of the nation-state can simply be prolonged and extended in order to explain global developments. If, as they say, differentiation of life areas will be the future in the process of globalization, the building of institutions with universal tasks will hardly resolve the problem of the insecurity of global exchanges.

## Abstract

Domestic courts are quantitatively not an insignificant institution in the global arena—in the European member states alone some one hundred to two hundred international cases are filed annually in civil first instance courts. But possibly even more international disputes are taken to arbitration, mediation, or other alternative dispute resolution mechanisms. It is also possible, and even probable, that more international than national actors give up their claims early due to legal uncertainty and cost considerations. Regarding the characteristics of international cases, the data show a rather marginal role of domestic courts in complex and—in terms of money—important disputes. As regards the way international disputes are decided in court, the authors conclude from their studies that continental judges are less well acquainted with dealing with foreign elements of cases than U.S. judges. It seems that the common-law requirement of proving foreign law fosters research and the employment of expert witnesses. But even here the gap between civil-law and common-law systems is rarely bridged. The authors raise doubts as to the future of domestic courts as adequate and effective institutions for the global arena. Arbitration and the normative potential of third cultures may take over their role to a certain degree as regards dispute resolution. But a contribution to legal interpretation and change, to the maintenance of stable orientations and expectations, and to the development of basic common values is not offered by these institutions. The model of the European Court of Justice is discussed but discarded as a possible solution for multicultural jurisdiction. What remains as a realistic outlook is only the theory of the world society with its prospect of the differentiation of global life areas that may develop their own institutions—but it follows that the problems of the insecurity of global exchanges will not be resolved on a universal level.

## The Authors

Hanno von Freyhold. Lawyer. Research Assistant at the Centre for European Law and Policy at the University of Bremen (ZERP). From 1992 to 1993 Attorney at Law licensed in Berlin and practising on international matters in a law firm in New York. Currently conducts research on cross-border civil litigation as well as policy research for the European Commission.
*Address*: ZERP, Universitätsallee GW 1, 28359 Bremen, Germany.
*e-mail*: HVF@ZERP.uni-bremen.de

Volkmar Gessner. Degrees in Law and Sociology. Prior practice as lawyer and as judge. Currently Professor of Comparative Law and Sociology of Law at the University of Bremen, Germany. Research areas (mainly empirical) lie in the fields of litigation in national and international contexts, alternating forms of dispute resolution, legal culture and globalization of law. Heavy involvement also in policy research for the German government and the European Commission.
*Address*: ZERP, Universitätsallee GW 1, 28359 Bremen, Germany.
*e-mail*: VGESSNER@ZERP.uni-bremen.de

Vittorio Olgiati. Lawyer. Researcher at the Faculty of Law, University of Milan. Currently Reader on Sociology of Organization, Faculty of Sociology, University of Urbino, and Sociology of Law, Faculty of Law, University of Macerata, Italy. Extensive writings on sociolegal issues and legal professionalism.
*Address*: Istituto di Filosofia e Sociologia del Diritto, Via Festa del Perdono 7, 20122 Milano, Italy.